CLASSIC
GOLF LINKS
of GREAT BRITAIN *and* IRELAND

CLASSIC GOLF LINKS

of GREAT BRITAIN and IRELAND

DONALD STEEL

PHOTOGRAPHY BY
BRIAN D. MORGAN

CHAPMANS

ACKNOWLEDGMENTS

In a book of such magnitude and complexity, many people have contributed significantly to its make-up, not least the officials of the golf clubs represented in the book. Too numerous to mention individually by name, I am, none-theless, deeply grateful to them for their collective goodwill and co-operation, a sentiment echoed by Tim Jollands who has helped mastermind the entire operation.

It was a source of great pleasure when Brian Morgan agreed to join the team. All but three of the photographs were taken by him, the exceptions being those on pages 23, 133 (bottom) and 141, courtesy of, respectively, Richard Drew, Trevose Golf and Country Club and, my colleague, Tom MacKenzie.

Regarding the course diagrams, our prime source of reference has been the Strokesaver guides, whose series includes so many of the links covered in this book. I am indebted to their managing director, David Duckering, for allowing us to draw on their published material. Many other sources of reference were consulted and specific thanks are due to Eagle Promotions in this regard. No course is fixed in time and, although Tim and I have tried to keep abreast of changes, we offer our apologies if one or two of these have slipped the net.

Debbie Harper put the manuscript onto disc, handled endless corrections and generally perfected the chaos; Ken Lewis, who prepared the diagrams, and Philip Mann, who, as designer, created order out of so many different elements, remained unflappable to the last; Geoff Barlow, production consultant, worked miracles at various crucial stages; and Ian and Marjory Chapman, the former a considerable golfer, were the ideal publishers – to them all, I should like to express my profound thanks.

Finally, I must thank Peter Thomson, an old friend and a supreme exponent of our seaside links, for his Foreword and Hitoshi Matsuura, chairman of the Nitto Kogyo Group, for his Preface and also for his generous support which has been much appreciated.

Donald Steel, Chichester, May 1992

Erratum pages 195 and 223
For 'Robert Trent Jones Jnr'
read 'Robert Trent Jones'.

Chapmans Publishers Ltd
141-143 Drury Lane
London WC2B 5TB

First published by Chapmans in 1992
Copyright © Donald Steel and Jollands Editions 1992
Photographs © Brian Morgan 1992

A CIP Catalogue record for this book is available from the British Library

ISBN 1 85592 537 0

Editor Tim Jollands
Designed by Philip Mann, ACE Limited
Course diagrams and map by Ken Lewis
Production by Geoff Barlow
Printed and bound in Great Britain by Butler & Tanner Ltd, Frome

Uncaptioned photographs
Page 1, 6th hole, Royal North Devon
Pages 2, 10 and 50, St Andrews
Page 6, 17th hole (Ailsa Course) and hotel, Turnberry

CONTENTS

PREFACE

by

Hitoshi Matsuura

Chairman, Nitto Kogyo Group
and Turnberry Hotel and Golf Courses

Since the Nitto Kogyo Group began its association with Turnberry in 1987, it has been my express wish to do nothing that would erode the natural beauty and character of two true links. Turnberry epitomizes the splendour of seaside golf which is such a special part of the game in Britain.

It was on wild land by the sea that golf had its origins and, though Turnberry cannot claim the centuries-old traditions of St Andrews or Leith, its place in the modern world has grown in importance. The Ailsa Course's position as host for the Open Championship is a matter of great pride.

Nowhere else, except around the shores of Great Britain and Ireland, is there anything remotely comparable to the variety of courses which this book highlights so admirably. Seaside golf may not be to everybody's taste. In America and Japan, in fact, there is a preference for more sheltered settings adorned by trees and lakes but everyone recognizes that golf's real heritage belongs by the sea and that its preservation is vital

Although most of the golf course and leisure projects which the Nitto Kogyo Group own or manage are in Japan and the United States, I look forward to the opening next year of The Oxfordshire Golf Club, near Thame, the first development we have planned and built in Britain. Whatever claims there may be to the contrary, golf is a wonderful means of fostering international relations, goodwill, understanding and friendship – a sentiment in which I firmly believe.

As a consequence, we see our stewardship of Turnberry and The Oxfordshire as the ideal way of furthering that cause. At Turnberry the formula is both tried and successful. The future of traditional British seaside golf depends on the proper interpretation of what has made it so popular and in leaving well alone. It is in the role of loyal custodians of Turnberry that we are pleased to endorse this policy as well as the theme of 'The Classic Links'.

FOREWORD

by

Peter Thomson, CBE

Open Champion 1954-5-6, 1958, 1965

The origins of golf are lost in the mists of time. There is no 'Big Bang' theory about its beginnings, at least none that I know of. Yet it is widely and reasonably accepted that the game started as a small spark that eventually became a raging fire.

There is little argument that it all happened in Scotland. There are some ancient prints of some kind of ice game played in Holland, using a long stick and a puck. That was another matter. Playing a ball game over links territory is definitely Scottish and no other.

The evidence is there for all to see. The turf of the Old Course at St Andrews is the same piece of sward that entertained whatever humble sport took place as long ago as the 16th century. Happily, it has survived, virtually untouched, although there is sadly a certain amount of ravage caused by the modern popularity of the game. St Andrews is a Mecca to anyone religiously captivated by golf. The Old Course has every reason to be *the* original course. Its known and written history reveals that it was, at an earlier stage, much narrower than it is now, and that it was played in both directions. Also it had more holes.

For practical purposes, it was refined down to 18 holes and the course widened by cutting back the whins to allow for traffic in both directions. Two cups were cut in the double greens so that players would keep out of each other's way. It settled down to become what it is today.

Being the original course, it therefore follows that all other courses are copies, at least to fundamentals. Why else would we settle for 18 holes in the middle of Australia, or the mountains of America, or the swamps of Florida? Why, indeed, do we go to the trouble of building sand bunkers far from the coastlines, if they are not in imitation of those made by nature at St Andrews?

The copies vary widely, even enormously, from the master print. Of the thousands of new courses that are being built today, few have followed anything like the St Andrews principles.

There are many reasons for this. In most cases, the land is not conducive. In others though, layouts that pass for courses are no more than caricature: absurd creations that attempt to take the game into some supposedly new orbit. Such apologies distort the dimensions of a tried and proven noble sport. Indeed, golf is in some peril of being led down the garden path!

It is timely and important therefore to remind ourselves of what is valuable and classic with regard to those arenas on which golf is played at its enjoyable best. Donald Steel, with his intimate knowledge and experience, has put together this impressive list of the best and most precious in Great Britain and Ireland.

Not all of golf's classic courses belong to Britain and Ireland, and Steel does not claim such a thing, but there is no other place on earth where so many of high calibre exist in a pristine state. This book is therefore at once an entertaining passage across the old countries and a lesson in principles and problems.

For example, it can easily be seen that almost all classic courses have flat greens, or at least a flat area for the purpose of holing out. This is a vitally important part of the game that is now being overlooked. Modern designers seem to have a fear of providing anything like a level putting area. This, in its turn, stems from the fear that today's professional players will make courses look ridiculously easy. And herein lies a serious stumbling block.

Courses today are being put together by property developers and land sellers. In byegone days, most courses were built by groups of enthusiastic players who wanted a new, perhaps more convenient, links upon which to play their golf. Often, the village would encourage golf on the common land (linksland if it was available). In this way, courses grew along lines that followed classic principles. Courses were designed and built to suit everybody. Courses that were practical, pleasurable, free of humbug (as Alister MacKenzie put it) of losing balls. Courses that looked like a golf course should!

The property developer has no such motive. His request to the course designer is to produce something that is stunning, photogenic – something the glossy magazines will pick up and feature. Something extravagant, outrageous – even impractical. In short, something that will 'sell my land'. They like bright lids to their chocolate boxes.

No such course features in this book or any other that claims to present all that is 'classic' in golf. Beauty is always in the eye of the beholder. Links courses owe more to wild nature and Mother earth. That, to many of us, is beauty itself.

Another aspect of classic golf that stands out is the bunkering. A bunker can be a feature of wonder if a little of nature is tempered with the small touch of a rake to formalise its presence. Bunkers come in an infinite variety of size and shape. I cannot think of bunkers without recalling some of the efforts of constructors in Japan where bunkers normally come in set patterns, uniform in depth (if any) and dimension.

The only variation accepted is what most of us would call an ordinary deep bunker, but which is called in Japan – an Alison bunker. The Alison bunker was introduced to Japan by Charles Alison, the famous English architect, who went there in the early 1930s to work on Kasumigaseki and Hirono Country Clubs. His bunker work must have stunned the local people because his name went on that type of bunker and adheres to the present day!

My experience of playing many of the classic links mentioned in this book has been an enormous pleasure to me. The thrill of squeezing a ball against the firm turf, trying to keep it low into a buffeting wind, is something that lingers in the mind forever. It reminds me, too, that a good deal of golf is played on the ground, or at least it should be. Classic golf provides this. There is a lot of chipping and long putting to do. Approaches can be made with straight-faced irons, running the ball up little banks and through shallow hollows. It is an important part of the game, alas little understood and appreciated and now, in modern design, virtually ignored.

This is a precious book for its message. Many of these courses are treasures that, like any other items of long term value, are under attack. Sometimes from neglect or ignorance, or even from overuse, they show signs of deterioration. They need to be preserved like ancient buildings for their aesthetic beauty and grand value. For if they are not, and golf courses follow 'down the garden path', then the very essence of what the game of golf is all about will have been lost, perhaps forever.

I commend the book and its message to you.

Peter Thomson

INTRODUCTION

This book is not meant as a scholarly explanation of how or why, by some geological quirk of fate, the seas around the shores of Britain and Ireland receded over hundreds of years to leave natural land, ideal for golf. It is acknowledgment and celebration of the fact.

One of the unique charms of the game is that it is played in a variety of settings, on a variety of terrains, not one of which is the same. In Britain and Ireland, the choice is infinite. There are sheltered parks, open heaths, lonely moors, enclosed woodlands, exposed downland and the ancient links by the sea where golf has its roots.

Many believe our traditional links are the only true form of expression and that anything else is second best. Their love of them amounts almost to a passion. Nowhere in the world is there anything else that compares; indeed, nothing that comes close. All our great championships are contested by the sea and, happily, no change of policy can be contemplated in the foreseeable future. Several inland courses might be considered worthy of the Open in a playing sense. The shortlist might include Woodhall Spa, Hollinwell, Wentworth, Woburn, Ganton and Walton Heath but none could cope with the non-golfing needs of modern championships, demands that have led to Prestwick and Hoylake, great names of the past, being relegated to the sidelines – Prestwick long ago.

Although Royal Lytham & St Annes is confined within four suburban walls, so to speak, there is a joyous sense of space and freedom about most seaside links, a feeling of escape that makes you glad to be alive. Only a tiny handful of golfers play purely to meet the game's essential, competitive challenge. The vast majority do so for reasons of health, exercise, exploration and the sheer enjoyment of the beauty in which they find themselves.

Courts or pitches for other sports must adhere to prescribed dimensions, often surrounded by banks or stands to house the crowds who come to watch. Cricket grounds are perhaps exceptions that may rejoice in the glory of a setting but golf courses are not bound by set standards, rigid acreages or minimum or maximum lengths. They come in all shapes and sizes, a variety of architectural styles and many different balances between the holes.

Golf course architects have a duty to arrange their layouts in the way they think makes best use of a particular piece of land and the best use of the budget available to them. There are a few unwritten 'rules' to which the best of them conform but there has been a growing belief among developers of new courses in recent years that so-called championship courses, a much misapplied and misunderstood term, must have a par of 72 with four par 5s and four par 3s – two in each half. That makes no more sense than regularizing the size of a potato.

Take the Old Course at St Andrews which is still regarded as the model at whose feet architects rightly worship. It has only two short holes, the first of which is the 8th, and two par 5s. Turnberry's par is 70, Muirfield's and Bally-bunion's 71. Royal Lytham begins with a short hole, Royal St David's ends with one. Of other fine courses, Ballybunion, Cruden Bay and Cypress Point have successive short holes while many clubs have successive par 5s. Royal Birkdale can arrange its finish to include four 5s in the last six holes. Royal County Down and Saunton have mighty starts, Royal Troon a more modest beginning in which the first three holes are all between 364 and 391 yards. There are no rights and wrongs.

A list of 'design oddities' which I once prepared to illustrate some of the quirks turned out to be far less odd than expected. However, one general peculiarity of design of our links is the fact that many have nine holes out to a distant point, in more or less single file, and nine holes back. There is little or no change in direction of the holes, the notable exceptions being Muirfield, Royal Birkdale, Royal County Down, Carnoustie, Portmarnock and Royal St George's. It is surprising that, in the courses that do go out and back, nobody thought of positioning the clubhouse in the middle.

A much discussed point in the study of our sea-side courses is the actual definition of the word 'links'. Whether mine is correct or not, it is certainly logical and convenient. It refers to the land that, quite literally, links the sea with the more fertile plains that may be only a couple of hundred yards distant. It is land with no agricultural value. The only vegetation it supports are the fine, wiry grasses that, on top of a sandy base, make an ideal playing surface, especially for iron play.

As this special land sometimes forms such a thin strip it explains the configuration of those links laid out no more than two holes wide. If they followed a more regular pattern, there would be only a limited number of seaside holes. The rest would be of much less stimulating character.

Character, after all, is the most important ingredient on any golf course, the joy of links being that they are entirely natural. That is why, before architects lent a hand, they were merely adopted as they were found. What God created, man implemented.

Greens were made out of clearings, plateaux and dells. Tees were flat though undefined, fairways following a path between sandhills, gorse or

across more open tracts, sometimes traversed by burns or streams which found their way to the sea as channels formed by the action of tides advancing and retiring over centuries.

The sea's withdrawal left sandy wastes which, with the help of winds, were built into dunes, hills, ridges, furrows and gullies in which birds began to nest and breed. It was their droppings which later produced a mild form of manure that, allied to the regurgitation of the birds, established vegetation – the fine bents and fescues. In addition, the huge sandhills that grew up were stabilized by the roots of sturdier grasses and stout bushes such as gorse or buckthorn – thereby preventing sand blow and, more vitally, giving protection. On the other hand, tide and wind patterns change, bringing the threat of erosion along shorelines and, worse still, causing invasion from the sea. Clubs such as Royal North Devon, Royal Troon, Royal West Norfolk, Ballybunion, Royal Portrush and Royal Cinque Ports have found that restoring their defences can be both problematical and costly. Others need to be forever watchful.

Although some land near the sea is flat, it became generally accepted that the best foundation for golf is the gently rolling sandy linksland which is why developers, in various parts of the world, give their blessing to spending millions of pounds shaping fairways in order to try and achieve just that. On any course, the ground needs to have enough movement in it to make it interesting yet not too much abrupt rise or fall to render it exhausting.

Most links have something in between, the undulations that give pockets of humps and hollows making an even lie or stance less likely. Traditionalists jump for joy, modernists tear their hair out.

Those professionals who want everything predictable, with shotmaking geared to a stereotyped level, expect perfectly straight drives to be teed up in the middle of the fairway in full view of the green and the bottom of the flag. They would prefer the term 'rub of the green' eliminated from the dictionary, but adherents to links golf contend correctly that the powers of invention necessary to overcome any unexpected situation plays straight into the hands of the more gifted. Reducing everything to a common denominator brings success within the range of the many.

The 8th hole at Tralee, the
most recent addition to
Britain and Ireland's links

On American courses, any player 120 yards short of the green will think of playing only one club – a wedge that must carry all the way to the flag. On a British or Irish links, he may have the choice of four or five clubs and can execute the shot with every club two or three different ways. When the wind whips up, he may need four or five clubs more than the day before but winds are an almost in-built hazard at the seaside and constant change of wind direction makes courses seem like four-in-one.

It is interesting and entirely relevant to this debate that in 1991 there were grumbles from eminent figures in American golf that US tournament courses are dull and artificial, producing a generation of young professionals less good than their European counterparts. Their argument was based on the lines that Americans are only used to playing in perfect conditions. On British courses that are less manicured, improvisation is essential. You hit the shots you can, not the shots you want.

There was criticism of Americans for not being innovative enough. A tough wind on a links calls for punching shots low with two or three clubs more than a yardage chart may indicate. It is no good selecting a 7-iron, hitting it into the heavens and complaining when it comes up short.

Tom Watson, who was as innovative as any, said of Ballybunion that it was a course on which many golf architects should live and play before they build golf courses, hinting no doubt that links demand a wider range of shotmaking than any other type of course. He was too modest to say that is why he has won the British Open five times but, if the purpose of any Open is to produce the best champion, it is unarguable that over the last thirty years the British Open has been more successful at doing that than its American counterpart. The reason? Links courses.

If the wind can change as regularly as it does, there can also be several seasons in one day, a lasting appeal of the seaside being the speed with which the weather changes. Everyone who has ever been stranded at the far end of a links as rain, driven on a strong wind, sweeps in from the sea will know what desolate places they can be. Mighty men can be turned into midgets as the knack of flighting shots low becomes vital to survival.

In those circumstances, yardage charts are not worth the paper they are written on, but as welcome as the dawn is the shaft of sunlight, in the wake of dark cloud, that signals the weather is on the mend. Tranquillity descends and all is right with the world again.

On the rare occasions when there is no wind, the ground is receptive and the greens putting true, links can represent the easiest form of golf but, to be seen at their sporting best, they need to be fast-running with emphasis on the low pitches, the putter working overtime from off the green – occasions when the wedge is blunted.

Acute powers of observation and familiarity with as many courses as possible confer on architects the qualification to sift good features from bad. They must visualize everything through the eyes of players of all standards, another way of saying they should have experience as golfers themselves. Thoughts of duplication must be rejected but architects are bound to be influenced by the attributes that make courses great and recognize that enjoyment is a pre-requisite in all they strive to achieve. Their doctrines may vary but seaside links have governed their thinking more than any other type of course. Golf course architecture is a battle of wits, the architect acting as the examiner and the golfer the pupil trying to fathom the answers.

Golf is a continuous process of decision-making, a strategic exercise that must explore the options on every shot on every hole. It then becomes a test of manoeuvrability and control rather like a game of snooker; the more skilfully the current shot is played, the more straightforward will be the next. Architects should never ask players to embark on impossible missions – that would be too simple. They, for the most part, explore the fine dividing line between what is challenging and what is unfair. If players are able to unravel the knot, architects are delighted; but, if they fail, then it is a case of let the devil take the hindmost.

Where architects fight a losing battle is with the advances in the manufacture of clubs and balls over which they have no control and to which officialdom pays insufficient heed. Changes from the feathery ball to the gutta-percha ball and from gutta-percha to the rubber-cored ball brought about dramatic shortening of holes but it is the further improvement in the ball in the last twenty or thirty years – together with little restriction on materials for the shafts and heads of clubs – that threaten the game. Unless a tight rein is kept, golf course architects may become powerless.

It may be one argument (that of the R & A in the mid-1960s) to say it doesn't matter how low scores become as long as it is the best players who produce them, but nobody wants 8000-yard courses in order to establish a status quo. What about those existing on 90 acres or so in the middle of town? They are already stretched to the last inch.

Some architects have tried to combat the trend by building modern courses that are impossibly difficult, completely losing sight of the fact that 80 per cent of all golf is played by those of more than 15 handicap, and that their pleasure is paramount. Losing half a dozen balls per round is not everyone's idea of fun.

Hiring household names to produce something more shocking, more spectacular, is not the answer. The highly respected and highly skilled band of men who, early in this century, replaced the top professionals – whose designs were geometric and artificial – and created the profession of golf course architecture, still have a message.

The likes of Harry Colt, Alister MacKenzie, Herbert Fowler, Tom Simpson, James Braid, A.W. Tillinghast, Donald Ross, Mackenzie Ross and Sir Guy Campbell realized that golf courses have an air of permanence and that that air of permanence depends upon a knowledge of how to build as well as how to design. In spite of a few understandable adjustments, their work has retained an incredible freshness, a state of affairs that has resulted in the British Institute of Golf Course Architects introducing a programme of education and examination for would-be members.

Although it is intended to safeguard clients, several choose to ignore the fact and end up with expensive blots on the landscape. However, the basic truth is that a study of British and Irish seaside links remains the finest way to understand the principles of golf course architecture.

They teach us how avenues between dunes reward straightness and accuracy. They show the thinking behind the placing of bunkers. They expound the virtues of positional play which can erode the priceless weapon of power. They reveal the importance of the proper angling, shaping and contouring of greens – the ultimate centrepiece on every hole on every course. They emphasize that subtle variations of level add to the interest and appearance. Above all, they underline the vital need for architects to possess those abstract qualities you cannot teach – imagination, attention to detail and eye for land.

That is what separates the good from the also-rans, the truly authentic links by the sea from others that are, at best, only thin imitations.

CHAPTER ONE

WEST OF SCOTLAND

When it comes to a discussion about the county in Britain which can boast the golf courses in which quality matches quantity, the field can be narrowed to Surrey, Lancashire, Ayrshire and East Lothian. This is neither the time nor place to fuel the debate but it is the moment to emphasize the blessings of Ayrshire, which can fairly be classified as the golfing heart of the west of Scotland.

Described once as golden links on an endless chain, Ayrshire's courses even inspired the verse,

Troon and Prestwick-Old and 'classy'
Bogside, Dundonald, Gailes, Barassie.

Prestwick St Nicholas, Western Gailes,
St Cuthbert, Portland-memory-fails-

Troon Municipal (three links there)
Prestwick Municipal, Irvine, Ayr.

They faced the list with delighted smiles –
Sixteen courses within ten miles.

Dundonald, Prestwick Municipal and Bogside may be no more but new courses have appeared in their place and the train journey from Paisley still has passengers with a golfing eye straining this way and that to spot the succession of courses on either side of the track. There is a station to serve the Gailes (Glasgow and Western), a stretch alongside Troon onto which even competitors in the Open deposit their stray shots, and two platforms at Prestwick which suffer much more

frequent bombardment from the 1st tee of Old Prestwick.

In terms of seniority, precedence must be extended to Prestwick, cradle of championship golf, where the Open was held on a regular basis until 1925. Two years earlier, Troon entered the list and, in 1977, Turnberry became the third west of Scotland course to house the Open. However, Prestwick's demise doesn't make it any less important and no keen golfer worthy of the name should pass it by. It conveys the atmosphere of what golf was like in more primitive days of gutty ball, long-nosed spoons and Norfolk jackets but it is still a substantial test with modern equipment. I should love to see today's professionals meeting up to its demands of patience, ingenuity and invention. If you are looking for an opening hole worthy of a scholarship question, Prestwick's fits the bill better than any and, though the Cardinal and its sleepers at the 3rd have lost some of their menace, the 4th, one of golf's first doglegs, retains a freshness that is all too real.

Further south, round the Heads of Ayr and down past Burns country and Culzean Castle, Turnberry ranks in the top three or four in Britain for a mixture of golfing challenge and compelling beauty. The Ailsa and Arran's precarious wartime experiences make their survival and reclamation a story in themselves. The Ailsa's elevation to the golfing peerage, so to speak, owes everything to the handiwork of Mackenzie Ross, a golf course

In the great galaxy of the Ayrshire courses, Western Gailes shines as brightly as its more famed neighbours, Prestwick, Turnberry (left) and Royal Troon.

architect to rank with the finest, but, for generations of Glaswegians and Ayrshire men, Troon has been a veritable home from home.

Western Gailes, scene of the Curtis Cup match in 1972, is a charming links between the railway and the sea in which dunes and heather are prominent features. Glasgow Gailes, Kilmarnock (Barassie) and Irvine are similar in character and complete a network of good courses as concentrated as any in the world.

Southerness on the Solway Firth, though not in the west of Scotland, qualifies in this bracket by being as near as makes no difference. It qualified for exalted status when the Scottish Amateur Championship was taken there in 1985. However, the true joy of the west of Scotland lies in its courses in out of the way places that, on a fine day, can be heaven on earth. There are other courses overlooking the Clyde, courses on Arran that, if not entirely seaside in the true meaning of the term, have exhilarating views, and courses like

Dunaverty, Machrihanish and Machrie that are further jewels in a glittering crown. Machrihanish and Dunaverty, home of Belle Robertson, are set in the curve of sandy bays, Machrihanish the more serious test but Dunaverty full of fun.

Machrie on the island of Islay is a seaside links of the original type, a stirring prelude before machinery eliminated blind shots and greens in dells. There are daily flights from Glasgow and many opportunities to explore an idyllic island when not playing golf.

Machrihanish has some wild, billowy dunes accentuated in the stiff winds that are common but, in spite of the dwindling number of distilleries, it is perfect for holidays and a friendly welcome is guaranteed. In 1990, Machrihanish housed the Scottish Ladies' Championship, a much deserved honour which emphasized how much in demand it would be if more accessible. What variety is provided by the west of Scotland – contrasts unique in the British Isles.

SOUTHERNESS

Nestling along the quiet waters of the Solway Firth, in an area associated with fishing nets and smoke houses for salmon, is to be found Southerness, a superb course largely undiscovered by golfers. It is the most modern of British seaside links, dating from the immediate postwar years when Mackenzie Ross was bringing about the reincarnation of Turnberry. He must have been a busy man, nipping to and fro across a corner of Scotland not as well known for its golf as others.

Southerness bears all the hallmarks of Mackenzie Ross's work, a series of challenging, natural-looking holes that reflect his imaginative eye for land. It was built, what is more, for £2000 and was turfed not seeded, the local soil being identical to that found in the Fens of England. Initially, the course was looked after by one man, a stalwart named Paterson, who mowed all the greens by hand.

On my first visit in the early sixties, a notice invited visitors to pay their green fees in the village shop across the road from the clubhouse which resembled a small rustic cricket pavilion. Catering was supplied in the Paul Jones Hotel, named after the famous admiral who also gave his name to the dance, although quite how or why is less clear. A new clubhouse was built in 1974 at a point near the old 6th and, in 1985, the distinction of the course was recognized by the staging of the Scottish Amateur Championship there. It also housed the 1990 British Youths' Championship, but it remains essentially a peaceful haven for golfers seeking a pleasant day out in a setting of heather, gorse, sea and distant hills. A diversion from Dumfries by way of a winding road is well rewarded.

It has no hole over 500 yards and only two par 5s in all over 475 yards but there are eight holes between 405 and 470 yards, an indication of the stern note it strikes, particularly as the clever angling of some greens emphasizes the importance of being in the right spot from the tee. The subtlety of its five short holes will also impress the advanced student, notably the well defended 4th on the westernmost tip of the course.

Driving is important because gorse and heather swallow up anything wayward but it is not intimidating. There is a tough start, the first two holes calling for two fine shots and the 3rd, influenced by bracken on the left, pushing the drive over

SOUTHERNESS Card of the course					
Hole	Yds	Par	Hole	Yds	Par
1	393	4	10	168	3
2	450	4	11	390	4
3	408	4	12	421	4
4	169	3	13	467	4
5	494	5	14	458	4
6	405	4	15	217	3
7	215	3	16	433	4
8	371	4	17	175	3
9	435	4	18	485	5
	3340	35		3214	34

Total 6554 yards, par 69
Course record • 65,
Mathias Grönberg (A), 1990

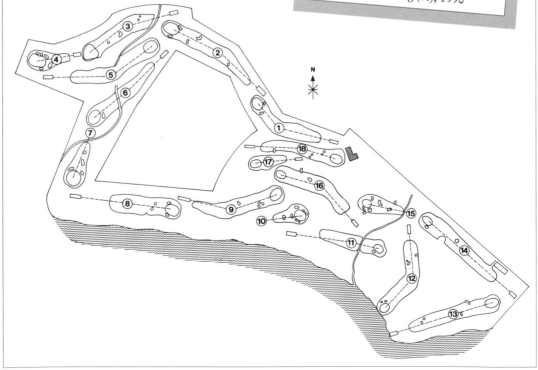

The view from the 9th tee, looking back across the 8th green along the coast of Kirkudbright and towards the hills of Galloway.

towards twin bunkers on the right. The 5th is the longest hole, its special feature being a green resembling an elevated vaulting horse, but the 6th, with its second over a narrow brook that is, nevertheless, more a problem for a long drive, turns back towards the Solway and is followed by a short hole that more often demands wood than iron against a background of sandhills.

The first seven holes circle around a large expanse of pasture. The 8th, taking aim on the lighthouse, is the start of a stretch along the shore towards the old clubhouse. A long, gradual uphill approach is the highlight of the 9th, and, of the shorter 4s, the 11th offers a second calling for accurate judgment over a ditch to a cleverly raised green. A significant change of route takes place

at the 12th, a sharpish dogleg to the right with bunkers on the pivot and a green, with a well channelled apron, enjoying the best of the view. Golden sands follow the coast of Kirkcudbright but attention is needed for the finish in which there are two par 3s in the last four holes.

The 13th, the old 18th, is a formidable 467 yards in a cross or head wind whilst gorse and heather form a gentle curve in the 16th before a cross ridge occupies the mind for the second shot. The short 17th has a long distinctive green and the 18th doubles back in the form of an encouraging par 5 to end a round which, if not dominated by dunes in the manner of Silloth, which is visible across the Solway, is absolutely first-rate.

TURNBERRY

TURNBERRY
Card of the Ailsa course (Open Championship tees)

Hole		Yds	Par	Hole		Yds	Par
1	Ailsa Craig	350	4	10	Dinna Fouter	452	4
2	Mak Siccar	428	4	11	Maidens	177	3
3	Blaw Wearie	462	4	12	Monument	448	4
4	Woe-be-Tide	167	3	13	Tickly Tap	411	4
5	Fin' me oot	441	4	14	Rish-an-Hope	440	4
6	Tappie Toorie	222	3	15	Ca Canny	209	3
7	Roon the Ben	528	5	16	Wee Burn	409	4
8	Goat Fell	427	4	17	Lang Whang	500	5
9	Bruce's Castle	455	4	18	Ailsa Hame	431	4
		3480	35			3477	35

Total 6957 yards, par 70
Course record • 63, Greg Norman, 1986 Open Championship

If it is true that the setting is as important to a course as a glittering frame to a celebrated painting, Turnberry is unsurpassable. It is impossible to write in less than superlatives of a spectacular links on the sea's edge in surroundings that make Scottish exiles dream of home. Robert Louis Stevenson described the Californian coast near Pebble Beach as the 'greatest meeting place of land and water' but Turnberry can beg to differ. The scene, as a summer sunset dips behind Arran, makes glad the heart of man. Behind the huge mass of Ailsa Craig can be detected the distant form of Ulster seemingly merging with the Mull of Kintyre, the remote fingertip of Argyll. To the north can be seen the splendour of Culzean Castle and to the south the Ayrshire hills but the wonder of it all is not the unchanging beauty as much as the reminder that golf at Turnberry was twice on the brink of extinction.

It was condemned in two world wars to be a Royal Naval Air Station with miles of concrete runway, the glorious contours of fairways flattened and lost without trace. There can have been few more depressing sights in 1946 than that from the terrace of Turnberry's incomparable hotel, whose future was just as much in doubt, but the battle for government funds was fought and won, a plan of reincarnation was drawn up and slowly Turnberry rose again Phoenix-like from the ashes.

That the Ailsa course acquired a nobility grander than before, one later bestowed the ultimate accolade of the Open Championship, was due entirely to the genius of Mackenzie Ross who, at about the same time, was creating Southerness near Dumfries and planning grander things for Castletown in the Isle of Man. It is distinctly easier to convert fairway into runway than it is to turn it back again but, by diligent study, a clear imagination and the making of plasticine models of greens, he conveyed to machine operators exactly what he wanted, and they responded to his behest as men happier at creating than destroying.

Mercifully, the magnificent coastal stretch, now occupied by the 4th to 11th holes, was untouched and it provides the much photographed centrepiece of the links. The 9th along the rocky outcrop by the lighthouse, near Robert the Bruce's Castle, is Turnberry's emblem, but the Ailsa is far from being an eight-hole course. Though contrasting in character, the other 10 contribute every bit as much to the severity of the examination.

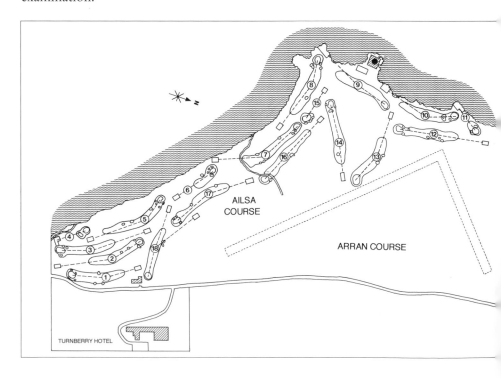

Turnberry's spectacular signature hole, the 9th. The carry of some 200 yards from the championship tee to the safety of the stone cairn may not be enormous for the top players but, in the context of the tee's setting high above the rocks, it can be an unnerving prospect.

A new clubhouse is planned for 1994, the year of Turnberry's third Open, and there are to be changes to the Arran course which will suffer little by comparison with its illustrious neighbour. Gorse is the Arran's main feature, a prickly hazard from which the Ailsa is largely free. The Ailsa embodies the virtues of typically tumbling seaside fairways, a clinging rough, a raging burn in evidence on the 7th and 16th and a susceptibility to the wind which attacks from all quarters.

No second or fifth greens on Open courses are closer to the clubhouse than those on the Ailsa, the first three holes running parallel; the 1st along a road lined by neat bungalows and the 3rd down a shallow valley with no bunkers to taunt the drive but several guarding the green. In between, the 2nd also has more feature to catch the second shot than the drive which, nevertheless, must not be pulled down the bank into rough shared with the 3rd. It can be wild and woolly.

The 4th is a beautiful short hole where the penalties for missing the pulpit green are too awful to contemplate. Years ago, the sea used to penetrate the little cove on the left and lap the base of the bank. Now it is dry land although the green can often look alarmingly small from the tee with the right side shut off by a hill.

Dunes rise up on the left to give an enclosed look to the dogleg 5th where the temptation is to err to the right, away from two strategically placed bunkers. A controlled draw is the shape for the second shot unless the drive is long enough for skilled players to pitch to the green.

There aren't many longer short holes than the 6th, the green perched up at the end of a sharp rise and hemmed in by bunkers. Roon the Ben is the descriptive name for the 7th, a par 5 from a high tee with a commanding view to a fairway below that breaks almost at right angles to the left. The second, with the lighthouse to act as a guide post, then surmounts a long, gradual slope to a long, sloping green.

Difficulties abound on the 8th, a bunker frustrating the efforts of driving into the perfect spot before tackling a long iron or wood that has to have flight, line and weight gauged to perfection.

The green has a stimulating view of Turnberry Bay although the first-time visitor has no clue what lies in store on the lonely back tee of the 9th. From here, rock dominates a more rugged shoreline that attracts oyster-catchers, cormorants and gannets – ever hunting for a meal. On a lovely day it is an idyllic scene, the lighthouse glinting white and colourful patterns etched over Ailsa and Arran.

In the 1977 Open, when Tom Watson and Jack Nicklaus rewrote the records for low scoring, a thunderstorm brought temporary relief to the glorious still weather that prevailed for much of the week but, at other times, it may be all you can do to stand on the tiny square of tee let alone concentrate on reaching the safety of the cairn on the hill ahead. Its slightly angled green with bold shoulders favours a drive on the left but the right is the side from the 10th, an exhilarating hole that has a large deep bunker short of the green. The 11th marks the end of the coastal section, a pleasant short hole with glimpses up the Firth of Clyde but, in a boisterous south-westerly breeze, it is a long haul home.

A granite war memorial on the hill overlooking the 12th green is an echo of Turnberry's turbulent past but the second shot is the forerunner to a variety of demanding strokes that characterize the

The short 4th is fully exposed to the elements, with a large bunker blocking the approach from the right and trouble all the way down the left. Only a direct, holding shot to the pulpit green will suffice.

The aerial route is the only way to the 16th green, guarded as it is by a steep-sided ravine containing Wee Burn which gives ample warning of the consequences of underclubbing.

finish. The best are the tee shot at the short 15th, a gaping chasm to the right, and the tantalizing carry over Wee Burn in front of the 16th green. It calls for decisiveness, courage and accuracy. A narrow waist of fairway causes problems on the 17th for those not long enough with their second shot on the second of the par 5s while the 18th, against a background of the hotel, has a green with no bunker to help identify it.

Mackenzie Ross's work meant that the Ailsa course became highly fashionable as a staging post for important tournaments and International matches. The Amateur Championship and the Walker Cup gave the lead along with the old News of the World Matchplay Championship, a sad victim of the absurd modern bias among professionals for strokeplay. Turnberry was the ideal stage for Celebrity Pro-Ams before the proper accolade was bestowed with the award of the Open but it is at its best when the crowds have gone, and the evening colours are reflected on land and sea. There is nowhere lovelier.

PRESTWICK

Having been the birthplace of championship golf, it might seem that Prestwick's banishment to the Open wilderness in 1925 cast upon it an air of 'the glory that was Greece, the grandeur that was Rome'. Its most celebrated days may have been long ago but, like antique clubs and feathery balls, the fact of it being no longer the rage has not lessened its value. Very much the opposite. Prestwick is as alive as ever, a monument to the past but a lasting symbol for future generations to admire and study. Its influence lives on. It was only circumstance that denied Prestwick a prominence that once was taken for granted.

Access, crowd movement, car parking, practice facilities and accommodation, essential ingredients to modern championship venues, were below par here well over half a century ago, but the cramped nature and shortness of the last four holes really sounded its death knell. Not everyone, however, would agree that the famous finishing loop had outlived its effectiveness. Some saw it as the greatest part of the links, particularly the 17th, the Alps, a hole that shaped the destiny of many an Open – and still would today.

Prestwick is no stranger to controversy, fierce debate having surrounded some of its blind shots and the decision to extend the links beyond the old wall that used to be the boundary. Bernard Darwin was a definite opponent, even going as far as maintaining of the wall's eventual removal, 'I still want on a charger the head of the iconoclast who took it down.'

Horace Hutchinson, on the other hand, took the contrary view. Writing in the Badminton Library *Golf*, he noted that 'the flatter holes might be duller', but asked 'were they not a truer test of golf?' He felt blind holes induced uncertainty and 'though uncertainty is the salt of the game, such a degree of uncertainty as this is not conducive to bringing to a fine test relative golfing merit'. Blind shots, such as are found at the short 5th and the second to the Alps, might be ruled out if the course were being designed today but that is neither

reason to eliminate them nor criticism of them.

However, Prestwick still has several truly memorable holes, notably the 1st and 4th. The 1st is as daunting as any opening hole, while the 4th introduced the principle of the dogleg, a principle to which every golf course architect has since resorted – many in abundance.

The early Opens were all held over the 12-hole course, which began with a hole measuring 578

PRESTWICK Card of the course (championship tees)					
Hole	*Yds*	*Par*	*Hole*	*Yds*	*Par*
1 Railway	346	4	10 Arran	454	4
2 Tunnel	167	3	11 Carrick	195	3
3 Cardinal	500	5	12 Wall	513	5
4 Bridge	382	4	13 Sea Headrig	460	4
5 Himalayas	206	3	14 Goosedubs	362	4
6 Elysian Fields	400	4	15 Narrows	347	4
7 Monkton Miln	484	5	16 Cardinals Back	298	4
8 End	431	4	17 Alps	391	4
9 Eglinton	458	4	18 Clock	284	4
	3374	36		3304	36

Total 6678 yards, par 72

Course record • 68, Billy Andrade, Peter Deeble, Paul Mayo, 1987 Amateur Championship

One of golf's great opening holes, demanding the straightest of drives between the stone wall on the right and gorse and heather on the left.

yards and was distinctive for the amount of cross-fire that was necessary on holes traversing each other. The club holds an annual competition re-enacting as far as possible the terror of that original layout, but today's 1st and 4th were not part of the original 12.

Many believe that the 1st would be a better hole if it came later in the round, but it is my favourite opener – an example of where only the fairway will do from a tee looking right down the stone wall next to the station. Any thoughts of making sure to avoid the out-of-bounds by going left are foiled by heather and gorse – one of the most distinguished victims being Eric Brown who, six strokes ahead in the 1956 Dunlop Masters, began his final round with a prickly 7. The first part of

the fairway is reasonably level but ripples develop on the approach to a green whose right edge also rubs shoulders with the wall.

A bunker at the rear of the green on the short 2nd reinforces one at the front, making club selection and assessment of wind vital but, by now, some of Prestwick's best and most hallowed ground beckons. The Cardinal bunker with its deep, sleepered ramparts at the 3rd is renowned as one of the world's most famous hazards, a mammoth obstacle to surmount in days when James Braid became ensnared by it and took three attempts to disentangle himself. Darwin described him 'as playing a game of rackets against those ominous black boards', but it didn't prevent him winning. Nowadays, it is easier to sail over them

but those going boldly for a quaintly shaped green must probe a narrow entrance – anything right running the risk of an early acquaintance with the Pow Burn which dominates the 4th. As with all great doglegs, the brave line across the corner of the burn – fortified by a long, thin bunker – leaves a shorter and easier second. Yet, for all the brave thoughts on the tee, it is so easy to bail out once the swing is in motion and settle for keeping the ball in play.

Whatever the feelings surrounding the 5th, the Himalayas, it rewards the good shot and punishes the bad. There is also a sense of expectation lacking on holes where the green is visible from the tee, of rushing over the hill to see if a shot is as good as was hoped. On the 6th, 7th and 8th, which indulge in a certain amount of up and down, the features to remember are a plateau green at the 6th

and approaches to the 7th and 8th that are never easy to judge. The 9th green is another eccentric beauty and the 10th, back across the Himalayas and the Pow Burn, is as appealing as it looks.

In keeping with St Andrews, the 11th sees the last of the short holes, a fine specimen in the dunes. Then it is back down the hill to a par 5, the best part of which is the green.

Sea Headrig, the 13th, is as good a contemporary hole as it ever was, two firm blows theoretically finding a long, angled and heavily contoured green that can be impossible to hold with a pitch. There is nothing remarkable about the 14th and its drive over the Goose dubs but there are several ways of playing the unique 15th which in the Boys' Championship of 1952 was played as the 1st. Whether you go left or right, short or long, the green is just as treacherous. Two

The cavernous Cardinal bunkers at the 3rd, an unforgettable feature of the course even if nowadays its intended purpose has been somewhat blunted by advances in equipment.

Beyond the 4th green lies Prestwick's infamous blind hole, the par-3 Himalayas. The white disc marks the line from the tee. Clearing the vast dunes and sleepered bunker is only part of the problem as five greenside bunkers await the misdirected shot.

putts can be more of an achievement than you might imagine.

Line, avoiding Willie Campbell's Grave and even the corner of the Cardinal bunker, is the secret of the 16th, which can be driven, but attention is now directed on the Alps which wouldn't be half the hole if the vast hill, which gives it its name, were removed and the green visible. There is a bit of a back wall to the green although the Sahara bunker in front, from which Freddie Tait hit his celebrated shot out of water in the 1899 final of the Amateur Championship against John Ball, is still a hurdle.

There are better 18th holes than Prestwick's, aimed on the clubhouse clock, and links that may be harder to score, but the return of the Amateur Championship in 1987 showed that the course has retained all its freshness and challenge although

Darwin's contention 75 years ago, that 'a man is probably less likely to be contradicted in lauding Prestwick than in singing the praises of any other course in Christendon', may not be quite so true today. Nevertheless, in 1987, it captivated with its charm as did the friendly spirit of the club which is second to none in its warmth. One large table in the dining room tells all about members who cannot pick and choose their neighbour and who invariably take pot luck with regard to getting a game. Not for them regular prearranged fours – and what a joy.

ROYAL TROON

After the demise of Prestwick and up until the advent of Turnberry, Troon carried the west of Scotland banner as a home for the Open Championship although, for some reason, it did not act as host between 1923 and 1950. In terms of character, it follows the middle ground, lacking the uplifting splendour of Turnberry and the old-fashioned traditional look of Prestwick, which people tend to love or hate.

Troon's best sandhills are at the far end of a links that has the 9th green at the furthest point, but the course has no lack of scenic beauty or the capacity to test modern professionals to the full. Changes made in the last thirty years have certainly kept it in the forefront.

One of the most major and significant alterations surrounded the 11th which used to be a drive and a pitch until it was straightened, lengthened and made into a par 5 along the stone railway wall which extends as far as the green and beyond. This was done in advance of the 1962 Open Championship to introduce an intimidating element, the sort of hole to play on the mind long

before it was reached. As such, it has been most successful, but nobody told Arnold Palmer. Characteristically, his policy at that time was all-out attack and he saw no reason to revise it just because of the odd danger. Rather the opposite. As he approached the turn, the smart spectator would make for the 11th in the same way that racegoers at the Grand National congregate at Becher's Brook. It was unquestionably worth the effort. In five rounds, four in the Open proper and one in the qualifying, Palmer had three birdies, an eagle and a par – the latter when his best second shot of all just overshot the green and he failed to get down in two. Day after day, he ripped into a 1- or 2-iron after first taking the daring option on a drive lined by gorse. It was this hole on the last day which cost the ever-watchful Jack Nicklaus 10.

Troon (bestowed the prefix Royal for its centenary in 1978) has a mixture of feature, from bunkers, rough and sandy hills to the relentless severity of a finish that has dented the hopes of many at the close of a championship. By contrast,

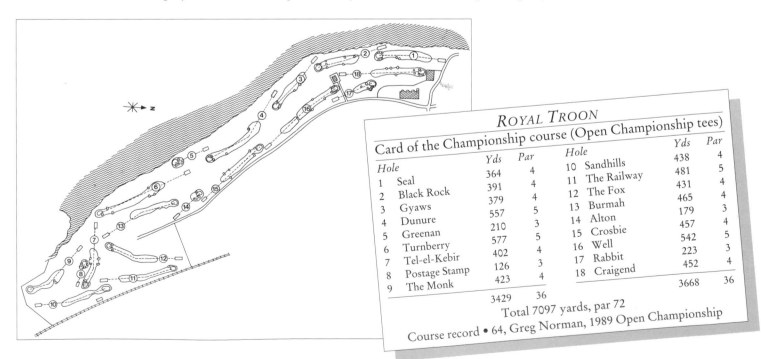

ROYAL TROON

Card of the Championship course (Open Championship tees)

Hole		Yds	Par	Hole		Yds	Par
1	Seal	364	4	10	Sandhills	438	4
2	Black Rock	391	4	11	The Railway	481	5
3	Gyaws	379	4	12	The Fox	431	4
4	Dunure	557	5	13	Burmah	465	4
5	Greenan	210	3	14	Alton	179	3
6	Turnberry	577	5	15	Crosbie	457	4
7	Tel-el-Kebir	402	4	16	Well	542	5
8	Postage Stamp	126	3	17	Rabbit	223	3
9	The Monk	423	4	18	Craigend	452	4
		3429	36			3668	36

Total 7097 yards, par 72

Course record • 64, Greg Norman, 1989 Open Championship

the start is relatively untaxing as regards length although Palmer found birdies hard to come by on the first three holes during his runaway victory in 1962. Paradoxically, he made hay on the way home.

The first three holes, indeed the first six, follow the line of the shore, the view from the 1st tee revealing the peaks of Arran, the Heads of Ayr, a distant Ailsa Craig and, looking northwards, a narrowing Firth of Clyde as it converges on Greenock, Gourock and Glasgow. None of the first three holes is more than 391 yards but two par 5s in the next three step up the tempo and are sandwiched by a fine short hole which, when played against the wind to the tightest pin position, demands a long iron to drop over a dominant bunker onto a small landing area. Both 4th and 6th greens have undergone 'surgery' in the last thirty years, the 4th minor, the 6th major. The 6th, the longest hole in British championship golf, is a shade harder with a new green closer to the dunes but it is the more rugged, middle part of Troon, the 7th to the 13th, which has particular appeal and merit.

The 7th, cutting inland, is a gentle dogleg to the right, the drive having to pierce the elbow between bunkers and the second mount a small ridge to the green. Then comes Troon's most celebrated hole, the Postage Stamp, so named for its meagre yardage and tiny green surrounded by bunkers and miniature dunes. In an age when so many short holes are depressingly long, it remains a symbol of defiance, its most recent triumph being to trip up Greg Norman in his final round of 64 in the 1989 Open. The only stroke dropped by one of golf's mightiest men was on easily the shortest hole of all. In the previous Open in 1973, Gene Sarazen, making a sentimental return after half a century, holed-in-one with a 5-iron, but, in 1950, it witnessed a different act of drama. Having declared his ball unplayable in a bunker, Roberto de Vicenzo hit a second ball from the tee to within two feet of the flag, as he could then, without penalty, and obtained his 3.

Until the 9th was changed for reasons of crowd control, the second shot used to be over a high hill to an unseen green in a slight dell but, after two or three attempts at a revision, its new position to

A potential card-wrecker, the lengthened and straightened 11th presents a sea of gorse, heather and rough. The out-of-bounds running alongside the railway line preys constantly on the mind.

In the lee of a large dune, the long and narrow 6th green is the ultimate target on the longest hole on the Open Championship rota.

Left Do not be misled by the tranquillity of the scene. The Postage Stamp is treacherous in any conditions. The tee shot can vary from a wedge to a wood, the green is both narrow and hard to hold, and five deep bunkers are ready to catch anything off-line or short.

the right is now visible provided the drive is aimed left and is skilful enough to avoid two bunkers. By gouging out part of another big hill, part of the 10th fairway is now visible from a tee that cowers under the final approach of noisy planes to Prestwick Airport. It requires a brave drive to the correct spot to counter some attractive slopes, and a long second must not waver if it is to hold a shelf-like green with a nasty drop to the right.

The 11th has been well documented but relief at averting disaster can be shortlived as both 12th and 13th are testing 4s, the 12th through a line of gorse and the 13th, with its green against the sky-line, favouring a drive down the left.

After a short 14th hole whose green is encir-cled by bunkers, the fairway at the 15th rises fractionally although not always sufficiently to see a green in a hollow. The same brook that adds menace at the 3rd reappears to stiffen the par-5 16th, the long drivers sometimes having to play short of it and then think twice about trying to get home in two. More often, discretion is the better part of valour as bunkers restrict the entrance and approach.

Hotel guests in the Highland Marine get a grandstand view of the 17th, a long short hole to a plateau green, but in length, character and dif-

ficulty, the 18th has much in common with Royal Lytham's, not least the fact that an overzealous second shot can break a window in the club-house. All the 18th's snares and good points were graphically illustrated in the final act of the 1989 Open and its play-off in which Mark Calcavecchia's triumph was outweighed by the disappointments of Greg Norman and Wayne Grady.

However, my abiding memory of Troon con-cerns the less glittering episode of a match I once played against Glasgow University and the story of my caddie, a former Ayrshire miner, a man of few words with little praise or encouragement in his vocabulary. My play for the first four holes was hardly deserving of either, the main feature being the fact that nearly every shot seemed to call for a 3-iron, the shaft of which had been bent by a previous misdeed. I had avoided using the damaged club but on the 5th tee the caddie was adamant that only a 3-iron would do. With no alternative therefore, I hit the 3-iron three or four yards behind the stick and, handing the club back to the caddie, thought that, at last, I might extract a smile or a compliment.

I received neither, merely the gruff aside, 'It's a pity a few more of your shafts aren't bent, Sir.'

WESTERN GAILES

Hole		Yds	Par	Hole		Yds	Par
1	Station	309	4	10	Ailsa	348	4
2	Railway	434	4	11	Plateau	445	4
3	Arran	390	4	12	Dyke	436	4
4	Irvine	400	4	13	Barassie	141	3
5	Bunker's Hill	453	4	14	Whins	562	5
6	Lappock	506	5	15	Heather	194	3
7	Sea	196	3	16	Camp	404	4
8	Burn	365	4	17	Ridge	443	4
9	Halfway	336	4	18	Home	377	4
		3389	36			3350	35

WESTERN GAILES
Card of the course (championship tees)

Total 6739 yards, par 71
Course record • 65, Bernard Gallacher, 1989

There was just enough room for Western Gailes to be fitted in between the railway and the sea, a fact that accounts for both being very much in play as major features.

The line of dunes running down the right from the 5th to the 12th is the part traditionalists love. It teases and torments in a manner no inland course could ever do and Western Gailes's place among the noble links is undoubted. In the great galaxy of the Ayrshire courses, it shines as brightly as its more famed neighbours. None can match the historical connections of Prestwick, the scenic splendour of Turnberry or the royal patronage of Troon. All have their advocates, but there are those who like Western Gailes best of the four and their allegiance is perfectly understandable.

Certainly, its setting is imposing in its own right and it is unique among seaside courses that are no more than two holes wide in having its clubhouse in a more or less central position. The arrangement of seven holes to the north and 11 to the south offers variety that is lacking on those going straight out and back, important when the wind direction is constant.

Western Gailes is ostensibly a private club although it has been in demand for big events and its praises have been sung by a variety of com-

petitors – including women, in spite of there being no lady members and no ladies' tees. It was something of a surprise therefore when the Curtis Cup was held there in 1972, but it was a great success, as was the PGA Championship of 1964 and several Scottish championships.

Western's defences are largely natural but a significant element in the difficulties it poses is the imaginative design of the greens which, to some extent, counteracts the relative shortness of the course by modern standards. Approaches to the pins are not solely a matter of picking a club and firing them in. They demand careful planning, a deal of versatility and a flair for improvization.

The first two greens set the tone. On the 1st, a modest opener, a sharp rise in fairway level sees a change to eccentric undulations that influence the choice of a low or high pitch, while long second shots to the 2nd have to contend with an appreciable drop onto the green. A new road has led to alterations to the 3rd and 4th although the 4th green remains a raised, angled, sloping target with a tight entrance round 'spectacle' bunkers.

Now begins the coastal stretch, the 5th, the longest of the 4s, having an even narrower entrance to the green and the 6th, the first of only two par 5s, being mighty hard to hit in two. The second part of the 6th has far more life and inter-

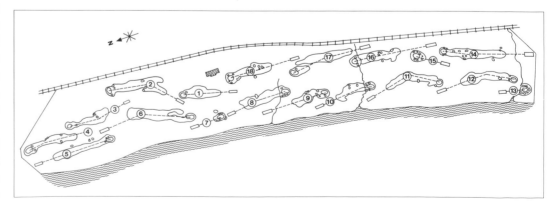

30

The short 7th depicts the attractive character of Western Gailes.

est than the drive, some characteristic sandhills and an attractive green in a dell being vintage seaside. So, too, is the short 7th which is dominated by dunes and has a tee with resplendent views of the Heads of Ayr, the peaks of Arran and the Firth of Clyde.

The next three holes are medium-length 4s, but the second to the 8th has to clear a burn in front of a sharply rising green and that at the 9th requires a spot-on approach to a hidden target. Both these holes and the three which start the inward half offer splendid drives but the feature of the 11th, Plateau, is a hog's-back green. On the 12th, a long

shallow valley channels the second shots – usually wood or long iron. Then follows a short hole against a background of gorse with seven bunkers encircling the green.

After that, it is home along the railway, the 14th, a dangerous hole, having a back tee just across the line from Barassie and three bunkers on the right near the green to taunt those who hit a good drive. A horseshoe-shaped bend in the burn defends the 16th green, a heather ridge shields a sight of the green on the 17th and three more bunkers on the 18th have to be avoided with the drive if a finishing 4 is to become a reality.

MACHRIHANISH

One of the greatest recommendations for any course is the light that comes into people's eyes and the infectious enthusiasm released at the mention of its name. With Machrihanish, I have known several devotees. One was a man not noted for excitement or overstatement but Machrihanish undoubtedly turned Dr Jekyll into Mr Hyde.

Part of its joy is its remoteness, a long road journey from Glasgow being necessary to probe the narrow strip of Arygll and locate the dot on the map near Campbeltown, a name once more familiar to distillers than golfers. For all the adage about 'better to travel hopefully', Machrihanish is a fine point of arrival. It also has, somewhat strange to tell, one of the longest runways in Europe and Glasgow Airport is only about 25 minutes flying time even in the square-shaped planes more used to landing on a pocket handkerchief.

On the return your neighbour is quite likely to be a box of kippers, but a glimpse from the air is a reminder of the splendour left behind. It is a course where the senses reel on a 1st tee that demands a daring drive, cutting off as much as you dare of a huge sweep of sandy bay. There is the stirring thought, too, that the next land to the west is Long Island although more practical information is given by the notice to non-golfers which reads, 'Danger, first tee above, please move farther along the beach'. In a less golfing conscious country than Scotland, the game might not be seen to have precedence.

Having negotiated Machrihanish Water and the shot over the crest to the 2nd green shaped like a saucer, the real duneland heart is penetrated. Every hole has an inviting look, the 3rd against the backcloth of the sea, the 4th, Jura, an intriguing short, short hole, and the 5th a sharp dogleg to the left. Good accurate driving is amply rewarded, partic-

ularly over a prominent ridge on the 6th and at the 8th, lined by hummocks and bents. There is a shallow crater to carry as well, a relatively simple task compared to the second over a high sandhill at the 7th, the hardest hole going out.

Just when the feeling emerges that everything is untouched by the centuries, the drive at the 9th comes alongside the airport, but even that has a welcome touch of informality. There are no blaring announcements, no mix-ups with the baggage, no bar and no interminable queues to check-in. The pilot is often glad of a chat and you can inspect the local lobsters bound for fashionable restaurants.

Right Machrihanish's spectacular opening hole, a legacy of Old Tom Morris. The direct line involves a carry of some 200 yards across the beach, which is in bounds. When the tide is in, the less adventurous would do well to give it a wide berth.

Bottom right The 16th, the second of consecutive par 3s, played towards the village and the distinctive Ugadale Hotel.

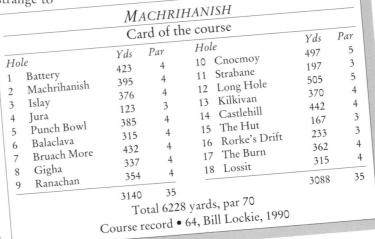

MACHRIHANISH
Card of the course

Hole		Yds	Par	Hole		Yds	Par
1	Battery	423	4	10	Cnocmoy	497	5
2	Machrihanish	395	4	11	Strabane	197	3
3	Islay	376	4	12	Long Hole	505	5
4	Jura	123	3	13	Kilkivan	370	4
5	Punch Bowl	385	4	14	Castlehill	442	4
6	Balaclava	315	4	15	The Hut	167	3
7	Bruach More	432	4	16	Rorke's Drift	233	3
8	Gigha	337	4	17	The Burn	362	4
9	Ranachan	354	4	18	Lossit	315	4
		3140	35			3088	35

Total 6228 yards, par 70

Course record • 64, Bill Lockie, 1990

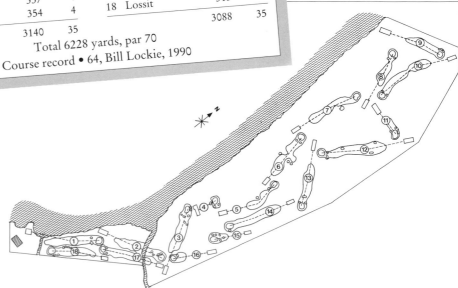

That digression over, the golf resumes with the first of two par 5s in three holes, the second short hole sandwiched in between presenting a difficult green to hit. The same applics at the 13th. All the time the pattern is changing, a move to the more inland character of the last few holes. The main talking-point is supplied by the 15th and 16th, consecutive short holes, if you can call the 16th (233 yards) short. It is a pattern shared, amongst many, with Cypress Point, Pulborough, Stoneham, Ballybunion and Royal Eastbourne. The theory of successive 3s to bolster the score is one thing, achievement quite another. Nor does the 17th offer unlimited hope. There is out-of-bounds along the left of a narrow fairway and not even a short par 4 to finish offers much comfort.

Competitors in the 1990 Scottish Ladies' Championship had no doubt heard a lot about Machrihanish yet wondered what to expect. Seeing is believing – it is a course that is living testimony to the wonders of nature.

MACHRIE

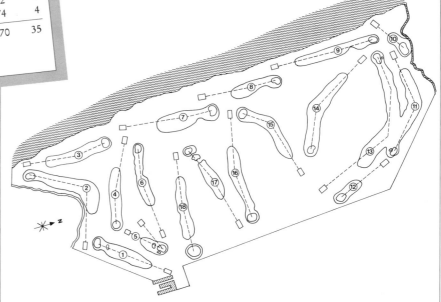

Hole		Yds	Par	Hole		Yds	Par
1	Anavon	308	4	10	Machrie Burn	156	3
2	Kintra	508	5	11	The Skor	357	4
3	Achnamara	319	4	12	New Mount Zion	174	3
4	Grannag	390	4	13	Lochindaal	488	5
5	Laird's Ain	163	3	14	Heather Hole	423	4
6	Lag	344	4	15	Willie's Fancy	335	4
7	Scot's Maiden	395	4	16	Druim	411	4
8	Manipur	337	4	17	Ifrinn	352	4
9	Glenegadale	392	4	18	Machrie	374	4
		3156	36			3070	35

MACHRIE
Card of the course

Total 6226 yards, par 71

Course record • 66, Iain Middleton (A), 1983

Building a golf course a hundred years ago on a remote island had to be a question of allowing nature to take the guiding hand. Machrie and Willie Campbell, its architect, were denied even some of the more primitive machinery that existed on the mainland but it was none the worse for that. It turned into a links with all the authentic elements – tumbling fairways, billowy dunes, punchbowl greens, a setting that can be wild and desolate yet an enchanting place to play. The locals, as it were, took it as they found it.

There is something romantic about island golf, especially on an island so full of character as Islay. It is a place of freedom and solitude. Sporting interests from shooting to deer stalking convey the scenic contrasts, but miles of golden sand along Laggan Bay provide the perfect framework to the golf. For years, the land beyond the 1st green was part of a layout that included a famous hole named Mount Zion, an area not for sale when new owners wanted to buy a full 18 holes. New boundaries were erected and new land taken in to the north where a small river runs into the sea. It served to make Machrie more complete, more

modern and more challenging. This fresh face of Machrie begins with the par-5 2nd which doglegs sharply to follow the path of a fast-flowing stream that later forms one flank of a tight entrance to the green.

Then follows a string of holes that exploit and enjoy the natural contours, none overlong but none straightforward in a golfing sense. The best of them is the 6th, a drive down the left opening up a sight of the green in a beautiful dell. The course makes for the turn hard by the shore, the 9th green at the furthest point from the hotel and clubhouse. All the while, high tees enhance the views.

For a hole of sheer, simple, unspoiled beauty, nothing could better the short 10th, the bold option on the tee being a direct line across a sandy inlet with the Machrie Burn plaguing the left and white irises the right. Then it is off into the more inland heart with views of lonely peat moor and mountain, the golf increasing as a test with the gently curving par-4 11th, a demanding long short hole and a par 5, the 13th, swinging left to an amphitheatre green. It is a stretch that, in quiet mood, finds golfers gloriously alone but, before the finish, there is a return to the traditional linksland of hummocky fairways and uneven stances and lies.

There is also a fine hotel with a variety of accommodation available, a little airport just down the road and the town of Bowmore and its distillery a few minutes further on. In days gone by, access to Islay involved a short sea crossing. Although an efficient ferry service still operates, the most convenient journey is by means of the appropriately named Islander aircraft which supplies an excellent geography lesson on its way from Glasgow.

There are few better places to enjoy holiday golf than Machrie. The course is in the finest tradition of seaside links, while its remote setting and sense of unhurried calm commands an affection both genuine and lasting.

CHAPTER TWO

HIGHLANDS

The thousands of visitors who head each year for the Highlands of Scotland do so for a variety of reasons. There are salmon to be caught, grouse to be shot and deer to be stalked. There is the splendour of hill walking and mountain climbing; and, in winter, skiing or skating.

The more sedentary pleasure is the motorized discovery of the sights, travel made so much easier in recent years by improvement in the roads, but the north-east coast of Scotland is as rich as any other region of Britain in the golfing treats on offer and many are drawn irrevocably by them. For those who plan their golf as an escape, the links here are particularly appealing. Scenically, they are a match for the much photographed parts of Scotland's heartland, the rugged dunes and wild seascapes – often framed by mountains – serving as reminders that the game had its beginnings in such settings.

In speaking of the Highlands for golf, it is important to emphasize that the focus is on the north-east. Scouring the west coast north of Oban, the map shows an almost barren pattern where good courses are concerned. Although the land is more suited to other pursuits, the main reason is a lack of population to bolster the demand. It only needs a relatively small town in Scotland for a demand for golf to be generated – amply explaining why the north-east claims a course every few miles along the coast.

Travelling north from Aberdeen, there is Royal

Aberdeen and Murcar, rubbing shoulders with each other, two mighty links, and another in Cruden Bay where students of architecture call to pay homage. Inland, courses are also thick on the ground but the coastal chain continues with Aberdeen's King's Links, Peterhead and Fraserburgh; heading west towards the Moray Firth, the list multiplies.

Moray and Nairn may constitute the pick but Buckpool (Buckie), Spey Bay, Cullen, Royal Tarlair and Hopeman are all part of a varied tapestry that makes British golf the envy of the world. Fortrose & Rosemarkie, redesigned by James Braid, is the first of the seaside courses north of Inverness, the start of another romantic journey in which Dornoch, Golspie and Brora represent the rainbow's end. However, even then, there are half a dozen other courses for those bound for John O'Groats – a geographical target rather than a golfing one.

Late spring and early autumn are the best times for golf, when the colours are at their best and the roads a little less crowded. Overseas visitors are frequently amazed that there are virtually no restrictions about who may play and when, and by the sight of locals in high summer setting out on a round as late as eight o'clock in the evening.

It is heaven for golfing insomniacs, the twilight never really giving way to nightfall and many clubs organizing midnight competitions. The Scots are also justifiably renowned for not wast-

For students of golf course architecture, north-east Scotland is required visiting. Royal Dornoch, characterized by its raised greens (such as on the renowned 14th, Foxy, left), is the undoubted jewel in the crown, while Cruden Bay scores heavily for sheer fun and variety. Its narrow 14th green sited in a dell and approached blind from the right is a welcome reminder of byegone days.

ing time on the course and expect others to follow suit. This means that, unlike other parts of the world, it is perfectly possible to play two rounds in a day and, for the hale and hearty, three.

One thing is certain: exploring the whole region takes several visits and should not be attempted in less if a real study is to be made. Different conditions are necessary to appreciate a course to the full and, though it is not unknown for Scotland to sample three seasons in one day, there can be many surprises in store. It is true that, when Dornoch housed the Amateur Championship in 1985, snow flurries greeted the first week of June. On the other hand, it is also susceptible to the benign influence of the Gulf Stream.

Dornoch's fame has spread to America largely through the name of Donald Ross, who left Scotland at the end of the last century and designed so many marvellous courses in the New World. Curious to see what it was that inspired his work, a pilgrimage to Dornoch is regarded as an essential part of any respectable American package tour. Nevertheless, a day should also be found for a game at Golspie and at Brora.

Concentration on Dornoch has detracted perhaps from the merits of the north-east's other gems – and gems they are. Nairn and Moray are

a must and don't be in too much of a hurry to head for Aberdeen. Spey Bay once afforded a sane refuge for me when stationed at an Army Cadet Force camp at Fochabers and is the authentic thing – if not quite as long as some of its distinguished neighbours. Royal Tarlair has some spectacular holes which are more clifftop and meadowy than true links but Cruden Bay, Murcar (excluded from these pages but not to be missed) and Royal Aberdeen fit the category perfectly.

Royal Aberdeen – or Balgownie, as the course is more shortly known – is ranked as the sixth oldest in the world, an entry in the Aberdeen Town Council register dated 1598 protesting against 'playirs on the links during the time of sermones'. It may have been the first official note of displeasure recorded about Sunday golf but Royal Aberdeen has played host to several Scottish Amateur Championships, two British Boys' Championships and the Scottish Professional Championship.

Cruden Bay's reputation is based more on its holiday appeal but the remoteness of the region, while making it less likely to be chosen as a home for championships, is undoubtedly its trump card. There is no better place for top-class golf in beautiful surroundings with variety and solitude thrown in.

ROYAL DORNOCH

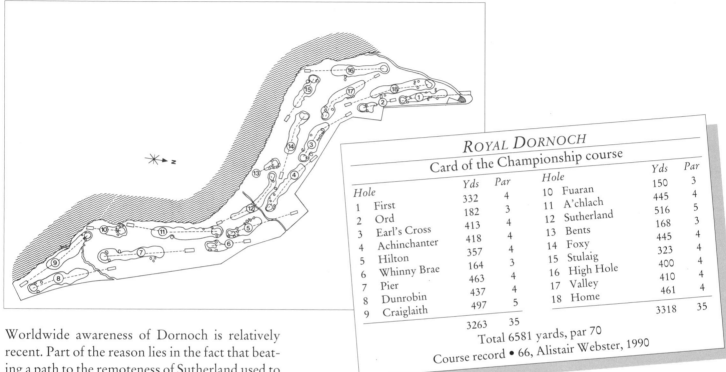

Hole		Yds	Par	Hole		Yds	Par
1	First	332	4	10	Fuaran	150	3
2	Ord	182	3	11	A'chlach	445	4
3	Earl's Cross	413	4	12	Sutherland	516	5
4	Achinchanter	418	4	13	Bents	168	3
5	Hilton	357	4	14	Foxy	445	4
6	Whinny Brae	164	3	15	Stulaig	323	4
7	Pier	463	4	16	High Hole	400	4
8	Dunrobin	437	4	17	Valley	410	4
9	Craiglaith	497	5	18	Home	461	4
		3263	35			3318	35

ROYAL DORNOCH
Card of the Championship course

Total 6581 yards, par 70

Course record • 66, Alistair Webster, 1990

Worldwide awareness of Dornoch is relatively recent. Part of the reason lies in the fact that beating a path to the remoteness of Sutherland used to be very much more arduous than it is today, but there was also a strong desire among those familiar with Dornoch's charms to keep its secrets to themselves. There is no surer way of incurring an invasion of the peace than to tell everyone what they are missing.

Locals have never needed any convincing of its greatness. For centuries, they have been sworn disciples of the gospel now preached far and wide and, in truth, always treated tales about it being so far off the beaten track with more than a grain of salt. As the course helped develop the celebrated talents of Roger and Joyce Wethered, when on holiday from the south, Royal Dornoch has been not so much discovered as rediscovered.

Nevertheless, there has been an enormous boost to its popularity in the last three decades, stemming, in fact, from the day in 1963 when Dick Tufts, captain of the United States Walker Cup team at Turnberry, insisted that one or two of his team undertake the long journey north. Billy Joe

Patton, than whom there is no greater enthusiast, was ecstatic about what he experienced and was persuasive enough to make me see for myself.

More than most Americans, Patton's game was wonderfully suited to seaside links but it must be admitted that Tufts was prejudiced in his recommendation in the first instance. When Donald Ross, son of a Dornoch stonemason, emigrated to Boston in 1898, it was Tufts' father, James, who appointed Ross professional at his new course in Pinehurst, North Carolina. What is more, Tufts encouraged his blossoming as a golf course architect and commissioned him to design Pinehurst No 2, the course by which Ross is perhaps best known and which is undoubtedly one of the finest in the world. After that, as golf spread through America like a prairie fire, Ross designed hundreds of courses but was always faithful in maintaining the importance that his upbringing at Dornoch had had in influencing his work and

helping him distinguish between architectural right and wrong.

Since 1963, a steady stream of admirers of Ross as well as new generations of architects have travelled to Dornoch to worship at the shrine. In addition, Tom Watson, Ben Crenshaw and Greg Norman have taken time off from their preparations for the Open Championship to play a round, taking advantage of the private airstrip by the shores of Dornoch Firth to alleviate the problem of getting there.

All this heavily publicized travel had a dramatic effect. Suddenly all roads, metaphorically speaking at any rate, led to Dornoch. In fact, journeys were considerably aided by the improved road system north of Perth and by the bridge across the Cromarty Firth. A new bridge across the Dornoch Firth is now of further assistance.

More significant recognition came with the staging of the 1980 Home International matches and the 1985 Amateur Championship. This broadened its role from host to exclusively Scottish events and reinforced its standing in the opinion polls to which magazines resort more and more. For all the various readerships that they serve, the message was the same. Dornoch occu-

pied a firm place in the top 10 of courses in the British Isles; and, in spite of being the most northerly first-class course in the world – some 58 degrees north of the equator – its enormous popularity has not hampered its condition, although rabbits added to the greenkeeping problems for a while.

Dornoch, with a cathedral dating back 750 years, has long centred around the game of golf. The two courses lie just beyond the main square and remarkably little has changed since first mention was made of golf in 1616. Only St Andrews and Leith preceded it as a golfing nursery but it is puzzling that no club was formed at Dornoch until 1877. Thirty-two years later, several of its members distinguished themselves in the Amateur Championship at Muirfield. Tom Grant, a baker, defeated John Ball; W. Henderson defeated the great American, Jerome Travers, and John Sutherland, Dornoch secretary for more than 50 years, beat Harold Hilton. Obviously relations were good and Hilton and Ball, duly impressed, visited Dornoch later in the summer. The crusade had begun.

A good deal of remodelling followed the initial design of Old Tom Morris, under whom Donald

Ross served an apprenticeship. There was upheaval during the Second World War but the present championship course is a supreme example of a modern links in which nothing is hidden. There are no blind shots, reward lying in the basic arts of the game, punishment in the betrayal of them.

Dornoch has few eccentricities as Herbert Warren Wind hinted in a comprehensive article in the *New Yorker* magazine in 1964 entitled 'North to the Links of Dornoch'. More than any other publicity, it put Dornoch on the map and hastened the arrival of those anxious to put it to their own test. Wind is rare amongst Americans in his belief in seaside links and in extolling their virtues.

Dornoch is a course that is essentially natural, although the impression is not gained by looking out of the clubhouse. There are more variations of level than on most links and this enhances the feeling of being away from it all. While on some other links the sea is never seen, its presence at Dornoch

is readily apparent even if neither beach nor sea comes into play.

The 1st and 2nd are forerunners of what lies ahead rather than memorable holes although the raised green at the short 2nd is a good one to hit and a bad one to miss. However, as you leave the 3rd tee, having driven to a narrow shelf of fairway below, the course unfolds in all its splendour. On the left runs a vast bank of gorse that dominates the setting of the next few holes which comprises a sterling sequence.

Correct aim on the 4th is on the giant statue of the Duke of Sutherland on the distant hill above Golspie and on the 5th it must thread its way down a shallow valley. There is a demanding second shot on the 4th from a humped-back fairway to an extensive plateau green surrounded by a deep hollow; and at the 5th, a slightly shorter shot must hold a green that is pulpit shaped. The 4th is probably Dornoch's finest hole, one rated only just outside

The short 10th which, along with the 9th, makes one most aware of the sea. It may be of modest length on the card but guardian bunkers and a two-tiered green make it a difficult target, particularly into the face of the prevailing wind.

Long drives may carry over the steep ridge that is such a feature of the 17th fairway but the best view of the green is from the high ground.

their best 18 by H.N. Wethered and Tom Simpson.

Because Dornoch's greens are more raised than many, it makes them appear smaller than they really are. They are typical, in fact, of the plateau greens beloved of Donald Ross. The pitch-and-run approach, so characteristic of links golf, is less effective at Dornoch, the raised greens demanding the well struck and well judged pitch that often has to be made to stop on a downslope. It is a skill that serves a golfer in good stead anywhere but it is one of the secrets to conquering Dornoch. Another is the ability to control the ball in the wind from lies and stances that are far from flat.

The 6th is the second of a noteworthy cluster of short holes, a mid-iron to a green, bunkered left and on the approach, blending so well into the hill that it is hard to believe man had a hand in its creation. The 463-yard 7th and the drive at the 8th runs atop an elevated ridge but the second shot to the 8th plunges down to a green near Embo Point.

The next few holes turn to follow the left-hand curve of the bay. The 11th is another long par 4 and the 12th the longer of the two par 5s; but the hole by which Dornoch is best known is the 14th, or Foxy, as it is appropriately named. It calls for players to adopt their strategies according to their strength, the drive running straight out from the tee before breaking sharply left and then right to a prominently raised green. One unusual feature of this double dogleg hole is that it has no bunkers.

For all the number of downhill strokes, the 16th involves a sharp climb, the only one. The 17th reverses direction with plunging fairway, the finish to the round taking the form of a 4 that, if not the best on the course, is pleasing to achieve.

Dornoch has no peers as a demanding and inspiring test but the abiding memory is the beauty of the setting, the hills of Sutherland, Tarbat Ness lighthouse standing guard on the Dornoch Firth and endless leagues of golden sands.

NAIRN

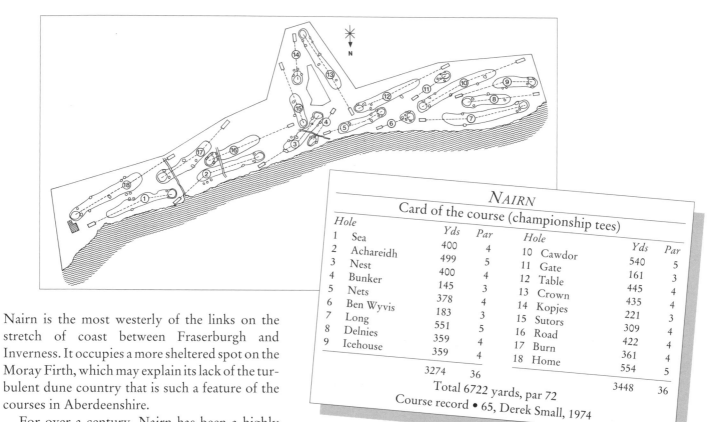

NAIRN Card of the course (championship tees)						
Hole		Yds	Par	Hole	Yds	Par
1	Sea	400	4	10 Cawdor	540	5
2	Achareidh	499	5	11 Gate	161	3
3	Nest	400	4	12 Table	445	4
4	Bunker	145	3	13 Crown	435	4
5	Nets	378	4	14 Kopjes	221	3
6	Ben Wyvis	183	3	15 Sutors	309	4
7	Long	551	5	16 Road	422	4
8	Delnies	359	4	17 Burn	361	4
9	Icehouse	359	4	18 Home	554	5
		3274	36		3448	36

Total 6722 yards, par 72
Course record • 65, Derek Small, 1974

Nairn is the most westerly of the links on the stretch of coast between Fraserburgh and Inverness. It occupies a more sheltered spot on the Moray Firth, which may explain its lack of the turbulent dune country that is such a feature of the courses in Aberdeenshire.

For over a century, Nairn has been a highly regarded course and a highly fashionable holiday resort known as 'the Brighton of the North'. Its fame has been helped by an association lasting almost 70 years with Lord Whitelaw who, in winning the Junior Championship of 1933 with a round of 73, set a record that was not bettered for more than 50 years. In his foreword to the centenary history of the club, he emphasizes how it is possible to slice into the sea at six of the first seven holes. This tendency of favouring the right may coincide with his political allegiance but it highlights the problems of the outward half which, for seven holes, follows the line of the beach.

On the 2nd and dogleg 3rd, a lateral burn is an added hazard. The 3rd breaks left sufficiently to leave the short 4th to be played in the opposite direction to a narrow green, the tee shot having to carry a large dune. Of the first three holes, the 3rd is by far the best on account of its interesting raised green, a central bunker on the approach and a large

Contrasting views of Nairn: on the one hand the holes along the coast, looking towards Inverness, and on the other the distinctive inland appearance with a heathland flavour.

bunker guarding the left of the putting surface. The drive at the 6th runs the greatest risk of finishing on the shore but gradually gorse begins to play an increasing hand, making it all the more important to hit the fairway.

On two holes coming home, the gorse reminds one more of Ganton but there is no doubting the links traditions. There is always sight and sound of the sea with the accompaniment of heather, gorse and the burns which come back into play on the 16th and 17th. Only on the 435-yard 13th and the 221-yard 14th are there any appreciable changes of level, the second to the 13th requiring an uphill approach to a two-tiered green and the 14th, in the opposite direction, needing the help of a downslope to bring the green in range for most golfers. The 13th, 14th and 15th are the only holes which do not run either west to east or east to west. The modest par-4 15th, to a green close to the 3rd fairway, runs on more or less the same lines as the 14th but the course then straightens out for home with three demanding finishing holes, more gorse flanking the 16th and, all the time, the fine new clubhouse, opened in 1990, drawing closer.

The course's appeal is strengthened by the nearness of the Firth, the ever-changing patterns of Black Isle and the splendour of the distant mountains that conjure thoughts of Dornoch. The call of the Highlands is unmistakable but the golfing joys of Nairn stand on their own and are exemplified best by the memory of Major David Blair, an elegant Scottish amateur, who developed his great skills on a links he loved. It is easy to understand why.

MORAY GOLF CLUB

My first awareness of Moray Golf Club and its delightful links was from the somewhat unlikely distant perch of an exposed hockey pitch at Gordonstoun School. As one with an eye for such things, it was pointed out as one of the landmarks in which there was obvious local pride although my chief memory was of the noise of the aircraft from RAF Lossiemouth which, even in 1955, created an alarming disturbance of the peace. In keeping with the traffic in and out of Leuchars which can detract from a round at St Andrews, it is a hazard one has learned to accept but it speaks volumes for the attraction of golf at Moray that it does little to dim the enjoyment. It is indestructible.

For more than a hundred years, Moray has served the needs of golfers and established a reputation that is recognized far and wide. It is a fame based on the true foundation of the classic links elements of glorious views and the unmistakable character of the firmness of a sandy 'carpet' underfoot.

Historically, there is the tale of Ramsay MacDonald being excluded from the club in 1915 on account of his pacifist views and of his refusal to re-join when he later became Prime Minister. There is also the proud claim of Meg Farquhar, a local lass, in becoming Britain's first lady professional at a time when Lossiemouth was a fashionable place for holidays. In that, it had much in common with Nairn, Dornoch and Cruden Bay.

The decision to build 16 holes at Stotfield was taken in 1889 and there the club has remained ever since. Within 12 months, the course had increased to 18 holes and in 1906 a new Ladies/Relief course of nine holes was added. At about the same time, changes were made to the original course which measured, according to the custom of the day, 3 miles 688 yards. John McConachie's marvellous history of the club mentions that the amalgamation of the existing 6th and 7th holes creating the present 3rd has, beside the green, a bunker referred to as 'Joyce Wethered's bunker'. In the absence of any explanation as to why, one must assume it is because it once caught one of her few shots that erred; a rarity, indeed.

Today's course enjoys a fairly gentle opening hole, inclining towards the shore, but from the 2nd the outward half heads inland amongst the heather and gorse, the holes changing direction more than on most links. The 3rd, 5th, 7th and 8th are stout par 4s, the 5th and 8th with a profusion of bunkers.

There is scenic contrast on the 11th and 12th, the 11th aiming at Covesea lighthouse, a resplen-

MORAY GOLF CLUB
Card of the Old course

Hole		Yds	Par	Hole		Yds	Par
1	Mt Lebanon	333	4	10	Tom Morris	314	4
2	Cup	493	5	11	Lighthouse	415	4
3	Table	400	4	12	Beacon	402	4
4	Coulart	203	3	13	St Gerardines	422	4
5	Kinneddar	419	4	14	Sea	417	4
6	Gordonstoun	141	3	15	Short	190	3
7	Ring	439	4	16	Road	359	4
8	Heather	460	4	17	Long	497	5
9	Ditch	316	4	18	Home	423	4
		3204	35			3439	36

Total 6643 yards, par 71

Course record • 66, Tony Minshall, 1981; David Huish, 1988; Frank Coutts, 1991

dent landmark, and the 12th, making an abrupt about-turn, setting its sights on the low outline of Lossiemouth. The 15th tee marks the beginning of a three-hole stretch along the shore although it is not such a daunting prospect as, say, the first few holes at Nairn.

The 15th, the last of only three short holes, is severely guarded by bunkers but Moray saves its best until last. The 423-yard 18th is as good a finishing hole as any. It is tightly bunkered down the left, the right side lined by out-of-bounds and a sloping bank. Positioning of the drive is impor-

tant but the raised green, nestling below the old stone clubhouse, can be elusive when a 4 is essential and there is the added worry that your efforts are in full view.

When Moray's New course, designed by (Sir) Henry Cotton, was opened in 1979, there was a good deal of relief that the 18th had been saved. Cotton's original plan was to sacrifice it to accommodate the New course but that would have been akin to levelling off the Valley of Sin or filling in the Barry Burn. Good sense happily prevailed.

One of golf's best finishing holes, as seen from in front of Moray's clubhouse.

CRUDEN BAY

Cruden Bay's most fashionable days were between the wars when there was a luxurious hotel, opened in 1899, built out of pink Peterhead granite, and a direct railway link with London – courtesy of the London and North Eastern and Great North of Scotland Railways. It marked a thriving era for the little village of Port Erroll with definite comparisons with Turnberry. The hotel was perched on a height but the 'palace in the sandhills', as it was known, never reopened after the Second World War. It was later sold for demolition although the present clubhouse now commands the same panoramic views.

As with Turnberry, there were doubts about the future of the golf club but mercifully the course was bought in 1950 for £2750 thereby saving one of the most authentic examples of true linksland and keeping Cruden Bay firmly on the map. The view from the simple clubhouse, though bettered elsewhere on the course, is stunning, serving to illustrate the remarkable phenomenon whereby a narrow strip of sandhills can be sandwiched between the sea and the more fertile, raised territory two or three hundred yards distant.

Cruden Bay has never earned full championship recognition although it might well have done but the pleasure it has given is incalculable. It offers the most exciting holiday golf with burns to cross, hills to carry and hidden dells to drop into. As befits a course approaching its centenary, some of the shots are blind but are none the worse for that. Some 'modernization' has occurred but the course is a reminder of bygone days, a study for golf course architects anxious to see what nature is really like. Pete Dye considers it, with Prestwick, to be his favourite in Scotland. Cruden Bay's greatest charm is its remote seclusion and the feeling that you have it to yourself. The course may be crowded but you would never know as the dunes cleverly hide one hole from another.

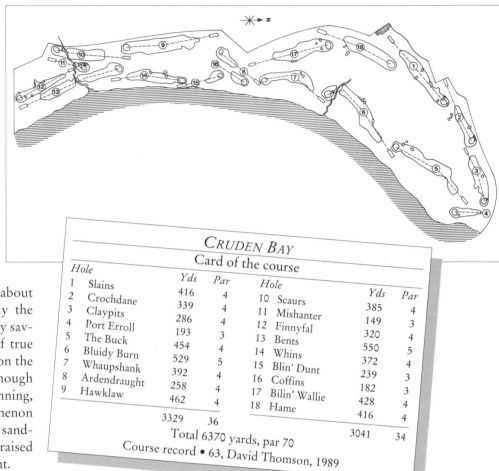

Hole		Yds	Par	Hole		Yds	Par
1	Slains	416	4	10	Scaurs	385	4
2	Crochdane	339	4	11	Mishanter	149	3
3	Claypits	286	4	12	Finnyfal	320	4
4	Port Erroll	193	3	13	Bents	550	5
5	The Buck	454	4	14	Whins	372	4
6	Bluidy Burn	529	5	15	Blin' Dunt	239	3
7	Whaupshank	392	4	16	Coffins	182	3
8	Ardendraught	258	4	17	Bilin' Wallie	428	4
9	Hawklaw	462	4	18	Hame	416	4
		3329	36			3041	34

CRUDEN BAY
Card of the course

Total 6370 yards, par 70
Course record • 63, David Thomson, 1989

Tom Simpson is the architect who masterminded Cruden Bay, many believing it to be his finest work. Simpson himself included the 1st, 8th and 18th among his selection of the best 18 holes in Britain and Ireland, the 1st calling for a well placed drive and a good second to an angled, well bunkered green. The more daring the drive close to the gorse on the right, the easier the second.

There is a huge plateau on the 2nd and a punchbowl green at the 3rd – a hole of 286 yards where the good players seek a birdie. Following this is a charming short hole across the valley with the inlet of a stream and a white bridge to embellish the scene before a marvellous view from the elevated 5th tee introduces us to a fairway running between

The first real hint of the dunes is provided by the setting of the 4th green. The tee shot, which involves quite a carry, is bordered on the left by the old fishing cottages of Port Erroll.

the highest dunes. The 6th, a par 5, demands a difficult pitch over a burn to a green guarded by a devilish bunker thereby making getting home in two a Herculean task. On the 7th, there is a narrow entrance to the green among the sandhills, a long iron having to be well flighted to reach its target, while the 8th, flanked by the highest hills, is a hole Simpson described as 'mischievous, subtle and provocative'. It has varied from a long par 3 to a short par 4 with a green made difficult to hit by the land falling away to the right.

Another panorama unfolds on the next two tees, the 9th compensating for its comparative plainness with its breathtaking position. It leads on to the lower land to which we descend from the 10th tee and to the shorter inward half, which, nevertheless, contains the longest hole, the 13th, with a burn crossing the fairway about halfway down and the green hidden by a large bank.

This is the peculiarly characteristic part of the course, the lovely 14th with the sea on the right, huge gorse bank to the left and a second over the

red and white post to a green in a dell. The narrowness of the course at this point dictates the nature of the play and the 15th, Blin' Dunt, which for those not accustomed to the Scottish tongue can be translated as blind shot, continues this wonderful stretch with a long short hole. Another short hole, more visible, follows at the 16th but the strength of the golf is that it keeps you on your toes with a variety of decisions to make and a series of shots to match if even modest success is to be claimed.

The course is a perpetual battle of wits but it is all unmistakably fun and, since golfers are inclined to take themselves and the game too seriously, that is a great compliment. Majestic is almost too weak a word to describe it all although Simpson's high ranking of the 18th might be considered a little overdone. However, with out-of-bounds on the left, a burn running across the fairway and a rumpled fairway culminating in a diagonal ridge in front of the green, it underlines the need for a sharp cunning and judgment.

ROYAL ABERDEEN

Royal Aberdeen, whose links at Balgownie consist of superbly rolling duneland, is ranked as the sixth-oldest club in the world. It started life in 1780 with the founding of the Society of Golfers at Aberdeen, fostering the local interest which was plentiful, and moved to its present site in 1888.

On the northern outskirts of the city, it is typical of the old type of links layout, running out to a distant point along a thin channel two holes wide. Much depends upon the strength and direction of the wind. Played against the wind, the 2nd, 3rd and 4th are particularly formidable following a downhill opening hole which heads straight out towards the North Sea. There are cross bunkers on the long par-3 3rd, while the name of the 4th, Valley, speaks for itself.

This is the prettiest stretch, with occasional gorse – as on the drive to the 4th – and frequent views of sea and coast from elevated tees but, for

ROYAL ABERDEEN
Card of Balgownie Links

Hole		Yds	Par	Hole		Yds	Par
1	First	409	4	10	Shelter	342	4
2	Pool	530	5	11	Short	166	3
3	Cottage	223	3	12	Plateau	383	4
4	Valley	423	4	13	Blind	375	4
5	Road	326	4	14	Dyke	390	4
6	Scotson	486	5	15	Well	341	4
7	Blackdog	375	4	16	Hill	389	4
8	Ridge	147	3	17	Pots	180	3
9	End	453	4	18	Home	434	4
		3372	36			3000	34

Total 6372 yards, par 70

Course record • 64, John Fought (A), 1971

all the 'out and back' design, there is a pleasant degree of variation. The fairways give the impression of playing along valleys between the dunes but a number of greens are sufficiently raised to make them stiff targets. The two-tier green at the 7th is a case in point.

Balgownie's 2nd hole runs along a valley between the dunes. With the wind against, its 530 yards can be hard going at the start of a round.

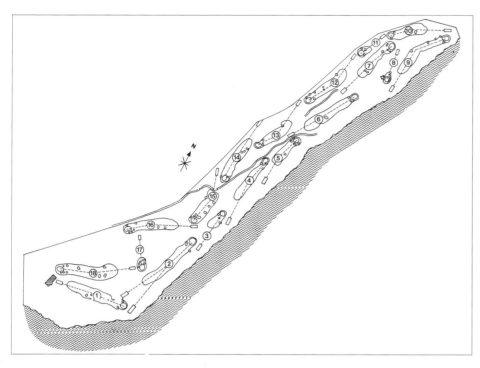

green on a rise that can only be hit by a shot precisely struck and perfectly shaped. It is here that the course rubs shoulders with its neighbour, Murcar, a group of visitors once believing it to be part of Balgownie and continuing before ending up at the wrong clubhouse. They should have turned back along the 10th over the crest and curving slightly left-handed at the start of the shorter inward half which, nevertheless, can be more difficult in the prevailing wind and because of the threat of out-of-bounds on the right of the 10th, 11th and 12th. The 11th has an unusually tiered green and the 13th, Blind, one in a hollow.

The lighthouse is the target from the 15th tee where the fairway remains obscured, the start of a tough finish in which a stream comes into play on the 15th and 16th. The 17th is another cracking short hole and then it is a walk through the gorse to a long, testing two-shotter to finish beside a clubhouse that surveys a glorious scene. Let the footnote be provided by Bernard Darwin who, in confessing on his first visit that Balgownie had remained a gap in his education for too long, described it as, 'much more than good golf, a noble links'.

The message at the short 8th is unambiguous; stray off line at your peril.

The short 8th, with its plethora of bunkers (10 in all) turns back towards the shore before the 9th completes the outward journey with the longest of the par 4s, a right-hand dogleg where the longer the drive the easier the second to a

CHAPTER THREE

EAST OF SCOTLAND

It may be possible on a fine day in high summer in the neighbourhood of Gullane to play one course before breakfast, two more before lunch and two or three between lunch and a late dinner. That is provided you get a clear run at them, which is doubtful in view of their popularity. In a week, you could only just scratch the surface of all the delights on offer in the east of Scotland and it would take years to claim any close familiarity. To know them all well demands a lifetime's study. But what a life.

At the exalted head of the list must come St Andrews, Muirfield and Carnoustie: the Home of Golf, the course most polls place top most often, and the one which, from the championship tees, is perhaps the hardest in Britain. They represent the scholarship questions, so to speak, but no symphony can be all crescendo. There must be passages of light relief and they are often preferable. The east of Scotland's support cast is second to none.

In terms of geographical convenience, the area can be divided, like Gaul, into three parts: East Lothian; the central region of Fife; and the land beyond the Tay that takes in Carnoustie, Monifieth and Panmure. Passage between the three is vastly easier now than it was 25 or 30 years ago before the days of the Forth and Tay road bridges. Dependence on ferries could upset calculations on how long to allow to meet starting times. The journey, for instance, from St Andrews to Muirfield used to take three or four hours but now it can reasonably be achieved in about an hour and a half with the help of the motorway north of the Forth Bridge and the bypass round Edinburgh which begins close to the airport.

The most celebrated, if sad, journey between North Berwick and St Andrews took place by boat. At the end of a foursomes challenge match in September 1875 between Old and Young Tom Morris of St Andrews and Willie and Mungo Park of Musselburgh, held at North Berwick, Young Tom was handed a telegram informing him that his young wife was dangerously ill. In the absence of trains, he chose to return to St Andrews by boat but, almost before he had left the harbour at North Berwick, a further message was received that his wife and their newborn child were dead. It was a tragic story made worse by the fact that Young Tom himself died on Christmas Day the same year – it is said of a broken heart.

North Berwick, which has much in common with St Andrews in that its courses begin and end almost in the middle of town, is one of the oldest clubs in East Lothian, the flavour of the golf being unmistakably full of fun and ingenuity. Some of the names of the holes, such as Redan and Perfection, are world famous and any serious student of the game should pay his profound respects to them.

Although the Honourable Company of Edinburgh Golfers dates from 1744, Muirfield,

their third home, is relatively modern. They moved there in 1892 to a chorus of comment, much of it unfriendly in the minds of the loyal lovers of Musselburgh whence they came. In spite of a friendly rivalry, it is possible to mention North Berwick, Gullane, Muirfield and Luffness in the same breath on account of their close proximity, Gullane and Muirfield lying on opposite sides of Gullane Hill which is one of golf's great landmarks.

The three courses at Gullane, in fact, rub shoulders with Luffness and share the same natural character which is the envy of the world and which developers try, and fail, to copy. There is no lovelier sight than that from the 7th tee on Gullane No 1 of the distant outline of Edinburgh, the wide reaches of the Firth of Forth and the hills of Fife on the opposite shore. Gullane is a town that eats and breathes golf and is certainly something of a spiritual home for me. Six years at school in Edinburgh gave a rich introduction to Luffness, Muirfield, Gullane and North Berwick and even after having completed the journey from Edinburgh hundreds of times, there is still a tingling sense of expectation on each new occasion that I make it.

North Berwick used to be the home of the Scottish Boys' Championship, held in April, and in 1953, further down the coast at Dunbar, the Royal and Ancient staged the British Boys'

Championship won by Alec Shepperson who, six years later, beat Tommy Aaron in his Walker Cup single at Muirfield. Dunbar is a fine course in its own right and, before taking leave of East Lothian, mention must be made of Kilspindie and Longniddry, but visitors to Edinburgh with only a few days to spare face the difficult decision of whether to head down to Gullane or venture across to Fife or beyond.

St Andrews has the Old, New, Eden and Jubilee with a fifth course, the Strathtyrum, opening in 1993. There is also the nine-hole Balgove course and new practice facilities which it has long lacked. Pilgrims at the holy shrine have much to assimilate but Fife is liberally sprinkled with other courses that are full of appeal. They run off the tongue freely and easily: Scotscraig, Crail, Leven, Lundin Links, Ladybank and Elie, many having served as qualifying settings for the Open Championship.

They are the peripheral jewels in the crown of Fife but Monifieth, Panmure, Montrose and Carnoustie enjoy easy access across the Tay bridge, one of the main arteries to the heart of Dundee, and Carnoustie is equally hallowed ground. Renowned as the place where Ben Hogan won his only Open on his only appearance, it is one of the famous golfing centres of Scotland, many of whose sons helped spread the game far and wide.

MONTROSE

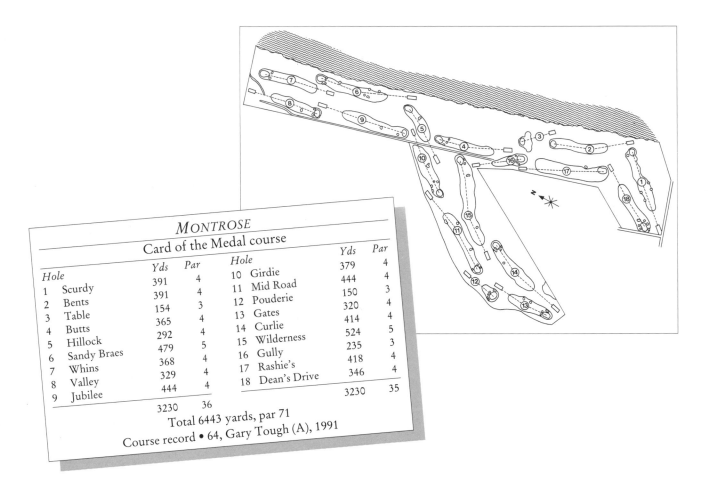

MONTROSE Card of the Medal course						
Hole		Yds	Par	Hole	Yds	Par
1	Scurdy	391	4	10 Girdie	379	4
2	Bents	391	4	11 Mid Road	444	4
3	Table	154	3	12 Pouderie	150	3
4	Butts	365	4	13 Gates	320	4
5	Hillock	292	4	14 Curlie	414	4
6	Sandy Braes	479	5	15 Wilderness	524	5
7	Whins	368	4	16 Gully	235	3
8	Valley	329	4	17 Rashie's	418	4
9	Jubilee	444	4	18 Dean's Drive	346	4
		3230	36		3230	35

Total 6443 yards, par 71

Course record • 64, Gary Tough (A), 1991

Montrose is a public links in the best Scottish tradition. In common with St Andrews and Carnoustie, three golf clubs enjoy the run of two courses under the administrative management of the Montrose Links Trust. The Medal course is the better of the two, the 1991 British Boys' Championship having been decided over an historical stretch of golfing country. It was an enjoyable and successful week.

Montrose is believed to be the fifth-oldest course in the world, situated just to the north of the ancient burgh which lies midway between Dundee and Aberdeen. As in many towns in the east of Scotland there is about Montrose an unmistakable air that golf is the focal point of life in the community with discussion of little else.

The Medal course follows the line of the mountainous dunes although there is a nice variation to the out-and-back theme. The shape of the layout is more that of a coathanger, with a central loop immediately after the turn venturing into a flat area, the holes making avenues through gorse.

There are three levels in all, but undoubtedly the most attractive is that in the vicinity of the dunes and there is an air of expectation as the 1st hole climbs gradually to the foot of the range. It is an appealing start with the 2nd enjoying all the typical seaside characteristics and the short 3rd, the only par 3 in the outward half, supplying a challenging shot across a huge, sandy hollow to a green that is wider than it is deep.

An exciting drive at the 4th, flanked on the right

Montrose's short 3rd, a vintage seaside hole set amongst the dunes. The temptation to overclub in order to avoid the deep chasm is countered by a green that is wider than it is deep.

by a long bank of gorse, drops down onto lower land which, nevertheless, has distinctive movement to it although not as accentuated as on the 5th. This is a short par 4 with a blind drive over a high ridge, the type of hole that fits in quite naturally on a seaside links. The green, guarded by knobbly mounds, is back on the higher ground, while the 6th and 7th occupy the heartland of the dunes. Par 5s at Montrose are limited to two, the better of them being the 6th which makes an appealing prospect from the tee, the fairway sticking rigidly to the path of the shore and the green visible from all parts.

A similar setting frames the 7th before the 8th – with another drop from the tee – signals the last of the vintage Montrose. There is nothing the mat-

ter with the final 10 holes; indeed, there are plenty of fine shots to be played and some may welcome the change, but there is nothing to match the special magic of golf in its classic setting even if Montrose's sandhills are so big that they hide a view of the sea.

The hook of the coathanger, as it were, follows the challenging 9th and includes greens with nicely revetted bunkers, the pleasant short 12th and the 15th, the longest hole on the course. The 16th, the last of the three short holes, joins up to form a thin artery with the 4th, the pattern on so many Scottish courses. The 17th is a tough par 4 and the 18th, if considerably gentler, concludes a round on a course which deserves recognition as a modern test as well as a monument to the past.

CARNOUSTIE

Carnoustie has been regrettably absent from the Open Championship rota since a young Tom Watson scored the first of his five victories there in 1975. This has nothing to do with its challenge as a test of golf. There are many who feel it has no peers, a course without a weakness. Its period in the wilderness relates purely to the speed with which the non-golfing requirements of the Open have grown, to the fact that its one big hotel has been lost and not replaced, and that access to the course by means of a low bridge under the railway is awkward to say the least. It is doubly sad because the Forth and Tay road bridges have made the major part of the approach march so much more straightforward.

Hope has not been abandoned that one day solutions to the problems will be found. Carnoustie looks as much to the future as it does to the past, but examination of its historical background reveals the immensity of the contributions of its sons to golf elsewhere in the world. It may have been its fame in this regard that gave rise to the comment that Carnoustie 'was a good place from which to emigrate'.

A high proportion of well over 300 Carnoustie men who became professionals headed for the United States. In its founding years, it is said that every state where the game was played had its title held by one of them. Certainly, they made their name as teachers, too. Stewart Maiden was famous as the man who helped Bobby Jones so greatly.

The best of the players were undoubtedly the Smith brothers, Willie, Alex and Macdonald. The eldest, Willie, won the US Open in 1899 at Baltimore, only the fifth time it was played, while Alex won twice, on the first occasion ending Willie Anderson's unique three-year run as champion.

For Macdonald, 18 years younger than Alex, there has always been the tag of the best player never to have won a championship. Before he was 20, he had tied for the US Open and lost a play-off to his brother, Alex; in the British Open between 1923 and 1934 he was second, third and

fourth twice each. In 1930, Grand Slam year, he was second to Jones in both Opens at Hoylake and Interlachen. His best chance came in 1925 when, needing a 78 to win, he took 82 in Prestwick's last Open, but equally disappointing must have been the final chance he had in 1931 in front of his old home crowd. The championship was won by Tommy Armour, another Scot who emigrated to America, but, in Carnoustie's first Open, Smith's involvement in a dramatic finish

CARNOUSTIE Card of the Championship course (championship tees)					
Hole	Yds	Par	Hole	Yds	Par
1 Cup	416	4	10 South America	452	4
2 Gulley	460	4	11 Dyke	358	4
3 Jockie's Burn	347	4	12 Southward Ho	475	4
4 Hillocks	434	4	13 Whins	168	3
5 Brae	393	4	14 Spectacles	488	5
6 Long	575	5	15 Lucky Slap	461	4
7 Plantation	397	4	16 Barry Burn	250	3
8 Short	183	3	17 Island	455	4
9 Railway	474	4	18 Home	486	5
	3679	36		3593	36

Total 7272 yards, par 72

Course record • 65, Jack Newton, 1975 Open Championship

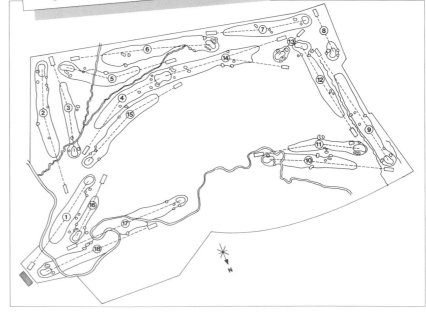

When the wind is blowing, there are few more demanding long holes than Carnoustie's 6th. Out-of-bounds down the left and fairway bunkers sited 200-220 yards from the medal tee threaten the drive, while Jockie's Burn snakes across from the right to dominate the second shot.

highlighted the worthiness of its elevation.

Carnoustie's five champions – Armour, Henry Cotton, Ben Hogan, Gary Player and Watson – confirm its ability to separate the men from the boys, one of the principal requirements of an Open, but its most celebrated moment was undoubtedly the triumph of Ben Hogan in 1953. Although he played so very few British courses, Carnoustie would have been the one many would have chosen to ensure that the greatest player of his generation won.

Carnoustie lacks the majestic beauty of Turnberry or Newcastle, County Down. However, a more plain, stern appearance sets the keynote for the golf which provides no let-up. Carnoustie conjures up an impression of burns, ditches and out-of-bounds, the latter perhaps lacking the scale of Hoylake but certainly enough to strike fear.

The 6th is the prime example, a boundary fence

running the full length on the hook side and a cluster of bunkers which a fine drive can reach. The drive poses the tantalizing question of whether to play short or to the side, the crucial rider to the second option being which side. As with all great holes, the advantage is to the side where the risk is greater. What is more, Jockie's Burn meanders in from the right to add substance to the second shot, the pitch that follows, for those who escape it, being relatively straightforward.

On the final day of Hogan's Open when two rounds were played, he suffered none of its torments. Morning and afternoon, he rifled two drives away past the right hand of the two bunkers, followed each with an unerring brassie and pitched up to make two birdies. Even for him, there was relief that an obvious danger had been averted although more menace lay ahead, particularly in the dreaded finish.

Not that Carnoustie's start is any push-over.

In the first round of the 1953 Open, Hogan needed a 2-iron to reach the 1st green off a characteristically impressive drive while the 2nd needs two Herculean hits if there is a touch of east in the wind. Braid's bunker dominates the drive. The next three holes are not of such formidable length but the pitch over the narrow stream to the 3rd green has to be cleverly judged, and positioning the drive is all important at the 5th. It was on this hole that Hogan, in his final round of 68, missed the green with a 5-iron out of a divot mark and then chipped in.

As on the Old Course at St Andrews, the first short hole is the 8th, the par out being 36 with the 6th the only par 5. The inward half begins with a hole named South America, a long 4 with the Barry Burn set a little way back from the green. Many interpretations have been put on how it derived its title, the true version apparently being that, in the days when so many from Carnoustie cherished ideas of the New World, a young man set out, no doubt after a few for the road, and got only as far as the spinney by the 10th before second thoughts, and the after-effects, got the better of him.

The 10th itself has got the better of a great many but the Barry Burn remains dormant thereafter until it returns to dominate at the 17th and 18th. The middle heartland of the course supplements the test admirably.

After the tightly trapped short 13th, the Spectacles beckons in the shape of a crested sand-hill into which two bunkers are set far enough back from the green to deceive even great players with yardage charts into misclubbing. In 1968, the

Carnoustie's finish is notorious. The 16th is a monster of a par 3 where it is all too easy to drop a shot. The typically Scottish bunker in the foreground is one of a pair that narrows the entrance to a long, undulating green which falls away on all sides. Often demanding a driver, it can be a fiendish hole.

hole decided the Open on the final day. With Jack Nicklaus breathing down his neck, Gary Player hit a glorious spoon up over the ridge to within two feet and went on to win by two strokes.

The 16th, which cost Macdonald Smith 6 in 1931, is the longest short hole on the championship rota, one made more awesome by a small entrance to a green on a shelf. The 16th ranks as part of Carnoustie's finish but it is the 17th and 18th that make the knees weak and the pulse beat like bongo drums.

There are many strategies to adopt at the 17th, all designed to keep the drive out of the burn that twists like a strand of spaghetti. This means a decision on the tee to suit the conditions, the ambitions, the state of play and the skill and power of the player. Even so, overhitting and over-exuberance can be a problem too. Control is paramount.

Having survived the 17th, the burn is again the central feature of the 18th, this time having to be carried twice and skirted down the left where out-of-bounds is an added line of defence. The drive has to be substantial, but the big decision is whether to play your second shot short of the burn in front of the green or to go for it.

It has been played in championships both as a par 4 and a par 5. In 1968 it measured 525 yards, Nicklaus carrying the burn in two, but in 1975 it was reduced to 448 yards. All the same, Watson's task was every bit as daunting, first in earning a place in a play-off with Jack Newton and then beating him in the play-off with a 71 to 72. Two days running on the 18th, the pressure on him, Watson's response was a 2-iron against Newton that won him the title and started him on a run of five victories in nine years.

In 1937, Cotton had no such worries but there could have been no more vivid drama than in 1931 as the Argentine, Jose Jurado, could have won if he had played the last two holes in 9 strokes – the sort of examination Open champions are expected to pass. In fairness to Jurado, scoring and communication systems were primitive in those days and he almost certainly never knew the exact position but, having hit a poor drive at the 17th and taken 6, he played short of the burn at the 18th, thinking a 5 might be good enough. Alas, he needed a 4 to tie with Armour and therefore made the wrong decision.

In any commentary on Carnoustie it is impossible not to return to Hogan who, needless to say, played the 17th and 18th holes on his final round as if the burn did not exist. He met every one of Carnoustie's demands except perhaps that he never quite mastered the greens which had no pace to them. Had he done so, the chasing pack would have lost touch. Carnoustie commands superlative play if it is to be tamed. There was nobody better than Hogan at supplying it.

The Barry Burn dominates the last two holes and provides the final challenge on a course that is generally regarded as the sternest test in golf.

PANMURE

PANMURE Card of the course					
Hole	Yds	Par	Hole	Yds	Par
1	289	4	10	416	4
2	488	5	11	171	3
3	398	4	12	363	4
4	348	4	13	398	4
5	147	3	14	535	5
6	387	4	15	234	3
7	418	4	16	382	4
8	360	4	17	401	4
9	174	3	18	408	4
	3009	35		3308	35

Total 6317 yards, par 70
Course record • 62,
Chris Moody, 1990

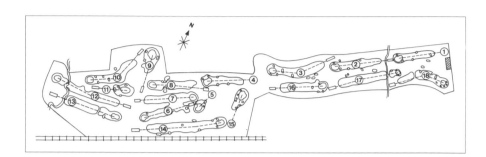

Panmure is first and foremost a member's club, its hosting of Open Championship qualifying rounds adding a truer clue to its honest potential. It is a relatively quiet backwater in an area whose golfing pedigree is rich, an obvious port of call for those not wanting to be overambitious. However, that is not to say that it commands any less respect or that it grants its favours lightly.

Its start is positively rural but the mood changes as the course blossoms on the other side of a dense pine wood, the transformation taking you somewhat by surprise particularly as the shores of the North Sea are a hefty stone's throw distant. Curious looking hillocks, resembling inflated beehives, hardly qualify as dunes but they look

For golfers who experienced a spell in the Army camp at Barry, a sneak round at Panmure may be their best memory. Barry lies between Carnoustie – whose infamous Burn is named after it – and Monifieth although the camp overlaps the links of Monifieth (well worth a visit) as well as Panmure on the sea side of the Aberdeen railway line.

Curious hillocks characterize the holes around the turn, a feature much in evidence on the short 9th.

The highly regarded 6th hole.

similar and their bite can be equally venomous with a helping of heather mixed in.

In terms of length, Panmure's 1st hole reminds one of the opening on Gullane No 1 and the 2nd carries the worry of out-of-bounds. The background to the green is a pleasant white cottage but the first signal of different terrain comes after the short 5th, the second to the 6th angled attractively to reveal a plateau green raised beside the railway. Interestingly rumpled fairways feature heavily on the 7th, where the green has a background of pines, and the 8th which drops down slightly before threading a way between two of the larger hills. This fine run of holes is continued with a pleasant tee shot over plentiful mounds on the short 9th and a drive that needs to be well placed on the 10th which doglegs to the right.

The 11th causes a change of direction, maintaining the trend of having all the par 3s on odd-numbered holes. The 12th and 13th are per-

haps the pick of the 4s – within the compass of nearly all, yet merciless in making a minor slip major. This applies more to the 12th and the tortuous burn that dominates thoughts of hitting an elevated green protected at the back by mounds but there is a lovely green setting at the 13th which is scarcely less demanding.

Then comes the longest hole by far, 535 yards alongside the railway on the right, the only time it really rears its head. A new green to the left breaks up its somewhat 'straightaway' appearance although there is virtually no elbow room on this side from gorse and finally trees.

The longest short hole, the 15th, plots a more diagonal path than most of the rest before the course straightens up for home on ground that returns to a flatter character. Three 4s take some achieving but the mind centres chiefly on the meat in the sandwich, the delightful part on either side of the turn.

ST ANDREWS
OLD COURSE

People have always argued about the origins of golf – whether it evolved from the Roman game of *paganica*, on the ice in Holland, or from the simple act of a highland shepherd boy aiming a blow at a pebble with his crook – but there has never been any doubt about the place of St Andrews in the hearts and minds of golfers. It is the home of a golfing world whose four corners and seven wonders radiate ever further from the Kingdom of Fife.

Nothing compares with the ancient university town; the shops of the clubmakers – that most noble of crafts; the hotels, or the railings round the first and last holes upon which critical observers lean. To generations of townsfolk, golf has always been a way of life. When their day's work is done, they shoulder their clubs and, in summer, the Old Course is full from dawn until the northern twilight conveniently holds the night at bay.

Every golfer has pictured himself standing on the 1st tee, eagerly aware of the historical connections, the traditions and the special quality of the golf. Yet what is so marvellous about St Andrews is that anyone can play on any of its four courses. The New, the Eden, the Jubilee and the queen herself, the Old Course: a simple stretch of land, a freak of nature which has had more influence than any other on the evolution of the game and the thinking of golf course architects.

However, like the game's beginnings, nobody knows who conceived the idea of playing in amongst the gorse and rabbit warrens; or when it all started. Quite possibly, anonymity was preserved intentionally. After all, golf was officially forbidden in the 15th century, and the playing of it punishable under an Act of Parliament.

The earliest written evidence dates from 1552 when a licence was issued permitting the community to rear rabbits on the links and 'play at golf, football and schuteing ... with all other manner of pastimes'. Except that other pastimes on the links have long since been frowned upon, the

ST ANDREWS Card of the Old Course (Open Championship tees)					
Hole	Yds	Par	Hole	Yds	Par
1 Burn	370	4	10 Bobby Jones	342	4
2 Dyke	411	4	11 High (in)	172	3
3 Cartgate (out)	371	4	12 Heathery (in)	316	4
4 Ginger Beer	463	4	13 Hole o'Cross (in)	425	4
5 Hole o'Cross (out)	564	5	14 Long	567	5
6 Heathery (out)	416	4	15 Cartgate (in)	413	4
7 High (out)	372	4	16 Corner of the Dyke	382	4
8 Short	178	3	17 Road	461	4
9 End	356	4	18 Tom Morris	354	4
	3501	36		3432	36

Total 6933 yards, par 72
Course record • 62, Curtis Strange, 1987

statutes and bylaws have changed about as little as the course. For centuries, golfers have enjoyed their rights and only as recently as this century has a modest green fee been charged. Golf used to be as free as the air.

Still, a few pounds are all that is needed for a round, plus maybe a bit of luck in the ballot for a starting time in the high season. But such small effort is worth it to see how the Old Course

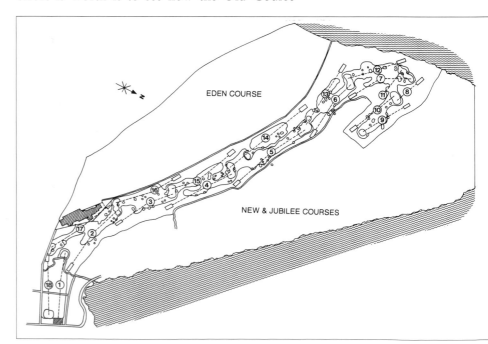

EDEN COURSE

NEW & JUBILEE COURSES

A graphic example of the peculiar humps and hollows of the Old Course as it stretches towards the Eden Estuary. In the foreground can be seen the double green of the 2nd and 16th; on the left, the old railway line marks out-of-bounds on the 16th.

remains a monument to the game as played on links by the sea – to many, the only true golf. Its critics call it a museum-piece, a test of golf that has outserved its usefulness, but all the great players, harbouring thoughts of success in an Open Championship, would still most like it to be at St Andrews.

Although architects have tried to copy its holes, it is impossible to duplicate the atmosphere at the close of such a championship, hundreds leaning from windows and thousands more flocking below. Nonetheless, the Old Course, like whisky, is an acquired taste. With most, it is hardly love at first sight. Bobby Jones, for instance, committed

the act, unthinkable to him in later life, of tearing up his card during the third round of the 1921 Open. As Bernard Darwin remarked, 'Legend declares that he relieved his feelings by teeing up his ball and driving it far out into the Eden. If he did, it was a gesture deserving of sympathy; and, if he did not, I am very sure he wanted to.'

What matters is that, from that moment, hatred turned to love and when, in 1958, Jones received the freedom of St Andrews and was made an honorary Burgess, he publicly confessed his sin. 'The more I studied the Old Course, the more I loved it; and the more I loved it, the more I studied it, so that I came to feel that it was for me the most

Although the Swilcan Burn makes the 1st predominantly a second-shot hole, one competitor in the final round of the 1970 Open Championship suffered the agony of putting back into the burn. Fortunately the story had a happy ending. Having dropped out on the far side, he then chipped in for a 5.

favourable meeting ground for an important contest. I felt that my knowledge of the course enabled me to play it with patience and restraint until she might exact her toll from my adversary, who might treat her with less respect and understanding.'

This truth hasn't changed even if times have. Strategy has been diminished by the distances the ball can now be hit, by the improvement in clubs, by automatic irrigation of the greens and, more recently, fairway watering as well. There will be much turning in the grave at that but it was needed to help the recovery of the course from the ceaseless invasion of golfing pilgrims whose skill rarely matches their enthusiasm.

But, for all the open appearance of most of the holes, a feature that astounds those from overseas, there remains a right and a wrong place to be.

Sometimes you can pitch where once a run-up was essential but character hasn't been totally blunted, and one thing which is very definitely the same is the outline of the course: the start in front of the clubhouse of the Royal and Ancient Golf Club, that square citadel of Scottish stone; out along the thin ribbon of double fairways to the waters of the Eden; round the famous Loop, arranged to give the course the shape of a bishop's or shepherd's crook; then back the way you came. Not that sheep may safely graze. Use of the same

fairway going out as coming in, and the huge double greens, make a unique combination not without points of danger.

In the early days, golfers played 11 holes out to the distant turn and 11 back, a round thus comprising 22 holes. In 1764, the Royal and Ancient suggested omitting two on the way out and therefore two on the way home. So, in a purely arbitrary way, a round of golf became 18 holes.

Greater playing numbers also brought the need for separate fairways and greens for outward and homeward journeys although at St Andrews the solution was still to share. Two holes were cut on the double greens, leaving only four holes with greens of their own.

The modern par is 72 made up of fourteen 4s, two 5s and two 3s. For an Open Championship it measures over 6900 yards, but its main defences are the wind and its bunkers. Nearly all of these have names; some are hidden, and some not much bigger than a decent-sized saucepan. You couldn't possibly locate or remember them all. Some have sinister names like Hell, Coffin and Grave; others are christened after men whose gallant deeds or calamities made them worthy of remembrance.

If the bunkers are constant, the wind is more fickle: one moment from here, the next from there. Often it is in your face all the way round in fact, and is rarely the same two rounds in a row. A

The Eden Estuary tends to mask the short 11th, dominated by the Hill, Strath and Cockle bunkers. A much copied hole, the Strath protects a fiendish pin position on a heavily sloping green.

knowledgeable caddie is therefore a help in steering you along the right course to avoid the coral reefs.

At least, there is no trick about the opening drive. It is innocence itself, the widest fairway in the world and nothing to worry about with the out-of-bounds. Or so you might think. It is so easy that it becomes hard. Balls fly daily over the white railing to the right but it is an enormous help to middle one, perhaps as far over to the left as the stone bridge if nerves get the better of you.

It is easy to wonder where the mystique lies, but it is a second-shot hole over an inglorious little stream, the Swilcan Burn, and it is much

easier played with an 8-iron than a 4-iron. The burn stretches with a serpent's twist across the front of the green, making it easier to play for the back and easier still to take three putts when the pin is at the front.

The 2nd is one of the best of the par 4s and nowadays 411 yards from the very back. A decision is needed on the tee, a decision between courage and fear. The first of many. You can play away to the broader reaches on the left, not quite as far as Cheape's bunker; or you can take the bolder line down the right and risk the gorse. With the pin on the left, cut close to a destructive pot bunker, the second is impossible. All you can do is to aim for the right of the green and hope to leave as hazardous a putt as golf possesses somewhere near the hole. From the right, a medium iron has far more scope.

By now, the open nature of the course will already have made an impact. It is this which makes finding the correct line puzzling, like a river pilot navigating in open sea. At the 3rd, usually only a drive and a pitch, there is 100 yards' latitude. However, the ideal place for the second is as far to the right as you dare.

Good players are looking for a 3 but the 4th is made of sterner stuff. Ginger Beer, to follow the old custom of giving the hole its name after the refreshment stall that greeted golfers in olden days, is a far more genuine 4. You have another choice on the tee: this time whether to hoist the drive over the bank on the left or aim for a narrower channel – the more direct line between a grassy bank and bunkers. A large mound can hide the view of the flag and deceive the second.

The 5th is the first of the two par 5s, and it is better treated as such unless the wind is helping. A cluster of bunkers on the right of the drive makes life difficult if you are in them and bunkers in the hill at the 5th also dominate the second shot, the less powerful players laying up short and the longer hitters chancing their arm hoping to clear a deep hollow in front of the green as well. If you pitch short, or if you overshoot on the vast double green, the result could be as long a putt as any in the world but tales of bad putting are less valid than elsewhere and success at St Andrews depends largely on the knack of rolling three putts into two. Each green has a vast backcloth, a feature which baffled Arnold Palmer during his first sight of St Andrews in the Open Championship of 1960. But not so Tony Lema four years later.

He defied all the laws of St Andrews which call – or used to – for an intimate knowledge of all its nooks and crannies. With only two days' preparation, he adjusted his game miraculously; playing the low, running pitches as though born in Granny Clark's Wynd, continually laying the ball dead or better still, holing it; and, above all, listening to the advice of his caddie – Tip Anderson – who has walked the links man and boy.

The 6th drive is one where advice is called for. From the back tee, the fairway is hidden by a heathery bank but it is only really formidable in what the locals call the Guardbridge wind.

Now comes the start of the Loop which invariably makes or mars a score, the 7th, so typical of what you find at St Andrews, and nowhere else: a generous choice of lines off the tee; the 11th crossing at right angles further down and a demanding second over a steep bank to one of the many plateau greens.

Unusually, the Old Course has seven holes to play before there is a short hole, and there are only two in all. The 8th has only one bunker to worry you and almost an acre of spare green – harder to miss than to hit it but so easy to take three putts and, for once, the tee shot is all carry.

In a less sacred spot, the 9th and 10th, running parallel, might stand to be condemned. Flat and featureless, they can be driven when conditions are right: nothing much to them except a lining of heather and a bunker or two to catch the drive. Nonetheless, the bunkers have a strange attraction and both pitches can have a player in all sorts of minds.

Indecision is a curse at St Andrews plus the thought at the 9th and 10th that here surely a 4 can be turned into a 3. The temptation is to try for more than is wise – abandoning the old advice of playing for a 4 and letting the 3 come.

After the artfully raised 10th green, the 11th slopes heavily. It is anything from an 8- to a 2-iron, depending on the wind, but it is never a short hole to be taken for granted and the terrors of the 11th are alarmingly up to date.

At the 12th, first impressions are deceptive. It's a modest 316 yards in length. The eye sees little – at first – that threatens disaster, but it contains all the hidden evil of a minefield.

The direct line to the green is a narrow channel between a heathery hill and venomous bunkers; or you can go away to the right. However, the key to the hole is the pitch, particularly when the hole is cut on the narrow shelf of green. The 13th begins the turn for home, an inspiring prospect with the spires and roofs of the town beckoning – a picture of which no one grows tired. But it can undermine the tasks ahead. The 13th drive must escape a row of bunkers including Walkinshaw's; the second to this excellent par 4 is over a heathery bank, and a low running shot is not what's called for.

The 14th is another of the really great holes, the

second par 5; and something of a twin to the 5th in the other direction though fuller of pitfalls. For the first time, the drive has no latitude. There are no options from a distant back tee to a shot between a menacing cluster of bunkers, the dreaded Beardies, and the grey stone wall over which a slice is out-of-bounds. The Elysian Fields, as the fairway is known, is indeed a promised land, but there is more to follow. Ahead lies Hell Bunker and there is the Kitchen also plus a sting in the tail. The Grave bunker tells its own story and before there is any thought of a putt for a birdie 4, there is another sharp plateau to surmount.

Don't grieve if you fall foul of the Beardies and have to play out only a few yards. Open champions share your grief.

This grief forms a sizable chunk of history. Many a high hope has run aground, never to be refloated, but one exception was Peter Thomson in the 1955 Open. A 7 at the 14th – he was in the Beardies and the Grave – put his ascendancy in question. Sevens can be even more infuriating if you are a professional but Thomson is not a champion for nothing. He replied with a birdie at the 15th, settled himself, and won by two strokes.

The 15th, the first of four par 4s to finish, lacks the devilment of the 16th and 17th. Aim on the church spire to get a sight of the green with the drive and the hard part is done even if distances are hard to judge at St Andrews. A yardage chart,

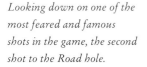

Looking down on one of the most feared and famous shots in the game, the second shot to the Road hole.

the professionals' bible, could be of some use but not generally at St Andrews. It may be a help at the 15th but certainly not at the 16th, another classic hole.

There is a clear choice between steering a drive down the perilous passage between the Principal's Nose and the old railway; or, if a promising score beckons, it is wise to give the Principal's Nose a wide berth on the left although that oversimplifies the case because it is a cluster of three mounded bunkers which constitute the Principal's Nose, and Deacon Sime, a handy accomplice, lies beyond. It is a simple choice but a big decision.

The 16th and 17th remain great holes because golfers will always make old-fashioned mistakes. The Principal's Nose caught Arnold Palmer in the 1960 Open and it almost certainly cost Britain victory in the first World Amateur Team Championship two years earlier.

The 17th, the Road hole, has been more praised and more abused than any other hole in the world. Many like it, most respect it and all fear it. It has earned its fame, or its infamy, by the road beside the green which gives it its name. Even today, in an age of more refined pitching clubs, recovery is by no means assured but it is wrong to put the cart before the horse – as many have done.

It is the one drive which has changed in appearance over the years: not the tee or the fairway but the part in between, the old railway sheds over which generations drove with anything from cowardice to daring. In their place has risen a hotel, hardly royal or ancient, which serves the purpose just as well but not with quite the same degree of romance.

The main problem is aiming correctly. The perfect position is on the right but sometimes it is better not to get high ideas. Settle for a 5. It's no disgrace. Against the wind, it can be out of range in two but for those with the nerve and technique, it can be a thrilling second shot. The angle is awkward, the road comes within feet of the green, down a sharp drop, and the left is guarded by the greedy little Road bunker. People lacking the inclination to pitch their thirds have been known to putt – yes putt – into the Road bunker. Treacherous slopes betray you, and then the thoughts occur that you might not get out or you might go too far, and it's too late to send for help.

The green has a narrow waist but not all is woe.

The penalties for finishing on the road are less than they were. It isn't sudden death any more. The bank isn't shaggy and the surrounds are more tidy. Traditionalists deplore these improvements as much as the passing of the little railway from Leuchars.

In any context, the 18th is a memorable sight since golfers are returning as much to the town as to Tom Morris's green. Ahead stands the headquarters of the Royal and Ancient, the most famous governing body of any game, to the left, the gold of St Andrews Bay – and, in the imagination perhaps, a 4 to win the Open.

The prospect is good: the same wide fairway that greeted the opening drive, a hole (354 yards) that has often been driven and a green big enough to house a game of cricket. Only the Valley of Sin plagues the timid. We cross the burn by the old stone bridge having aimed on the clubhouse clock, and determine to take enough club for our second. Judge the distance, decide on the type of shot, and a 4 is in the bag. Millions have achieved it but how much harder a game it is when things really matter, when a lifetime's ambition hangs on a pitch and two putts.

For a course that owes more to the hand of God than that of man, the Old is an acknowledged masterpiece. Its terrors are less now but it remains the queen of golf, containing, as it does, so many absolutely first-class holes. Played in a fresh wind off the sea, or from the Eden, it maintains its colossal reputation. But, as was suggested years and years ago, 'If there are those who deny any charm to the links, there must surely be none who can deny a charm to the place as a whole.'

Bobby Jones, without any hesitation, named the Old Course as the one he would choose were his golf limited to one alone. But the most glowing of the tributes he paid in what amounted to a love story came that same evening in 1958, the evening the town paid its own homage and gave him its freedom, the first American to be so honoured since Benjamin Franklin.

Having abandoned the notes which he had prepared, Jones ended what was surely the most moving ceremony of his life, more moving even than his Grand Slam, by telling a packed, emotional audience, 'I could take out of my life everything except my experiences at St Andrews and I'd still have a rich, full life.'

ST ANDREWS
NEW, EDEN AND JUBILEE COURSES

The 2nd green on the Jubilee course.

As an example of fitting a quart into a pint pot, the design of the Old, New, Eden and Jubilee courses take a lot of beating. They run roughly parallel with each other in thin ribbons across the most famous tract of golfing land in the world although the revised Jubilee and Eden have more twists and turns in their layout than their neighbours. The Jubilee is the most northerly and the Eden the most southerly of the four, the Old and New adding the tasty filling to the sandwich, the Old more than once rubbing shoulders with the Eden.

The New and Jubilee are conveniently paired together because they are controlled from the same starter's box. A modest opening hole greets golfers on the New which has perhaps more in common with the Old than the other two in so far as it has several holes amongst the gorse and others which have no clear shape or definition. There is a certain freedom off many of the tees but the revised Jubilee which is considerably longer than it used to be puts great emphasis on hitting the fairway. There is no hint of the double fairways that are so familiar on the Old.

Another unusual feature for St Andrews is that the Jubilee has more than one change of level and becomes embroiled with the only line of sizable sandhills. This applies on the 15th which was cut out of the gorse and at the far end on the 9th and 10th which took shape from what was the town's refuse disposal tip. In order to build the 10th fairway, all the debris had to be buried in exchange for excavated sand.

Scenically, the Jubilee commands the best views, the 9th tee offering contrasting splendour in all directions. There are subtle variations in the out-and-back formation characteristic of the Old and New but the Eden indulges in the unique luxury to St Andrews of having two loops of nine based on the clubhouse.

This has resulted from the recent changes that are part and parcel of the exciting new proposals by the St Andrews Links Trust to improve and enlarge the facilities that many have come to expect. In addition to the upgrading of the Eden and Jubilee courses, these include a conventional, modern driving range, the relocation of the Balgove – popular with the less ambitious – and the creation of an entirely new Strathtyrum course which is intended to fall somewhere between the Balgove and the other four courses which are, for the first time, far more on a par with each other.

In order to accommodate these developments, the first two and last two holes of the old Eden were sacrificed and new land purchased alongside the road from Guardbridge although it was land that was plain and featureless. The revised Eden takes in a small corner of this new land but still has holes along the estuary which bears its name. It is one thread in the varied tapestry of golf at St Andrews which, for the atmosphere it generates and the fun it provides, is second to none in the world.

CRAIL GOLFING SOCIETY

Far out on the most easterly tip of the East Neuk of Fife is the windswept Balcomie Golf Course, the modern home of the Crail Golfing Society, the seventh-oldest club in the world. It is open to all the winds that blow, stretching a course of relatively modest length to more sizable proportions, although the par of 69, with six par 3s, is achieved only by the very best players.

On clear, sunlit days, Balcomie, a couple of miles or so north-east of the little town of Crail, has commanding views – north to Montrose and south to St Abb's Head. Old Tom Morris had a hand in the early layout of Balcomie which replaced eight holes at Sauchope, scene of high revelling in days of celebration in the Golf Inn after the popular monthly dinner matches.

Fines of a half-mutchkin of punch for failing to turn up for a match are recorded in the society's minutes which have been faithfully handed down since their first meeting in February 1786. In preserving such enviable continuity, they have been more successful than some other early clubs who, in keeping perhaps with their masonic connections, may have preferred to keep their affairs secret. Considering his St Andrean roots, one slightly surprising statement of Old Tom's about Balcomie's links was that 'there is no better in Scotland', but he may have been applying the rule of thumb that none brought the rocky beach into play better than Balcomie, not even North Berwick on the opposite shore of the Firth of Forth.

The first five holes make a thrilling opening. The 1st descends from a high tee over two bunkers to a green beside the old boathouse – now a maintenance shed. There is room at the 2nd to err on the left without being immediately punished but the perfect line is between two hills, particularly as the slippery slopes of the small green can push any shot from the wrong angle irrevocably towards the rocks. The 3rd turns at right angles with the line of the shore, a pleasant short hole to an unusual green. The 4th and 5th maintain the spectacular coastal theme, the drive at the 4th offering a good dogleg's choice between playing safe or being greedy, and the 5th extolling the virtues of stout, straight hitting.

CRAIL GOLFING SOCIETY
Card of the Balcomie course

Hole		Yds	Par	Hole		Yds	Par
1	Boathouse	312	4	10	The Turn	209	3
2	Ower the Knowe	480	5	11	Lang Whang	500	5
3	The Briggs	179	3	12	The Burn	489	5
4	Fluke Dub	348	4	13	Craighead	215	3
5	Hell's Hole	346	4	14	The Cave	149	3
6	North Carr	334	4	15	Mill Dam	265	4
7	Breeches Buoy	421	4	16	Spion Kop	163	3
8	Dykeside	306	4	17	Road Hole	461	4
9	Castle Yetts	334	4	18	The Quarry	209	3
		3060	36			2660	33

Total 5720 yards, par 69

Course record • 63, Graeme Lennie, 1991

Balcomie's remote and beautiful setting as viewed from the 14th tee. Beyond the heavily contoured green stands the old boating house, beside which is the 1st green.

As players climb the hill to the 6th tee there is a tinge of regret that the best is over. The character of the next nine holes is more inland and up and down but they are undoubtedly fun. There is a second to the 6th over a track forming a ridge in front of the green, an out-of-bounds wall to haunt the slicer on the 7th and a nice slanting green beside more out-of-bounds on the 8th. The 9th involves an uphill pitch countered by a downhill tee shot at the short 10th to what is almost a treble green shared by the 12th and 1st. The 10th is the first of five short holes on the inward nine including two in succession at the 13th and 14th although these could hardly be more different. The 13th scales a rocky escarpment, the 14th drops

from a tee beside the 1st over central bunkers to a heavily contoured green.

The walk to the 15th resembles the path to the back tee on the 9th at Turnberry, but there the comparison ends. Although the 17th, the longest of the par 4s, is called Road Hole, it has little in common with its illustrious neighbour at St Andrews. The 15th can be driven and the 16th and 18th are one-shotters.

Obtaining a better balance between the nines has deficd strenuous efforts but it is remarkable that the outward half, with only one par 3, is a mere 400 yards longer than the inward half which has five. All it emphasizes is the joyous fact that golf courses enjoy endless variety in their make-up.

GOLF HOUSE CLUB, ELIE

Take golf away from many of the towns, villages and hamlets around our shores and you might as well obliterate them from the map altogether. Turnberry, Machrihanish, Saunton, Carnoustie, Gullane and North Berwick are cases in point, and so too is Elie on the coast of Fife.

Elie's golf is very much in keeping with the place itself, a holiday atmosphere emphasizing a delightful informality with enjoyment the main priority. St Andrews inevitably casts an historical shadow over the many other links of Fife but centuries ago Elie was a Danish settlement and there seems little doubt that there was some golfing activity for well over a century before the Golf House Club was formed in 1875.

Around that time James Braid, son of an Elie ploughman, was honing his game on a course that earned rapid fame, to which Braid contributed in abundance. There are only about forty Scottish courses older than Elie, which developed a little world of its own. Braid, locally recognized as record holder and medal winner, soon added to a reputation it had already gained for producing famous golfers. It was so marked that Braid once said that he felt Elie could challenge the rest of the world.

Oddly enough, his father was one of the few citizens who did not play golf. Braid, nevertheless, was typical of children taking to the game almost as soon as they could walk and developing skills to last a lifetime. It is noteworthy that Elie's tradition in encouraging the young has lived on in the shape of the children's course, additional nine and practice ground that form a separate golfing centre.

Those who carried the fame of Elie far and wide included the six Simpson brothers, of whom Jack and Archie were the best known, and Braid's own cousin, Douglas Rolland, commonly regarded as one of the finest players never to have won the Open. It was said he hit the ball distances it had never been hit before, often with clubs he had borrowed.

In its earliest days, Elie (formerly the Earlsferry and Elie Club and then Earlsferry Thistle) consisted of 9 holes; it later became 11 and then 14 but in 1895 Tom Morris stretched it to 18, Braid (who else?) making alterations in 1921. The clubhouse stands at the top of a narrow walled lane and the round begins with a blind drive over a sharp rise, the starter giving the instruction to 'play away' after looking through his submarine periscope

GOLF HOUSE CLUB, ELIE
Card of the course

Hole		Yds	Par	Hole		Yds	Par
1	Stacks	420	4	10	Lundar Law	267	4
2	High Hole	284	4	11	Sea Hole	120	3
3	Wickets	214	3	12	Bents	466	4
4	Provost	378	4	13	Croupie	380	4
5	Doctor	365	4	14	Suckielea	414	4
6	Quarries	316	4	15	Coalhill	338	4
7	Peggy's	252	4	16	Grange	407	4
8	Neuk	382	4	17	Ferry	439	4
9	Martin's Bay	440	4	18	Home	359	4
		3051	35			3190	35

Total 6241 yards, par 70
Course record • 62, Kel Nagle, 1971

Elie's 13th was once described by James Braid as 'the finest hole in all the country'. The hole follows the sweep of the bay and ends in a raised, angled green.

which gives him a view of the fairway. In nautical terms, the first two or three holes occupy relatively quiet waters although the 1st green requires a second shot played down to it and the 2nd green a shot played up to the skyline.

The 5th follows the row of pleasant houses at Earlsferry but once the drive at the 6th has scaled the brow of the hill, Elie's views turn from landscape to seascape although it is not a duneland course. As you pitch down to the 9th green and perhaps attempt to drive the 10th green by the water's edge, a map unfolds on a good day with North Berwick, Muirfield and Gullane all visible across the Firth of Forth.

The 11th (Sea Hole), the shorter of the two par 3s, is a quaint hole with an eccentric green but the 12th (Bents) and 13th (Croupie) follow the rocky beach towards MacDuff's cave set into a mountainous cliff. It is probably the finest hole on the course, a long second in a crosswind having to find a raised, angled green which, though large, is no easy target.

It is the stretch from about the 7th to the 13th that gives the real flavour of Elie, a wind from the Forth lifting the demands and leaving no doubt about its seaside character.

From there, it is a case of setting sail for home with more drives to undulating fairways and a variety of shots to subtle greens. The description often used of holiday golf strikes the right tenor but it does less than justice to a course that combines the best of both worlds – one to give pleasure yet one that, given the stiffish breeze mentioned, makes the best players pleased with a good score.

LUNDIN

Lundin's 4th green, the boundary wall with Leven in the foreground.

A master of mine at school used to contend that his idea of heaven was a round at Lundin Links. Although a modest and infrequent player, he was typical of golfers in knowing what he liked and his choice was perfectly understandable.

Fife is brimful of courses with historic pasts but none combine the pleasures of enjoyment, charm and beauty better than Lundin. Before 1868, it shared a layout that, in early seaside tradition, had nine holes out and nine back along the shores of Largo Bay. Leven Golfing Society was the instigator but in 1868 the land was divided down the middle, nine holes were added on each side of the fence and Leven and Lundin developed separate identities.

For old times' sake, the two societies join up once a year for a competition over the original 18 holes which had the beach as one boundary and the single-track railway line as the other. The railway used to transport golfers to Elie and St Andrews; in spite of the closure of the line, sentimental evidence of the track remains as the old out-of-bounds is preserved. There are still nine holes on one side and nine on the other.

The earliest holes comprise the better part but there is no doubt that Lundin got the better divi-

LUNDIN
Card of the course

Hole		Yds	Par	Hole		Yds	Par
1	High	424	4	10	Thorn Tree	353	4
2	Quarry	346	4	11	Racecourse	466	4
3	Bents	335	4	12	Sunnybraes	161	3
4	Mile Dyke	452	4	13	Neil Shaw	512	5
5	Silverburn	140	3	14	Perfection	175	3
6	Spectacles	330	4	15	Heather	418	4
7	Burn	273	4	16	Trows	314	4
8	Aithernie	364	4	17	Station	345	4
9	Long	555	5	18	Home	442	4
		3219	36			3158	35

Total 6377 yards, par 71

Course record • 63, Andrew Hare, 1990

sion of the cake, as it were, than Leven with regard to the extra land it acquired, not least on account of its pleasant contour which enhances the views.

A glorious start beside the beach contains four par 4s. The 1st and 4th are the most difficult, the 1st fairway rising from a valley shared with the 18th to an elevated green with a lovely distant prospect and the 452-yard 4th involving a long carry over a burn snaking across the front of the green. For the majority, it has to be treated with healthy respect as a 5. A short hole turns at right angles beside Leven over the same burn, a less exacting feat of strength if not of judgment, and, having crossed the old railway, the 6th, 7th and 8th wend their way back to the clubhouse with three more 4s, the 8th bothered by a different burn.

A par 5 ends an outward half in which the 5th is the lone short hole but two short holes on the second nine bridge the higher and lower land on this section of the course. From the 13th, the second par 5, which runs along the road at the top, the full extent of the splendid view unfolds. Across the Forth, there are clear traces of the landmarks of Gullane and North Berwick, the outline of Edinburgh and, nearer home, the coast towards Kirkaldy as the 13th doglegs round the trees. The short 14th descends in enticing fashion before the last four complete the circuit, reunited with the characteristic folds and hillocks of the ground that have made Lundin famous. They add extra skill and interest to the shots.

The 15th, 16th and 17th provide welcome variety until the 18th, from a point near the old station, brings us back to a long, narrow valleyed green in the shadow of the clubhouse that looks out on a classic piece of golfing territory untouched by the years.

LEVEN LINKS

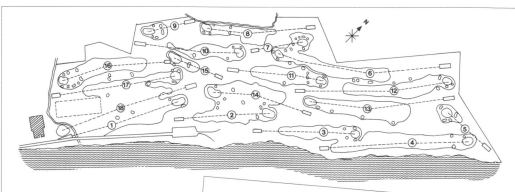

LEVEN LINKS					
Card of the course (championship tees)					
Hole	Yds	Par	Hole	Yds	Par
1 Table	413	4	10 Cattle Creep	325	4
2 Knowe	381	4	11 Boundary	363	4
3 Bents	343	4	12 Silverburn S.	482	5
4 Sea	449	4	13 Seg	482	5
5 Valley	157	3	14 Dykeneuk	332	4
6 Silverburn N.	567	5	15 Railway	188	3
7 Corriemar	184	3	16 Circus	386	4
8 Bing	348	4	17 Howe	414	4
9 Pavilion	164	3	18 Scoonie	457	4
	3006	34		3429	37

Total 6435 yards, par 71
Course record • 63, Paul Hoad, 1984

Leven and Lundin Links are inextricably entwined both in terms of having a common boundary and, for years, having shared the same course. In its earliest days, the Leven Golfing Society held its competitions over the Dubbieside Links, its Standard Assurance gold medal claimed by some to be the oldest open amateur trophy in the world.

In 1852, the Standard Assurance Company of Edinburgh bought the Lundin estate and did much to develop golf in a district that saw the coming of the railway and the building of Methil harbour for the coal trade. The quest for suitable land led to the demise of Dubbieside and brought a new home at Scoonie for the merger of Innerleven and Leven Golf Clubs into the Leven Golfing Society.

Leven claims to be the 11th-oldest club in the world, Young Tom Morris winning the first tournament on the new course whilst at the height of his powers. In 1909, it was agreed that Leven and Lundin would form separate clubs, Leven taking over the football ground and acquiring new land on the other side of the then railway line.

There is much in common between the links of Leven and Lundin, not least the fact that the first four holes on each are par 4s along the beautiful sands of Largo Bay although they run in opposite directions. There is certainly not the change of levels at Leven that there is at Lundin but the 1st and 4th are formidable in length and the 2nd unusual in offering two distinct ways of playing the hole. You can play safe to the right down a valley from which you cannot see the green or aim for the plateau of fairway to the left from which everything is visible provided you make a sizable carry over twin bunkers in the face of the hill.

The short 5th runs parallel with the short 5th at Lundin on the other side of the fence, reminding one of Murcar and Royal Aberdeen. Another

Whatever comes before, a good score can never be assured until the Scoonie Burn has been carried on the 18th. As can be seen, its dimensions are considerable.

change of direction comes at the long 6th which has out-of-bounds to the right. The next four holes form a neat rectangle before the 11th, 12th, 13th and 14th occupy a central heartland with far more interest than may be apparent from afar. The short 7th has 10 bunkers, the 8th is characterized by a lovely bank of gorse and the Scoonie Burn along the right.

A green by the corner of a row of houses marks the 15th, the fourth short hole although the only one in the second nine. The 16th and 17th go up and back, reacquainting you with the 'demonic'

Scoonie Burn which laps behind the 16th green. It doesn't really come into play on either of these holes, but it dominates the second (or third or fourth!) to the 18th, making it, at 457 yards, as formidable a finishing hole as you can find. Everything about the hole revolves around the passage over the burn which is both wide and deep. It needs a long drive for the carry to be tackled with certainty and safety in two but laying up and pitching over can send a shiver down the stoutest spine-teasing end to a round on historic ground.

LUFFNESS NEW

From a distance, the three courses of Gullane and the one at Luffness are indistinguishable from each other. They occupy those vast acres of incomparable linksland around Gullane Hill so beloved of golfers everywhere – a monument to the school of architecture that believes in leaving well alone. Accepting and working with nature is a strength, not a weakness; as, indeed, is the awareness that only a handful of golfers measure quality by a string of impossible par 4s.

Although Luffness has housed the qualifying rounds for the Open, it is a classic of the gentler kind. A round elicits the feeling of escape that golfers seek. It is an entrancing place to play.

Sentimentality has a strong pull in shaping judgments and I plead guilty to an unashamed sense of attachment to Luffness. Dull sermons in school chapel – as well as some not so dull – provided ideal opportunities to relive the enjoyment of rare Sunday afternoons on the links and to mull over where things went wrong or might have been improved upon. Luffness taught me, too, how good greens should be: lest that be thought an exaggeration, Bobby Locke, than whom there was no greater putter, believed there were none better. Its famous head greenkeeper, James King, had no time for Green Committees and preferred his results to speak for themselves. There is a salutary lesson to be learned if people would only listen.

The greens' beautiful surfaces and relatively small size mean that, when you hit them, you are nearly always putting at the hole but Luffness undoubtedly possesses a challenging note.

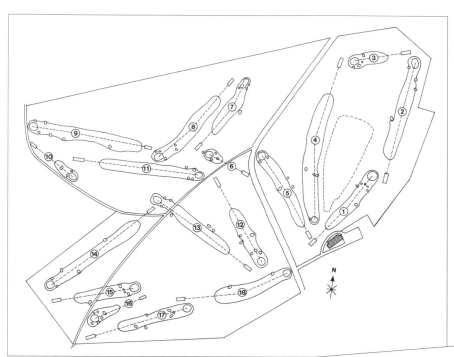

Hole		Yds	Par	Hole		Yds	Par
1	Luffness Mill	332	4	10	Benty	176	3
2	Saltcoats	420	4	11	Peffer Bank	445	4
3	Gullane	196	3	12	Luffness	336	4
4	Long	531	5	13	Well	393	4
5	Milestone	326	4	14	Aberlady	435	4
6	Quarry	155	3	15	Road	346	4
7	Hill	293	4	16	Warren	163	3
8	March	383	4	17	Plantation	349	4
9	Inchkeith	427	4	18	Home	416	4
		3063	35			3059	34

LUFFNESS NEW
Card of the course

Total 6122 yards, par 69
Course record • 62, Christy O'Connor Snr, 1962

A general view of some of the most natural golfing land in the world and a more specific view of the 6th (foreground) and 11th, showing Luffness's beautiful small greens and deep bunkers.

There are five holes on the clubhouse side of the busy main road from Edinburgh and 13 on the other, a relic of bygone days being the short 6th, a blind shot over a quarry. Now the angle is different and the green in full view but the green at the 1st, a shortish 4, is hidden by a hill into which are set a row of bunkers. The 4th is the only par 5 but the best of the golf occupies a peaceful stretch beyond the 8th out by Aberlady Bay. The 7th takes play up the hill, the 8th bringing it back down again.

There are many admirable 4s. The length of the course struggles to exceed 6000 yards but accurate driving is called for both to leave the best line for the second shots and to steer clear of rough that has claimed more lost balls than most. Luffness's other architectural defence is its network of bunkers: neat, well defined and well shaped, excavated into a base of bottomless sand. My favourite hole is the 9th, a stern par 4, but there really isn't a weakness on a course that, if not made to test the giants, never ceases to give pleasure to the rank and file of golfers who form the backbone of the game.

GULLANE

Of all the golfing centres that have sprung up throughout the world, Gullane remains the best and most natural. Schooldays are an impressionable time and there may be a hint of blind loyalty in such an assertion but I hope no more than a trace.

The great expanse of wild country has changed little since my introduction to it when an escape from lessons was a rare treat. In an era when conservationists, planners and ecologists are currently up in arms that golf strikes a discordant note in the environment, the three courses coexist happily with an area famous as a bird sanctuary. What is more, they have done so for years and will do so for years to come.

The little town nestles under the lee of Gullane Hill from which majestic views over the Forth towards Fife contrast with the more pastoral setting of East Lothian.

The 1st hole on Gullane No 1, which Joe Carr once drove in an Open Championship qualifying round, and the uphill 2nd, are a prelude to the panorama unfolding. The exhilaration generated permeates the play which, though authentic enough, has the dash of adventure to lend added spice. Over the next three holes the full range of par is seen before gradually the inviting 6th completes the climbing.

From an elevated tee at the 7th, there

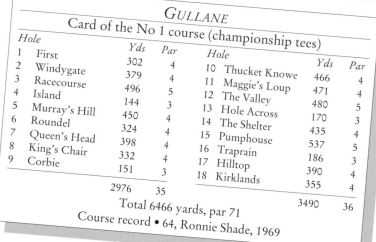

GULLANE
Card of the No 1 course (championship tees)

Hole		Yds	Par	Hole		Yds	Par
1	First	302	4	10	Thucket Knowe	466	4
2	Windygate	379	4	11	Maggie's Loup	471	4
3	Racecourse	496	5	12	The Valley	480	5
4	Island	144	3	13	Hole Across	170	3
5	Murray's Hill	450	4	14	The Shelter	435	4
6	Roundel	324	4	15	Pumphouse	537	5
7	Queen's Head	398	4	16	Traprain	186	3
8	King's Chair	332	4	17	Hilltop	390	4
9	Corbie	151	3	18	Kirklands	355	4
		2976	35			3490	36

Total 6466 yards, par 71
Course record • 64, Ronnie Shade, 1969

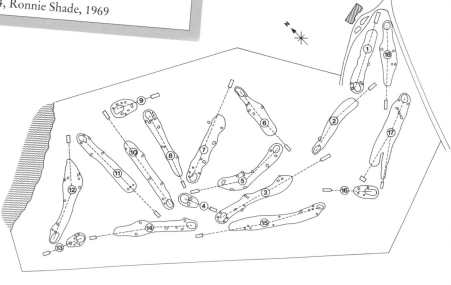

is a further racing of the senses. Of all the downhill holes in golf, none is more spectacular. There is a joyous urge to open the shoulders, much in keeping with the general freedom conveyed by the open nature of terrain with not a tree in sight. Not that too cavalier an attitude can be adopted. Gullane's rough can be all-engulfing.

The 8th edges play closer to the shore, while the short 9th and particularly the 10th are no place for those suffering from vertigo. There follow several marvellous holes with variety the essence. The layout is carefully plotted to test without torturing and to scale the peak of the hill once more without undue physical effort. A fine tee shot awaits at the 16th, the last of the short holes.

On the 17th there is another high tee, a majestic view and an opportunity to show off. Unlike

Like the 7th, the 17th offers an inviting downhill drive towards a green well framed by bunkers.

mountaineering, a sport in which ascent is the key, golf is a better game played downhill and few holes are more downhill than the 17th. Elevation, however, tends to foreshorten the task in hand and shots can be dropped by underestimating the need for precision with the approach. It is tempting to allow the slope to do the work for you. The 18th, levelling out for home, is another to guard against. Its length is more modest than its backlash.

Like St Andrews or North Berwick, the last green hovers on the edge of the town, bringing visitors by the score. In summer, the courses bustle from early dawn to the late twilight that is such a feature of Scotland, an attraction based on the simple love of playing the game as a source of enjoyment and fun. Gullane leaves no room for regret.

MUIRFIELD

The Honourable Company of Edinburgh Golfers had many chapters of history behind them before they eventually came by a real home of their own at Muirfield. They drafted the first code of rules, established themselves as the club which today has the longest continuous existence, and enjoyed lengthy sojourns at both Leith Links and Musselburgh. Overcrowding on courses shared by a variety of clubs and societies led to the decision to move and shaped what has, in many ways, been their most distinguished era. Muirfield epitomizes most people's idea of perfection.

Tucked along the shores of the Firth of Forth with resplendent distant views of Edinburgh and the Forth Bridge, Muirfield's present design is a masterpiece. A clockwise outward nine envelops an anti-clockwise inward nine, the constant change of direction of the holes being an exception to the rule that seaside links consist of nine holes out to a far-off point and nine back. No point of the course is more than about seven minutes walk from the clubhouse, making it ideal for spectators who may not want to be confined to one match.

As a test, its prime quality is that it is honest and straightforward. Muirfield's latest version bears the hallmark of Harry Colt and none could have a higher recommendation. He was one of the golf course architects who turned a somewhat haphazard exercise of 'arrangement' into a profession that rolls imaginative flair and technical knowledge into one.

Such architects set the fashion of hand-picking their positions for greens – angling, shaping, defending and contouring them rather than slavishly accepting what they found. They paid attention to the balance of the holes. They plotted the style and profusion of fairway bunkers which at Muirfield are highly distinctive. They worked on the small details, the fine tuning, and they realized the vital importance of good appearances and good condition.

Muirfield's universal acclaim and popularity owes much to all these factors; yet, in its early days, there was a reluctance to sing its praises. This was due partly to the in-built dislike of change among most golfers, partly to the fact that some critics – mainly the lovers of St Andrews – claimed it was not seaside enough and partly because its unveiling meant the demise of Musselburgh as a setting for the Open.

Curiously enough, Bernard Darwin denied it the compliments that in other cases guaranteed a course instant fame. Of Andrew Kirkaldy's claim about Muirfield being 'a water meadie', he remarked 'there was just enough truth in the aphorism to make it unforgettable'. Even after the Honourable

Hole	Yds	Par	Hole	Yds	Par
1	447	4	10	475	4
2	351	4	11	385	4
3	379	4	12	381	4
4	180	3	13	159	3
5	559	5	14	449	4
6	469	4	15	417	4
7	185	3	16	188	3
8	444	4	17	550	5
9	504	5	18	448	4
	3518	36		3452	35

MUIRFIELD
Card of the course
(Open Championship tees)

Total 6970 yards, par 71
Course record • 64, Rodger Davis, 1987 Open Championship

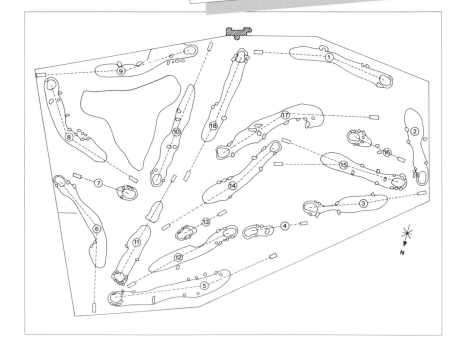

Muirfield's 5th, the first of its par 5s, shows an unusual feature on the green: it is on two levels, the right part higher than the left.

Company had acquired extra land nearer the sea, he felt 'Muirfield still retains, and always will, a certain inland character. We are always, or nearly always, playing our shots between two lines of rough.'

Darwin preferred St Andrews or Prestwick but there is no doubt that he was in favour of the alterations implemented by Colt which gave us the feel of the sandhills and opened up noble views. Previously, the course's northern boundary was marked by the stone wall which crossed near the present 6th green and ran in a more or less straight line to the 3rd tee.

Even today it has to be admitted that Muirfield is not the supreme example of a traditional links but it is about the only criticism that could be levelled at it. Discordant notes are rarely, if ever, voiced.

Muirfield presents its problems without undue complication. It keeps nothing up its sleeve. There are no fearsome carries, no water hazards and only the odd blind shot. Players know where they are meant to go without a second look. However, it is a wonderful test of good driving even if, in keeping with many courses, modern equipment has blunted its cutting edge in that respect.

During a stormy third morning in the 1987 Open Championship, Sandy Lyle returned an astounding 71 without ever once hitting a wooden club but that was more the 'fault' of the equip-

ment than the course. On the other hand, when Alf Perry became Open champion in 1935, his driver, brassie and spoon worked overtime – a daring second with a spoon from a bunker on the 14th in the final round probably being the difference between winning and losing.

One of the hardest tee shots is the first, which is invariably against the prevailing wind. The horseshoe bunker on the left has a magnetic appeal, while the fairway to the right always appears ribbon-like and remote. Having been a par 3 when Cyril Tolley won the Amateur Championship in 1920, the 1st has become one of the most demanding par 4s, a narrow entrance to the green giving due notice of what lies ahead. If putting casts doubt and fear in some, Muirfield ensures that it can also inspire. In spite of subtle slopes, its greens call for all the ideal qualities – judgment of pace, a delicate touch, a sure eye and a stout nerve. All the same, overborrowing can be just as great a problem on fast greens and the 2nd is difficult to fathom.

Positioning the tee shot correctly is important on the 2nd and vital at the 3rd if a sight of the flag is to be gained when it is tucked away on the right. The 4th, with its limited approach, is a fine short hole for there are varied penalties for missing the green and, in any wind, the clubbing must be spot-on.

The 5th is a par 5 on which Johnny Miller holed

his second shot during the second round of the
1972 Open Championship. Apart from a well
bunkered, well channelled fairway, the feature of
the hole is a split-level green where a birdie invariably depends on an inventive pitch.

Changes of direction at the 6th and 7th mean
that the first seven holes have boxed the compass,
the left-hand curve of the 6th alongside
Archerfield Wood offering a further variation for
the second shot. The best view of the green is from
the peak of the crest; while a long drive over the
top may obscure the target, it can make the difference of three or four clubs.

Hitting the green at the short 7th is not the same
thing as being near the pin on a hole which needs
a headwind to bring out the best in it even if it
lessens the severity of the 8th, and its network of
bunkers. There is a fearsome cluster on the right
to ginger up the drive and a fine old-fashioned
cross bunker short of the green. Unless the second is from the rough, this teases the members
more than the mighty. With such a combination
of hazards, small wonder that the 1990 Amateur
champion chose to bypass all the trouble by driving down the practice ground, an avenue barred

to contestants in an Open by out-of-bounds.

Fear of out-of-bounds haunts the mind on the
second at the 9th – always assuming the drive is
long and accurate enough to bring the stone wall
within reach. Simpson's bunker, a central hazard
marking a diagonal row of traps, plays a crucial
part in the equation, the ideal being the happy bal-

ance of erring a little to the left though not too much. It is the demand of making correct decisions and hitting the shots to support them that makes the 9th such a marvellous hole.

Failure to be able to see the 10th green for your second or the 11th fairway from the tee does nothing to lessen their impact or pleasure, the approach to the 11th affording the perfect opportunity of assimilating the scenic blessings of Muirfield. However, distraction can be fatal. Hopes of a birdie can be easily dashed by the most heavily contoured green of all.

The 12th is the only hole that gives the impression of driving downhill, a gently rolling fairway tapering gradually towards a narrow green surrounded by bunkers. From the tee, the line is on Gullane Hill, a landmark standing like a sentinel over the varied links under its gaze. The 13th offers swift contrast.

Innocent enough in length, it is, like as not, a shortish iron to a raised green – the only obviously uphill shot on the links. It is, however, a prime example of how short holes do not need to be a long iron or wood to make them difficult. Unseen from the tee, the green is deceptive at its narrowest point where all the hard pin positions are located, and there are four or five steep potbunkers from which recovery is not guaranteed. There is also a sharp slope from the back, conjuring up the prospect of an overeager approach putt slipping down off the green. This is one of the most recent changes, one shaped by men with

wheelbarrows and horses with scoops. Although this method of construction was slow, it was more controlled than modern, mechanized methods as a means of introducing subtle contour.

The 14th reacquaints us with the meat of the challenge at Muirfield, the long par 4s. A series of bunkers down the left tempts you to play a little to the right but the line of the second shot is easier if this inclination is not overdone. The prevailing wind adds a cubit or two to its dimensions, as it does to the 15th which changes direction just enough to reassess its effect. There is a new Open Championship tee to the right which takes out of play the cross bunkers that are such a concern for the less exalted, and the huge green has an awkward ridge in it.

The 16th completes the quartet of short holes, frequently catching unawares those thinking ahead to the 17th and 18th, the scene of so much drama in Muirfield's Opens. On the 17th, the temptation is to cut the corner and it is a big temptation. The angle to the green for the second is better if the tee shot is played to the left, but mounds and bunkers punish the pull. If in doubt, play to the right where there is more room. Except in the face of a stiff wind, the cavernous cross bunkers play less part than they used to for anyone hitting a solid drive but the secret of the hole is as much in the positioning of the second shot. Any shot hit too far right leaves a nasty pitch to a 'walled' green. The pitch from the left leaves more options.

Muirfield's finishing hole is a classic, a hole that under any circumstances rewards the man with the skill and nerve to summon up two long straight shots. The drive, slightly angled, must avoid bunkers and rough, left and right; then sights are set on the smoke room of the clubhouse, the green the only safe haven.

Encircled by bunkers, including two on the approach to gather the mishit, the 18th green has broken many hearts. On the other hand, it has crowned the efforts of many a champion needing a 4 to win. Jack Nicklaus (1966), Lee Trevino (1972) and Nick Faldo (1987) hit glorious seconds to the green when nothing less would have done, a reminder not only of the quality of Muirfield's Open champions but that the links extracted the best from them.

NORTH BERWICK

North Berwick is one of the finest examples of a course which, though full of stout challenge, has earned the reputation for holiday golf. It is part of the celebrated cluster that makes East Lothian world famous but North Berwick's historical connections make it especially hallowed ground.

Geographically, North Berwick is a short drive from Muirfield yet in style they are worlds apart. North Berwick tends to have the public watching the golf from beach, footpath or road and there are some quaint holes that have a whiff of eccentricity.

The West Links is a course of blind shots, shots over stone walls and shots found only at the seaside. Its challenge is much more ancient than modern but two holes, Perfection (the 14th) and Redan (the 15th), are renowned names. Every architect has studied them; indeed, some have copied them as a gesture of their esteem. Charles Blair Macdonald was their greatest disciple and recreated versions of both on his National Golf Links of America. Some believe that his Redan is better than the original.

However, let us not overlook the beginning at North Berwick. Point Garry is celebrated as a hazardous opening hole with a wickedly sloping green from which it is perfectly possible to topple onto the rocks. It is a typical North Berwick hole, entirely natural and virtually unchangeable even supposing such a sacrilegious thought ever occurred.

The early holes convey the scenic splendour of North Berwick, notably the rocky islands of the Forth that are a haven for seabirds. The 2nd, where it is all too possible to drive onto the beach, and the 3rd, with its second shot over a wall, follow the line of the shore but the short 4th switches with the homeward holes by turning inland.

There are attractive changes of level on the next few holes, the second to the 7th having to negotiate Eil Burn. The par-5 9th, turning at right angles with an out-of-bounds wall on the left, connects

NORTH BERWICK
Card of the West Links

Hole		Yds	Par	Hole		Yds	Par
1	Point Garry (out)	328	4	10	Eastward Ho!	161	3
2	Sea	431	4	11	Bos'ns Locker	499	5
3	Trap	460	4	12	Bass	389	4
4	Carlekemp	171	3	13	Pit	365	4
5	Bunkershill	373	4	14	Perfection	376	4
6	Quarry	160	3	15	Redan	192	3
7	Eil Burn	354	4	16	Gate	381	4
8	Linkhouse	488	5	17	Point Garry (in)	421	4
9	Muzzentop	492	5	18	Home	274	4
		3257	36			3058	35

Total 6315 yards, par 71

Course record • 63, George Laing, 1987

A wall protecting a green may be frowned on by modern architects but such features as shown on the 13th have always been an accepted part of the scene at North Berwick.

with the most distant point where dunes guard the holes from the sea. The 13th (Pit) is particularly quaint, a short dogleg to the left with the sunken green protected by a wall. Perfection has a lot to live up to in its title. Blind shots are not to everybody's liking and the second shot on the 14th is over a big hill to a green sited perilously close to the beach, but it is undoubtedly fun to play.

Redan is a short hole to a plateau green angled slightly against the line of the tee shot, a deep bunker protecting the putting surface. There is a ridge to the left but the ground over the crest assists the straight tee shot. A high shoulder marks the right-hand front of a green which falls away towards the back.

The 16th, alongside the grounds of the Marine Hotel, has a drive over a ditch and an unusually shaped green in the form of two plateaux separated by a deep gully. The 17th (Point Garry In) has a long uphill second to a green close to the 1st, but the 18th is of modest length and drivable in certain conditions. Its approach, on the other hand, is difficult on occasions for being so straightforward. It bears more than a passing resemblance to the 18th at St Andrews except that the out-of-bounds on the right is even more threatening.

DUNBAR

East Lothian is rightly famous for its seaside links and the last, though not the least of them, on the journey south is Dunbar, nestling along the rocky shore a few miles north-west of St Abb's Head. At one point, as the course weaves its way from the clubhouse to broader uplands, it is only just wide enough for two holes. It is a popular place to play and attracts Scottish professional tournaments and amateur events. In 1953, it housed the British Boys' Championship which produced Alec Shepperson as winner at the start of a celebrated career as an amateur.

Like many seaside links, Dunbar has something of a split personality, the first and last few holes, if never dull, lacking the quality and freedom of the holes which blossom after the 7th. In a golfing and an aesthetic sense, the latter are more memorable.

An unusual starting formation of holes sees the 2nd return to the clubhouse alongside a pleasant bank on the left, the short 3rd completing a triangle with the 3rd green occupying a fine position more commonly associated with the 18th. It provides a good tee shot that must avoid several bunkers. The 4th, on the other side of the wall, begins the stretch that must have given the original golf course architect quite a puzzle in squeezing in two holes to provide passage for players both on the way out and the way home. In keeping with St Andrews, he chose the right for the outward holes which develop encouragingly as the 7th arrives at a green between a high wall and a beautiful stone shelter

or barn. It is as much of a feature on the 14th, a hole which is named Mill Stone Den after it.

A slight climb off the tee and a second over a ridge are features of the 8th but the more exciting hole is the par-5 9th. Here the drive must scale the hill, missing the out-of-bounds wall on the right

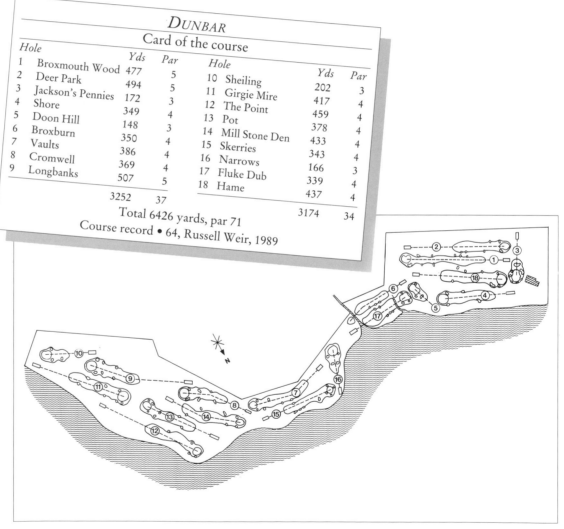

Hole		Yds	Par	Hole		Yds	Par
1	Broxmouth Wood	477	5	10	Sheiling	202	3
2	Deer Park	494	5	11	Girgie Mire	417	4
3	Jackson's Pennies	172	3	12	The Point	459	4
4	Shore	349	4	13	Pot	378	4
5	Doon Hill	148	3	14	Mill Stone Den	433	4
6	Broxburn	350	4	15	Skerries	343	4
7	Vaults	386	4	16	Narrows	166	3
8	Cromwell	369	4	17	Fluke Dub	339	4
9	Longbanks	507	5	18	Hame	437	4
		3252	37			3174	34

Dunbar
Card of the course

Total 6426 yards, par 71
Course record • 64, Russell Weir, 1989

The 2nd green in the foreground and a view of the short 3rd running parallel with the fence.

and, ideally, leaving a neat full view of the inviting second shot to a distant green with the curve of the bay beyond.

The 10th, a long short hole with bunkers left and right, reaches the furthest point of the course. The 11th turns up a slight incline after which the true splendour of the setting is unveiled on the 12th tee. Dunbar is past the point where the Firth of Forth becomes the open sea but the opposite coast is visible and it is an inspiring spot. This is just as well because the 12th is the most demand-

ing hole in relation to par, the green resting in a lonely position on a headland. The 13th green is very much more protected by hills and a ridge short of the green into which bunkers are set.

In terms of difficulty, the 14th, a long par 4 curving left to the Mill Stone Den, is a definite match for the 12th. Thereafter, the next three follow the line of the rocks before the 18th comes further inland, another long par 4 embracing the threat of out-of-bounds along the wall on the right.

CHAPTER FOUR

EAST OF
ENGLAND

I t is a peculiarity of Yorkshire, Britain's biggest county, that its coastline is largely clifftop, a fact which explains why there are no areas of linksland to warrant inclusion in these pages although Seacroft lies just to the south in Lincolnshire and Seaton Carew just to the north in Durham. They are authentic seaside courses.

The eastern seaboard's Open and Amateur Championship courses (with the exception of Ganton) are in the south-east corner but East Anglia has several worthy examples of links, Norfolk, in particular, boasting Hunstanton, Royal West Norfolk (Brancaster) and Great Yarmouth & Caister. As tests of golf, Hunstanton and Brancaster stand comparison with most.

Less has changed at Brancaster in a hundred years than anywhere else in Britain although the carries over sleepered bunkers and across the salt-marsh are less severe with modern clubs and balls. The remote setting is still the major attraction together with the call of the seabirds and the little sailing boats in summer streaming out of the harbour. The pace of life in Norfolk is more leisurely than elsewhere in England but Hunstanton, Brancaster's celebrated neighbour, is a club that has welcomed many championships on a course that sets a stern test. In an east wind from the Urals, it is even sterner.

Between Brancaster and Yarmouth lie Sheringham and Royal Cromer which, if not duneland, occupy breezy elevated perches above

the sea. They also have important historical con-nections, Sheringham as the venue of English Ladies' Championships and Cromer as the scene of the first women's international match between Britain and America in 1905 – the forerunner to the Curtis Cup. The Curtis Cup did not start until 1932 but the Curtis sisters, who took part in the match at Cromer, were so impressed by the good-will that was generated that plans for the Curtis Cup took shape from that moment. It is sad per-haps that it never took place at Cromer which has seen some changes in recent years. It has the odd weak hole but it is an invigorating spot with some famous holes. It is part of the richness of East Anglian golf.

Sheringham was the scene of the 1920 English Ladies' in which Joyce Wethered made her leg-endary remark 'What train?' when asked whether the noise of a passing train had disturbed her while putting at a crucial juncture of the final. Sheringham's course has more a hint of downland but Great Yarmouth & Caister comes closer to the definition of the real thing where seaside char-acter is concerned. It rubs shoulders with the racecourse to provide an unusual setting.

The Suffolk coast has its jewels although some of the county's best courses, Aldeburgh and Woodbridge, are just inland, conforming to the familiar pattern of heather, gorse and silver birch. Thorpeness is similar in spite of being by the sea but the oldest course in East Anglia is Felixstowe

The lofted perch of the 12th tee at Berwick-upon-Tweed.

Ferry. It was there that Bernard Darwin played as a small boy at a time when Felixstowe was a fashionable place. It has changed a good deal but it occupies a pleasant, gently sloping stretch of seaside territory and the holes beside the sea remain as an echo of the past.

North into Lincolnshire, the seaside theme relies almost solely on Seacroft near Skegness which, close to the shores of the Wash, runs largely down two valleys lined with sea thorns as well as more typical vegetation. It is the ideal combination of charm and challenge.

Seaton Carew at Hartlepool is the pick of Durham's courses, a club that has enjoyed playing on the same site longer than any other in the

north of England. Some alterations have inevitably been made but, in spite of being more or less encircled by industry, the seaside connection is unmistakable. It was once said that 'if the going out is a little tame, the home-coming makes amends'. Now, indeed, it may be the other way round.

Cleveland at Redcar is well worthy of a mention, the only links in Yorkshire, but, heading north again, the links of Berwick-upon-Tweed at Goswick beckon. It is a marvellous stopping place en route for Scotland, providing enjoyable golf in an enjoyable setting. It is a glorious piece of seaside terrain of which it is easy to become very fond.

The 9th hole typifies the appeal of Brancaster with its sea marsh, little boats and sleepered bunkers.

BERWICK-UPON-TWEED

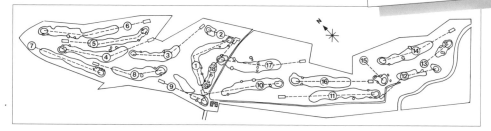

Berwick-upon-Tweed's ancient links at Goswick lie a few miles south of the town on a lonely stretch of coast within sight of Holy Island. Access to them is a pastoral one between arable fields and grazing sheep, the twisting lane gradually dropping down across the main railway line to a clubhouse that divides the course in two, front nine to the left or north, second nine to the right or south.

It is an even split in every sense because there are fine holes in both halves and uniform, sporty character in the terrain which has interesting movement everywhere. In places, fairways pierce the solid line of dunes that defend the land from the sea. There are elevated tees to display the grandeur of the setting and the greens are full of somewhat eccentric fun.

It is a trifle incongruous that the opening drive, doglegging round a gnarled copse with an artificial out-of-bounds to the right, leaves an awkward angle for the second shot to a green set into the dunes. The green position almost redeems the other shortcomings, and any quibble is forgotten as the short 2nd turns across a deep chasm on the crest of the sandhills and the drive at the 3rd drops down, turning right, at the start of a fine 4. A short par 5 follows on the lower ground which, for all that, is far from flat. The 5th tacks its way back up to the edge of the dunes and the 6th, a beautiful par 5, runs the gauntlet of out-of-bounds to the course's northernmost extreme.

Out-of-bounds governs the drive at the 7th and the strength of the 8th is its unusually contoured green but, in spite of a hefty start to the inward half, the true charm belongs to a quaint quartet of holes that make up in character anything they lack in length. They belong only on a links, providing puzzlement and pleasure in whatever conditions prevail.

At first sight, the 12th, Pilgrim's Way, is a trip into the unknown, a blind second over a rugged bank the sequel to a drive that must avoid a narrow, watery channel. A high, dropping second is necessary to hold the green at a lower level and the tee shot to the short 13th must negotiate a cluster of bunkers. The 14th, in an isolated alcove of the dunes, is a beauty for its natural simplicity. Flanked by hills on both sides, its green is a model

A dropping shot from a high tee is the requirement of the short 15th.

of cunning and subtle interest.

From there a path leads to a tee that surveys the coastal splendour and has a bird's eye view of every corner of the links. More immediately, the task is another dropping shot to a well protected green in a dell. Thereafter, the 16th and 17th involve substantial hitting that is more conventional but Goswick's chief joy is its ability to transcend the orthodox and ordinary. Its strengths are more cultural than cold-blooded.

The 14th, a hole that exemplifies Goswick's simplicity and wild desolation.

SEATON CAREW

SEATON CAREW Card of the Brabazon course					
Hole	*Yds*	*Par*	*Hole*	*Yds*	*Par*
1 Rocket	358	4	10 Gare	394	4
2 Long Trail	560	5	11 Chapel Open	471	5
3 Doctor	168	3	12 Beach	386	4
4 Dunes	385	4	13 Whins	559	5
5 Pond	373	4	14 Sahara	523	5
6 Mashie	165	3	15 Cosy Corner	203	3
7 Sandhills	354	4	16 Dog Leg	445	4
8 Road	355	4	17 Snag	397	4
9 Lagoon	371	4	18 Home	392	4
	3089	35		3766	38

Total 6855 yards, par 73

Course record • 66, Ian Garbutt (A), 1990

Rather like the American tourist's comment that it was a shrewd move to build Windsor Castle so near to London Airport, it is hard to think of Seaton Carew without its industrial cloak. Because, in 1874, the year of its founding, there were no other clubs in Durham or Yorkshire, it started life with the comprehensive title of the Durham and Yorkshire Golf Club.

In step with the subsequent development of the game in both counties, a more local name was assumed but Seaton Carew and Seacroft remain the only true championship seaside links in the east from Norfolk to Northumberland. It is ironic that such a classic stretch of coast is surrounded by factory chimneys, but Seaton Carew itself is first and foremost a holiday resort and the sight of sandhills close to the mouth of the Tees is a clear indication that its golf is something special. Fortunately a large embankment blocks out most of the chimneys.

A slender strip of undulating ground houses a rare challenge that, if deprived of the grandeur of more remote settings, deserves close scrutiny. The flat expanse of the practice ground bordering the right of the 1st hole is indication enough of how unusual is this thin strip. For all its masked surroundings, it is exposed to the winds that add to its devilment, and the four most recent holes, designed by Frank Pennink, capture a spirit that embodies more than a hint of greatness. They gave it a new dimension.

The 1st conveys the characteristic flavour with twin hills to frame the green although the 560-yard 2nd is somewhat mundane until bunkers enliven the scene. A series of four bunkers guards the plateau that marks the green on the short 3rd

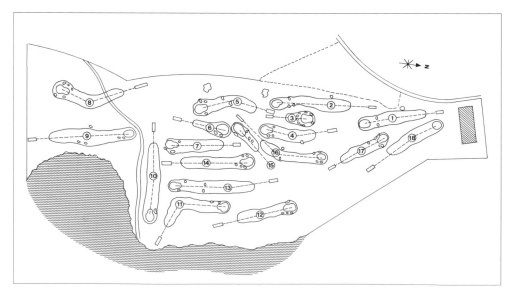

The Lagoon hole, played as the 9th on the Brabazon course and the 10th on the Old.

which turns back towards the clubhouse. After this, the short 6th is the only other variation of direction in the first eight holes.

Seaton Carew, in fact, maintains 22 holes, the club sometimes preferring to play the Old course which has a hole out and back beyond the 8th. The new holes contribute to the Brabazon course which was used for the 1985 English Open Amateur Strokeplay Championship and the 1989 British Boys' Championship – and great successes they were. Before the new holes are encountered, the first half ends with a fine hole extolling the principle of only being able to see the green if the most daring line is adopted from the tee – in this case skirting the lower marshy land to the right known as the Lagoon. The more cautious route involves the higher part of the fairway, with a sizable carry over sandy hummocks and only a glimpse of the top of the flag.

Of the four new holes, the best are the 10th, in a contrary direction to any other hole, the 11th, a fine dogleg to the right, and the 12th, penetrating lovely rolling ground on the edge of the dunes.

By now, the formidable sea buckthorn has made its spiky bow and the par-5 13th, 559 yards, runs the gauntlet of it on the right, but it is here to stay. Apart from the 15th, the only par 3 on the back nine, it dominates the drives on the last few holes, notably the long 14th and the 18th which is even more intimidating. The 14th is an avenue between heavy bunkering on the left and buckthorn on the right, the 18th having the added charm of a fairway punctuated by abrupt plateaux and plunging dells. However, the really memorable hole is the 17th, an Alister MacKenzie original – its title of Snag is a definite understatement.

There is some freedom from the tee, the preferred path for the drive being away from the central spine of hillocks that divides the opening and closing holes, but the fan-shaped green is an elusive target. Bunkered left and right, it rises at varying levels to a proud position that defies all except the bravest and best. A study of it alone justifies a visit to Seaton Carew.

SEACROFT

Seacroft lies in noble splendour as virtually the only true seaside links on the east coast of England between Hunstanton and Seaton Carew. This may explain why it is comparatively little known but it is an absolute gem and, if my words send golfers scurrying across the Lincolnshire Fens to see for themselves, it is no more than it deserves.

It occupies land reclaimed from the Wash a mile or two south of Skegness on the way to the nature reserve, Gibraltar Point. The furthest end of the course enjoys the sense of remoteness golfers love although the first two and last two holes are bordered by garden fences and suburban avenues. They strike an intimate note on the approach to one of the most distinctive of our links, the notable features being two contrasting levels to the holes and a sea of thorn bushes and trees acting as the division between them and posing prickly problems almost throughout.

Seacroft is a clear example of the pattern of so many links in having the clubhouse nearest the main centre of population and the holes running virtually in single file to the turn and in single file back again. The characteristic symes, ridges and mounds lend an engaging degree of undulation to fairways which occupy the thinnest of strips, the land to the right of the 8th being flat, agricultural, and far more typical of Lincolnshire.

By today's standards, an overall length of 6501 yards is modest but few courses, if any, pose a sterner test of straight driving. There isn't quite the impression of walking continually through a gateway of sandhills although a central spine of dunes always seems to limit the freedom to the left. In spite of the closeness of the outward and inward holes, no suggestion exists of double fairways and there is every opportunity on several holes going out of driving out of bounds to the right. Seacroft is no place to cultivate a slice. On nearly every tee, it is a case of looking down a gun barrel and, in a crosswind, it is the very devil.

Little hint of what lies ahead is apparent on the 1st tee on which the aim is on a large tree. The 2nd green on a hill slope gives a little more clue but, once the brow is scaled in front of the 3rd tee, expectation mounts. It is a pity that the 3rd green is not visible from the tee because the thin line between a bunker and a lone thorn needs to be carefully plotted. The elevation of the green setting is reflected by the difficult pitch from the right, if it is missed. The short 4th provides another elevated green, the first of four beautiful par 3s although the only one going out.

Only the fairway will do on the 5th which has a particularly enclosed look, a bunker on the left pushing shots towards the out-of-bounds. The feeling is matched on the 8th where, as well as being hemmed in left and right, a central bunker forces the long drivers to play short. In between, the 6th turns back, a short par 4 dominated by bunkers, and the 7th finds the green tucked in

SEACROFT
Card of the course

Hole	Yds	Par	Hole	Yds	Par
1	405	4	10	156	3
2	375	4	11	539	5
3	330	4	12	225	3
4	187	3	13	495	5
5	431	4	14	176	3
6	333	4	15	406	4
7	428	4	16	314	4
8	395	4	17	414	4
9	478	5	18	414	4
	3362	36		3139	35

Total 6501 yards, par 71
Course record • 68,
Simon Hatch (A), 1991

The short 14th, on an elevated ridge, which contributes substantially to the strength of the back nine. Seacroft's characteristic thorn bushes are clearly visible.

behind sandhills. A little ridge in front makes the angle or shape of the second shot all-important.

Another oblique second over a hill completes the outward half but the journey home begins with a lovely short hole over a valley to a green sitting up and looking justly proud of itself on top of an exposed ridge: it exemplifies the classic simplicity of links architecture. One of the hardest drives and the longest short hole follow, the 12th, turning at right angles and heading up towards the sea.

The 13th is one hole by which Seacroft is principally remembered, where a long drive and a long, daring second are essential if the green is to be reached. It stands defiantly on another ridge overlooking a marshy lagoon between it and the sea. Less ambitiously, the hole may be played more to position the second over a prominent hog's-back and then to pitch up over two bunkers on the slope.

It may be on account of the views over the Wash that Seacroft reminds me a little of parts of Hunstanton, but the next three holes preserve the heady standard and form the section of the course most vulnerable to crosswinds. They all follow the same long plateau although, after the fine 14th, the third par 3 in five holes, the drive at the 15th embraces a carry over a hill. The green, offset by a delicately chiselled approach and standing back to back with the 3rd, is the climax of another marvellous hole.

On the 16th, there is every incentive to take a bold line on a fairway that tapers down to a narrow neck in front of the green. Then it is back to the rows of houses and two holes of 414 yards. At that length, the 17th and 18th cannot be taken for granted but it would be asking too much if everything was as splendid as Seacroft's interior heartland. It is superb.

HUNSTANTON

Hunstanton and Brancaster are frequently mentioned in the same breath, largely on account of their close proximity to each other on the Norfolk coast. There are inevitable arguments about their respective merits although it is one argument into which I will not be drawn. My affections are shared equally.

One point that can be made in favour of Hunstanton is that it is the sterner test, particularly with card and pencil, the successful result of one or two attempts to upgrade it from days long ago when it had the reputation of being 'for the most part very good'. James Braid had a hand in devising some cunning bunkering and James Sherlock raised the course to new dimensions by adding the existing 9th, 10th and 11th holes.

The course straddles a long spine of dunes on the waters of the Wash, the lower-lying, inland part influenced by the River Hun and the higher part nearer the sea providing the best holes. In the cold easterly winds, the journey to the turn can be formidably difficult – even the drive over the magnificent bunker at the 1st.

The drive at the 2nd must be long and daring if there is any hope of reaching the green in two, while the 3rd and 5th are excellent 4s with the constant danger of slicing into the Hun. In between, the short 4th does an about-turn with a crisp iron shot called for, but the 6th and 7th are a pleasant foil for each other and for the rest of the outward nine which can be classed as 'big golf'.

After a drive onto a flat, almost meadowy, fairway at the 6th, the second has to be hoisted to a narrow raised green with some devilish contours. Crosshill or downhill putts can be positively hair-raising, reminiscent more of some American greens; but it gives a definite advantage to the approach that is well conceived, well struck and well judged.

Accuracy is everything on the short 7th, the tee shot having to carry onto the green over a deep sandy chasm and central bunker and then avoid the perils of overshooting or falling away to the

right. Out-of-bounds beckons on the right of the 8th but the true seaside flavour permeates the 9th, another par 5 where sandhills guard the left.

The drive at the 10th, parallel with the 9th, needs careful placing down the left to aid the passage of the second shot. At the 11th, passing through sandy mounds, precision is again essential with the second shot to a flatter green. The next three holes go back and forth, traversing the central ridge, the best of them being the 13th where a high plateau of fairway is the target for

HUNSTANTON
Card of the course (championship tees)

Hole	Yds	Par	Hole	Yds	Par
1	343	4	10	372	4
2	532	5	11	439	4
3	443	4	12	356	4
4	165	3	13	387	4
5	424	4	14	216	3
6	332	4	15	476	5
7	162	3	16	188	3
8	483	5	17	446	4
9	508	5	18	398	4
	3392	37		3278	35

Total 6670 yards, par 72
Course record • 65,
Malcolm Gregson, 1967; Steven
Robertson (A), 1989

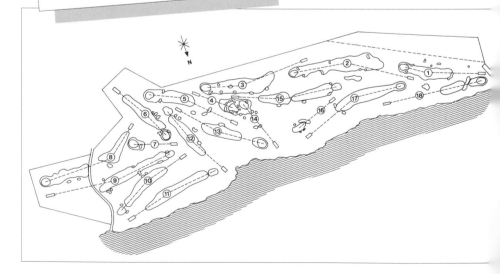

One of the keynote holes, the short 7th. The carry over the dominant bunker can be formidable in a headwind but gauging the strength of the shot downwind can be almost as demanding.

the drive and a green at a lower level the aim for the second shot.

A valley fairway forms the basis of the 15th before a climb and a high tee have us looking down on the short 16th, perhaps the pick of the par 3s, encircled by bunkers. In 1974, Bob Taylor, a member of the Leicestershire county team, holed-in-one there on three consecutive days, the first in practice with a 1-iron and the other two in competition with a 6-iron, but that gives the wrong impression of a shot that normally leaves one content to have hit the green.

Together with the 17th and 18th, it contributes a magnificent finish, the 446-yard 17th being the hardest of all the 4s with a drive to a rising fairway that inclines balls to the right if the line of the shot hasn't been carefully plotted. However, the best position is tucked under the slope on the left in order to obtain the most favourable approach to a green nestling on a narrow shelf. Too far to

the left and you are down over the hill; too far right and the ball cascades away down the slope, leaving a pitch that nobody relishes.

It is an unusual green but, by now, sights are set on the clubhouse. The 18th is an agreeable hole with the easy line down the right, away from the dunes and the rough that envelops them. Bathing huts lend a nice seaside note but a wide, sandy path crosses the fairway at the bottom of a sharp rise to a green that it is unwise to miss on the right. It is a spectacular ending.

Originally, the clubhouse was more the size of a shepherd's croft, a notice displaying the fact that horses could be stabled and tea obtained at Melton's Farm. Nowadays, the upstairs dining-room offers fuller fare but the view down the length of the links hasn't changed any more than the vast expanse of the Wash which, if grey and forbidding one minute, can be shining and inviting the next.

ROYAL WEST NORFOLK

In all golf, no course conveys a stronger feeling of remoteness and escape than Royal West Norfolk at Brancaster. There is a sense of timelessness in the bleak beauty of the saltmarsh, the vast expanse of sand and the distant outline of Scolt Head. It is a paradise for sailors, bird watchers and nature lovers, but, for a hundred years, golfers have blended happily and easily into the scene, content that so little has changed since their Norfolk-jacketed, starched-collared ancestors pursued their pleasure with hickory shafts and gutty balls.

There are few greater joys than a clear course, a light breeze to rustle the dunes' wild bents and the crisp contact of club on ball from ideal, firm turf. The club has never sought prominence, very much the opposite, so the true quality of the challenge has never been put to the test by the best professionals under competitive conditions. If only for curiosity's sake, this is a pity. Brancaster is decidedly a course that rewards shotmaking values and the powers of variation that some modern courses do not demand. As a result, many modern players think and play only one way.

Certainly, few have confronted the likes of Brancaster although the signal that it offers something special dawns as the lane turns down past the church and through the saltmarsh known as Mow Creek. During the highest tides it floods and the clubhouse is cut off, leaving Brancaster almost an island and enhancing its romantic character.

From the clubhouse, the way to the 1st tee is across a sandy path to the strand and through a wrought-iron gate. The first two and last two holes are not as memorable as those further out although the opening drive and the second shot to the 18th must have been terrifying when the ball did not fly as far as it does nowadays.

Brancaster is a course of carries and dark-faced sleeper bunkers on which good long driving is an asset – for that matter, it is an asset anywhere – in reducing the formidable nature of some of the second shots. They are much easier played with a short iron than a long iron. The 3rd, one of the

A notice beside the 1st tee that speaks for itself.

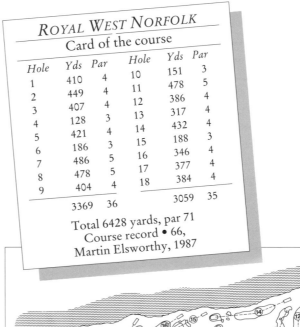

ROYAL WEST NORFOLK
Card of the course

Hole	Yds	Par	Hole	Yds	Par
1	410	4	10	151	3
2	449	4	11	478	5
3	407	4	12	386	4
4	128	3	13	317	4
5	421	4	14	432	4
6	186	3	15	188	3
7	486	5	16	346	4
8	478	5	17	377	4
9	404	4	18	384	4
	3369	36		3059	35

Total 6428 yards, par 71
Course record • 66,
Martin Elsworthy, 1987

The sleepered bunker guarding the 18th green presents the final of many such hurdles at Brancaster.

best par 4s I know, is a classic case in point, also serving as the perfect illustration of how a daring drive into the correct position is even more important. The marsh threatens the slice; yet the further you play for safety, the harsher and more impossible becomes the angle of the second shot which must carry over a raised sleepered bunker to a green perched on the skyline. A yard or two too far left and the shot is gobbled up by a hidden, sunken bunker; too far right and there is another nasty drop.

Proper judgment is necessary on the short 4th, which turns back over another sleepered bunker, and the 6th and 10th are more demanding short holes, both presenting attractive targets with suitable punishment for missing them. In between is perhaps the best stretch, notably the 8th and 9th which rank as great holes in any company even ignoring the aura of their setting. As the turn is reached, the gaze is caught by the harbour of Brancaster Staithe, the lovely shape of Scolt Head and the spread of the Saltings.

The 8th is certainly the hole by which Brancaster is chiefly remembered, although my preference is for the 9th which consists of a drive over the marsh and a second over a large bunker shored up by more black sleepers. The aerial route is the only means of reaching it. In a headwind, it

is a particularly satisfying green to hit, but there are no sleepers on the 8th which tests instead the ability to make clear decisions and hit the shots to match. There is nothing quite like it anywhere else.

The hole comprises three islands or tongues of land; the first is the tee and the third is the green and its long approach. In between lies the landing area for the drive which makes a diagonal attack over the marsh. There is then a second tributary of marsh which can be reached if the line of a really long drive hasn't been plotted correctly. The marsh is defined as a hazard but the hole is at its best when it needs a crisp hit to reach the fairway from the tee and another crisp hit to get home in two on what is a short par 5 without bunkers.

Unusual green positions are the feature of the 11th and 12th but another hole distinctive of Brancaster is the 14th. The green is in a hidden hollow in a waste of sandhills and the second shot has to clear some sandy scrubland on the approach; it is often more sensible to lay up. The 15th and 16th greens are up in the dunes, then the 17th crosses down to the lower ground again. The 18th is on the old clubhouse all the way, a building on the edge of the shore that is almost exactly as it was originally designed and furnished. It is functional as opposed to luxurious but none the worse for that.

GREAT YARMOUTH & CAISTER

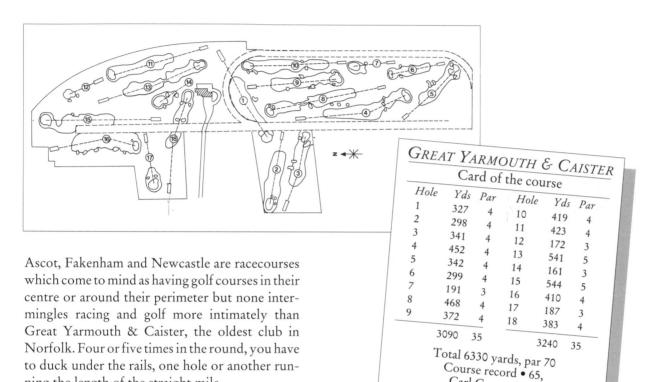

Hole	Yds	Par	Hole	Yds	Par
1	327	4	10	419	4
2	298	4	11	423	4
3	341	4	12	172	3
4	452	4	13	541	5
5	342	4	14	161	3
6	299	4	15	544	5
7	191	3	16	410	4
8	468	4	17	187	3
9	372	4	18	383	4
	3090	35		3240	35

GREAT YARMOUTH & CAISTER
Card of the course

Total 6330 yards, par 70
Course record • 65,
Carl Green, 1988

Ascot, Fakenham and Newcastle are racecourses which come to mind as having golf courses in their centre or around their perimeter but none intermingles racing and golf more intimately than Great Yarmouth & Caister, the oldest club in Norfolk. Four or five times in the round, you have to duck under the rails, one hole or another running the length of the straight mile.

This means that, in order not to impede the view of racegoers, the terrain consists more of hummocky mounds than mountainous dunes. Although the sea is within earshot, sight of it is obscured by low hills on the back nine and a wretched caravan park on the front. However, in addition to more than a smattering of gorse, many fairways undulate to give a liberal feeling of a links that is firm underfoot, the character of the shotmaking further influenced by the near certainty of a wind. Other parts of the Norfolk coast may be more exposed but Yarmouth, a famous fishing port, is hardly well protected either.

Apart from an unusual opening drive that cuts across the turn on the racecourse, the start is unremarkable, taking in the lower, flatter land whose only real feature is a winding ditch that makes itself known twice on the 3rd. At 341 yards, this is the longest of the first three holes but the 4th, 452 yards, raises the heat a notch or two: a deep cross bunker and an approach with nice movement highlighting a stern second.

By now the grandstands cast their shadow, the dogleg on the 5th diverting away from the winning post, but the stretch that completes the outward half is full of good things. A substantial carry over a sandy dell is a tough introduction to the 6th which, if drivable downwind, presents a narrow entrance between bunkers to a raised green that is wider than it is deep.

By contrast, the green at the 7th, the only short hole on the way to the turn, is long, two-tiered and drops away on either side. The 8th and 9th are excellent 4s – notably the 8th which verges on a 5. A slight rise in ground level adds interest and intrigue to the 10th which returns to the clubhouse, while another change at the 11th is signalled by the first and lone impression of a valleyed fairway.

Another good short hole, similar to the 7th, follows in the form of a raised target and then comes the first of two par 5s in opposite directions, the

Against the background of the rails of the racecourse, the 14th green occupies a pleasant hollow guarded by a sleepered bunker.

15th green embellished in the front by a large, grassy hollow. In between is the lovely short 14th, bunkers (one sleepered) causing quite a headache. After the 15th, which reaches the most northern point lined by houses, the finish is a trifle tame although the 16th has three bunkers on the right of the drive and the 18th ends as we began with a shot to hurdle the rails.

Not a bunker to be seen on the long par-4 11th – natural hillocks and gorse form an ample defence.

FELIXSTOWE FERRY

Felixstowe Ferry is historic ground, the oldest club in East Anglia – an area of so many golfing riches. Its other distinction is its precious connection with Bernard Darwin who, in his wonderful *Golf Courses of the British Isles,* wrote, 'I have the tenderest and most sentimental association with Felixstowe, because it was there, in 1884, that I began to play golf.'

That book also contained a watercolour depicting the scene at Felixstowe, the pebbly beach, the famous martello tower and a pleasant view of the course that ran almost to the Ferry at Bawdsey across the mouth of the River Deben. If Darwin were alive today, he would notice much change but, in respect of the tower and the beach, things are exactly as they were a hundred years ago.

In the early days, when a first-class return rail ticket from Liverpool Street cost 17s 6d, the tower was the starting point; the first course laid out by Tom Dunn included holes named Eastward Ho, Bowling Green, Orwell and Cork Light. Because of congestion, the course that started as 18 holes was reduced to 15 and later to 9. Felixstowe was, in every sense, a fashionable place whose fame and popularity were undoubtedly enhanced by its links.

Interruption to play came with the advent of the First World War and it did not resume until 1920, but the course suffered a worse fate in 1939 when it became part of the defence system against invasion. In 1946, there wasn't much evidence that it had ever been a golf course but superhuman efforts (not helped by the floods of 1949) led to its re-opening in 1950 although the building of the sea wall led to the loss of a fine short hole facing out to sea. It is easy to understand how the exhibition match to mark its relaunch was a matter of great rejoicing. The latest version of the layout embraces holes on both sides of the road but the ground nearest the shore is still the best and most interesting. From the clubhouse, the aspect is delightful with almost the entire course in view and an inviting tee shot on the 1st to launch the round although a hole of 432 yards makes a stern way to start. There are all sorts and lengths of opening holes, and each architect and player has his own fixed ideas, but a long par 4 can be just about the most forbidding.

The first three holes take you out to the furthest extent of what might be termed the old land,

Hole	Yds	Par	Hole	Yds	Par
1	432	4	10	509	5
2	501	5	11	324	4
3	310	4	12	144	3
4	324	4	13	356	4
5	138	3	14	320	4
6	423	4	15	404	4
7	491	5	16	220	3
8	498	5	17	446	4
9	159	3	18	325	4
	3276	37		3048	35

FELIXSTOWE FERRY
Card of the course

Total 6324 yards, par 72
Course record • 65,
I. Richardson, 1979

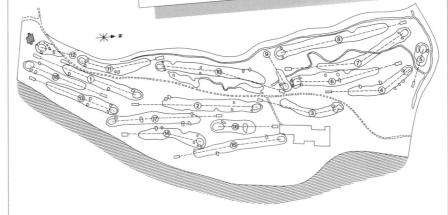

The symbol of Felixstowe Ferry, the martello tower, looms over the 13th green.

the 2nd, a good par 5 with two bunkers short of the green, swallowing up most of that stretch. Then a dogleg to the left makes the introduction to the lower-lying land on the other side of the road, a run of eight holes of which the 10th, another par 5, is perhaps the pick. It has a lake to influence the drive but it is another lake on the left approach to the green that narrows the landing area of the second shot fairly alarmingly. Out-of-bounds on both sides dominates the 11th before the short 12th involves a tee shot that has to clear wire netting, the road and three bunkers to a green in front of the clubhouse. Such hazards make it unique in my experience.

The 13th is the start of the nicest part, a finale that brings the closest contact with the sea and a variety of challenging strokes. The 13th, 14th and 15th run parallel with the first three, the 15th out to a pleasant green set by a charming white house.

There are reminders of Deal in this hole, particularly the sea wall. The 16th, the last of the short holes, has to surmount a broad cross bunker and the 17th is a mighty 4, with a beautifully contoured green as the recipient of a long second that passes the martello tower which, in most people's eyes, is the emblem of Felixstowe.

Felixstowe embodies the quality of survival that many of our links have had to possess although the Rt Hon. A.J. Balfour, Prime Minister three years after being captain of Felixstowe, in 1889, may well have had Felixstowe in mind when he wrote, 'My ideal in life is to read a lot, write a little, play plenty of golf, and have nothing to worry about.' And so say all of us!

CHAPTER FIVE

SOUTH EAST ENGLAND

When Dr Laidlaw Purves and Mr Henry Lamb spotted the land on which Royal St George's was later built, they must have been on the verge of despair. Anxious to escape the over-crowdedness of some London courses and find a seaside links to accommodate their Scottish instincts, they began their search in the Bournemouth area, working their way eastwards along the south coast. Knowing now that no suit-able terrain lies between Sandwich and Norfolk, they had reached the end of the line.

As Hayling had already been founded, the only serious quibble one could find with their judgment is perhaps their overlooking the glories of Rye and its then unplanned and uncharted dunes. What they eventually found from the tower of Sandwich church was incomparable country and they were right if they congratulated them-selves on their perception.

1894 saw Sandwich's first Open and, after a period in exile, so to speak, it has deservedly regained its position on the roster. Some changes were necessary to the course but Sandwich is only one of a tight cluster of championship links unmatched in their concentration even in Lancashire or Ayrshire.

Deal and Prince's housed far-off Opens, Deal in the days of hickory shafts and Prince's in the days immediately following the abdication of Bobby Jones. Jones's absence may have had some-thing to do with the sentimental victory of Gene Sarazen who, having failed to qualify as a young US champion in a storm at Troon in 1923, vowed he would return until he won – even if it meant swimming across. He left things late but his five-stroke triumph inspired him to such an extent that he returned home to capture the US Open for the second time by playing the last 28 holes at Fresh Meadow in 100 strokes. Golf had never known such scoring although two years later at Sandwich Henry Cotton played the first two rounds of the Open in 67, 65.

His achievement remains one of the landmarks in the history of the game, never mind the more parochial confines of Sandwich, but Sarazen's vic-tory next door was, without question, the highlight in the story of Prince's – the next chap-ter of which was near destruction in the Second World War. Those who knew Prince's in its heady days contend it was never the same again. Nevertheless, it is admirable golfing country which suffers only by its close proximity with two other such mighty links.

Deal is more straight out and back than Sandwich, which used to have a reputation for blind man's buff. Deal has its own blind shots, most notably on the 3rd, but it is less remote and solitary. There are echoes of the past in some of Deal's holes, high pitches to the 6th and 16th greens, a huge dell in the middle of the 5th fairway and a gathering green at the 12th with its sloping sides. There is little to protect it from the north and

The starter's hut at Royal St George's.

*Confine me to one course
and I would probably choose
Rye, which is unrivalled in
terms of character, setting
and atmosphere. This view
of the 7th green, nestling in
the sandhills and surrounded
by trouble, epitomizes the
natural challenge of our
traditional links.*

west winds and only the giant pebble wall to shield it from the east. Even that has, on three occasions at least, failed to keep the sea at bay but Deal has, without significant change, adapted easily from being a fine, old-fashioned test to being a fine, modern test.

Sandwich and Deal have their own decided advocates and there are usually no half measures although I find no difficulty in liking both equally after years competing in the Halford Hewitt, a tournament that is fortunate enough to play over both even if the headquarters are at Deal.

Littlestone is more like some of the little Scottish hamlets where there is little else except the golf course; or rather life tends to revolve around the club. It is not the most prepossessing place and the land for the course is a little flat but the sea is in the air and it is hard to resist the urge to play.

It is a convenient stepping-stone between Deal or Sandwich and Rye although Henry Longhurst felt it was not nearly as well known as it deserved to be. It is popular for holiday golf but it has had its big events and I remember it fondly for being open in 1963 when Rye was unplayable for the first time for the President's Putter. Littlestone enabled the show to go on, a fact that may have owed much to the statistic that it has the lowest rainfall (and, I presume, snowfall) in England. It was cold –

mighty cold – but there was much of the gallant knight in Littlestone's rescue act that was admirable.

Some of the bleaker parts of the Romney Marsh separate Littlestone from Rye, and a windy drive it makes, but Rye is a magical place, unique in the world of golf. It is a model of what a true seaside links should be, a test of imagination and ingenuity where bounce and run – the third dimension, as Peter Thomson has called it – are more valuable than raw power.

In spite of having only one par 5, the 1st, it never yields low scores easily, its combination of 3s and 4s representing something close to perfection. In the modern golfing world, it is a pillar of the past but it is still a paradise; and paradises are rare.

Rye, with one foot almost in Kent, wears Sussex's crown effortlessly but you are almost in Hampshire before confronting another worthy links. Littlehampton has its more inland side but there are some capital holes that take quite a bit of playing.

Hayling guards the western boundary of this south-east section, a fine course next to the Solent and the Isle of Wight which has delighted golfers since 1883. It has seen its share of changes but the turf and its character are as good now as they were then.

PRINCE'S

After its undignified use as a vital defence against invasion from Hitler, it is hardly true to describe Prince's as unspoiled. Lord Brabazon, a member of the War Cabinet, likened the pounding it received to 'throwing darts at a Rembrandt' but, in the restorative period, it has regained a standard that, if not quite of the excellence to satisfy the sentimentalists with long memories, has won a definite nod of approval from more recent generations.

The approach along Pegwell Bay past some of the holes at Royal St George's that look out to the cliffs of Ramsgate quicken the sense of escape evoked by Prince's. Tall wispy grass on low hills rather than high dunes gives a uniformity to the look of the golf. It has retained or regained a measure of the fairway undulations that are unmistakably part of great links, and many greens snuggle into the hills or are set on exposed ridges thereby accentuating the penalties for missing them.

The addition of a new clubhouse means that three roughly equal nines – Shore, Himalayas and Dunes – radiate from it, all three combinations to make up 18 holes having been used in important events of one sort or another. However, the great days of Prince's involved the staging of the 1932 Open Championship, which brought a romantic

victory for Gene Sarazen with a then record score of 283, and the 1956 Curtis Cup which witnessed a never-to-be-forgotten finish in which Frances Smith was the British and Irish heroine. The full significance of Sarazen's triumph is that, having tried to capture the Open on a number of occasions, it was seen as one of his last chances although, as things turned out, he went home to win the US Open as well.

One of the best references to that Open is contained in the book *Sport of Princes* by Laddie Lucas, who was born in the clubhouse. His father, the secretary of the club, had been responsible

PRINCE'S								
Himalayas			Shore			Dunes		
Hole	Yds	Par	Hole	Yds	Par	Hole	Yds	Par
1	377	4	10	420	4	19	440	4
2	376	4	11	485	5	20	147	3
3	172	3	12	161	3	21	484	5
4	319	4	13	385	4	22	400	4
5	380	4	14	377	4	23	406	4
6	570	5	15	393	4	24	487	5
7	183	3	16	538	5	25	363	4
8	407	4	17	176	3	26	200	3
9	379	4	18	412	4	27	416	4
	3163	35		3347	36		3343	36

Himalayas/Shore record • 65, Melvin Goodwin (A), 1987
Shore/Dunes record • 65, Joe Higgins, 1989
Dunes/Himalayas record • 69, Simon Wood (A), 1986

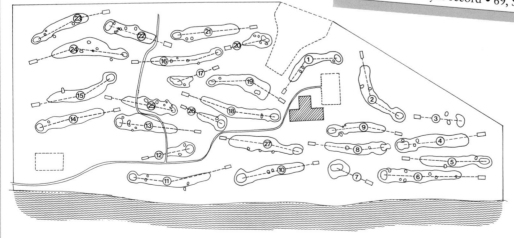

with Henry Mallaby-Deeley for laying out the course on which, in 1922, Joyce Wethered won the Ladies' British Open Amateur.

After the Second World War, the Australian, Aynsley Bridgland, brought Prince's back to life and, in spite of difficult times, it has survived splendidly. Preferences for each of the three nines are individual but all combinations are attractive.

Himalayas occupies the land to the north of the clubhouse, starting with a gentle right-hand dog-leg round two bunkers and a line of hills, followed by a sharper dogleg to the left.

Dunes also opens with a dogleg, a hole that has won acclaim for the awkward shape of its green, but it has other fine holes. The 4th demands five

bunkers to be carried to an elevated target; the green at the par-5 6th is not one to be missed on the left, while the 7th and 9th are tough 4s.

Shore, marginally the longest of the nines, has its best holes in the middle, the 4th boasting many pleasant rolls in the ground and a dominant central bunker guarding the green – somewhat reminiscent of the nearby 15th at Royal St George's. The 5th is the old postwar 18th and the 6th a par 4 on which hills on the left give the impression of a shallow valley.

One bunker makes the short 8th but the short holes, two on each nine, are not the least attractions of a modern Prince's that, for all its turbulent past, enjoys a solitude that is its trump card.

The 9th green of the Shore nine at Prince's. The old clubhouse can be seen in the distance.

ROYAL ST GEORGE'S

As befits a club bearing the name of the patron saint, Royal St George's has been very much a knight in shining armour to English golf. It is not the oldest club and some believe the course is not the best but nobody can deny its great and good influence or the historic part it has played in the development of championship golf in England.

It was the course on which the first Open was held outside Scotland, producing, incidentally, the first victory by an English professional. It saw the first overseas winner in the Amateur and the first American winner in the Open. Of all the subsequent victories in the Open, only two were as important in restoring British pride as Henry Cotton's in 1934, one of the others being that of Sandy Lyle in 1985.

By then, Europe, if not quite Britain, was the dominant golfing force in the world again but not the least happy aspect of Lyle's Open was that it reinforced Royal St George's as one of the finest championship staging-grounds after long years in exile. Between 1949 and 1981, it had to take a back seat as debate raged about its suitability to hold an event as big as a modern Open; or whether enough people would turn up to make it financially worthwhile.

Its geographical position as the only Open course south of Lancashire was a powerful argument but Sandwich is well used to controversy and change. Before the announcement declaring its return to favour, new 3rd, 8th and 11th holes were introduced and a bypass of the town built, but high on the list of reasons to take Sandwich back into the fold was the simple one that it is one of the truly great seaside links. On that, there has never been any serious disagreement.

It opened its doors in 1887, after Dr Laidlaw Purves spied the land from the church tower in Sandwich at the end of a coastal search that began in the area of Bournemouth. Royal St George's became, and has remained, London's own links, so to speak.

Looking out today from the church tower, the scene looks much the same, as do the ancient houses, narrow streets and toll bridge of the town. However, closer scrutiny of the course reveals that, whilst the feeling of wild, remote beauty persists, and the larks still sing, some of the original holes have departed. One of these, the 3rd, was a

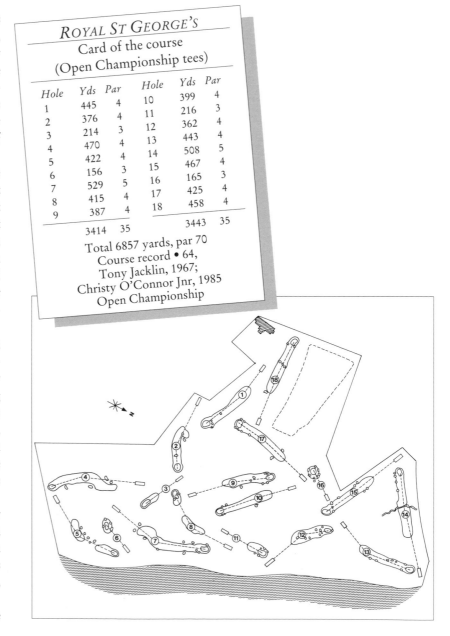

ROYAL ST GEORGE'S
Card of the course
(Open Championship tees)

Hole	Yds	Par	Hole	Yds	Par
1	445	4	10	399	4
2	376	4	11	216	3
3	214	3	12	362	4
4	470	4	13	443	4
5	422	4	14	508	5
6	156	3	15	467	4
7	529	5	16	165	3
8	415	4	17	425	4
9	387	4	18	458	4
	3414	35		3443	35

Total 6857 yards, par 70
Course record • 64,
Tony Jacklin, 1967;
Christy O'Connor Jnr, 1985
Open Championship

The carry from the tee at the 4th which can stretch the longest drivers.

hole of no architectural merit but there were many who mourned its passing.

Just as many perhaps questioned, years earlier, the temerity of the first changes that were brought about when criticism was levelled that Royal St George's was largely a driver's course and that there was more to golf than clambering up a hill to see where a shot had finished. These criticisms referred to the fact that there were long carries from the tees and a number of blind shots. The degree of blindness was further reduced when the course was prepared for its Open reappearance but two facts need emphasizing. The first is that blind shots are an integral part of golf at the seaside – and a vital element, too. The second is that

Royal St George's will always be a driver's course and, at a time when good driving, sadly, is not the art it was, any attempt to resuscitate it should be welcomed rather than condemned

After the 1985 Open, professionals complained that good drives could bound away into the rough: that was the fault of the rough not the fairways. Sandwich has a variety of humps and hollows virtually unmatched and you must therefore take it for what it is or not at all.

However, in spite of its severity from the tee, it has a more or less unrivalled range of second shots, an immediate example coming at the 1st where, after a drive over the Kitchen (why kitchen nobody knows), the green can only be reached by

a high shot over bunkers or along what is no more than a suspicion of conventional approach on the right.

The 2nd is a hole on which to gamble or play safe but there is not much future at the 4th and 5th if the fairway is not found, the 4th over a cavernous bunker and the 5th across typically undulating scrubland. Another feature of the 4th is a green with a wall-like slope to the top plateau. On the 5th, a small platform on the fairway allows the only sight of the green between two more hills. One of these might just be classed as a foothill of the Maiden, the name given to the famous mountain over which a short hole used to be played. Nowadays, there is a pleasant shot with a full view of the green from a different angle watched over, a mite disapprovingly perhaps, by the Maiden.

Views of Pegwell Bay and Ramsgate's white cliffs enliven the 7th, the first of two par 5s with the longer drives tumbling from high ground to a longer, lower expanse of fairway parallel to the sea. The 8th is the best of the most recent alterations of Frank Pennink, a searching par 4 with a knobbly cross belt of mounds and rough dividing a high rampart of fairway from the approach to a distinctive green. But two of my favourites are the 9th and 10th, holes that reward the virtues of subtle cunning, positional play and the ability to flight the ball in the crosswinds needed to show them at their best. They illustrate the infinite variety of the second shots at Royal St George's.

The elevated nature of the 10th green, etched against the skyline, can be an alarming prospect as, indeed, can be the task of preventing the sec-

The green at the short 6th, the Maiden, named after the hill from which the photograph has been taken and over which the hole used to be played.

The 17th, a hole that is often underestimated.

ond at the 9th slipping away down the slope on the right of the green. Missing it on the left is thoroughly inadvisable. Neither the 9th or 10th is particularly long but their formidable nature is always apparent.

After the 11th, a long short hole to replace an old 4, and the 12th, a short dogleg par 4 round a sandy ridge, the run home begins with an approach to Prince's; an altogether more formidable 4 with a slightly offset drive and a long second through something of a minefield of bunkers. This is followed by the second par 5, skirting the boundary with its neighbour and crossing the Suez Canal after which the 14th was christened. The hole is more interesting on the tee side of the canal which has lost some of its fearsomeness.

The 15th is a mighty 4 resembling the 1st with its second shot over a wide bunker. The short 16th is an 8-iron or 2-iron according to the wind, Tony Jacklin choosing a 7-iron when he holed-in-one in the last round of the 1967 Dunlop Masters. It is rare that holes-in-one help in winning or even contributing to low rounds but, for Jacklin, it

meant he needed to take no chances at the 17th or 18th, a fact which was no doubt a great relief to him. Both holes need good drives although it is the second shots that matter. The 17th green, wider than it is deep, is three feet higher than the approach, and the 18th falls away on either side, a perfectly placed bunker guarding the front right. The second shot must not waver an inch.

In 1985, Lyle's second to the 18th came to rest in Duncan's Hollow, so called after George Duncan who took three to get down from there at the end of his final round in the 1922 Open. Requiring a 4 for a 68 and a tie with Walter Hagen, he failed only at the last gasp. It seems decidedly unjust that his one blemish is remembered when his near-miracle is forgotten.

ROYAL CINQUE PORTS

For some reason, the film *The Big Country* makes me think of Deal, home of the Royal Cinque Ports Club. It needs strong, long-hitting golf to conquer a course more bleak than most, a battleground whose revenge is all part of a day's work.

The south-east tip is not the prettiest corner of England and Deal consists of a long row of unprepossessing houses creeping out to the edge of the links. It takes you somewhat by surprise, in fact, to find a clubhouse standing in splendid isolation but there is a charm about the terrain that has many fervent admirers convinced of its fairness in settling the outcome of important occasions. It rewards the virtues.

Nor is that an idle sentiment. Rather is it one based on more than thirty years participating in, and watching, the annual Halford Hewitt com-

petitions, the largest gathering of golfers in the world, which has brought greater fame to Deal than anything else. It is true that Deal has housed two Open Championships and, more recently, the Amateur Championship returned there after a gap of almost sixty years, but there is nothing like foursomes matchplay to highlight the strength and enjoyment of individual holes.

A whole book could be written about the triumphs and tragedies witnessed at the 1st and 18th or, more accurately, the 18th and 19th. Responsibilities of team play inflict terrible torture but the still, murky waters of the stream crossing the 18th fairway, and guarding the 1st green, make it a thousand times worse.

The stream at the 1st has much in common with the Swilcan Burn at St Andrews except that, at Deal, there is more room for error which paradoxically perhaps makes it harder. It does not concentrate the mind quite so effectively although the crossing of the Rubicon is the first hurdle – and a major one, too. It always helps to hit the fairway, and that is easier said than done. The 2nd, turning in the opposite direction, is a truer sample of Deal's seaside delights. The fairway has few flat lies or stances and judgment of the second shot is complicated by the approach, though not the flag, being obscured by a low ridge.

At the par-5 3rd, there is no sight of the flag at all until scaling the hill to descend on a punchbowl green that is wonderfully old-fashioned. It is not

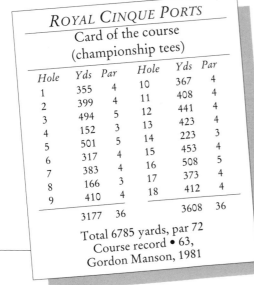

ROYAL CINQUE PORTS
Card of the course
(championship tees)

Hole	Yds	Par	Hole	Yds	Par
1	355	4	10	367	4
2	399	4	11	408	4
3	494	5	12	441	4
4	152	3	13	423	4
5	501	5	14	223	3
6	317	4	15	453	4
7	383	4	16	508	5
8	166	3	17	373	4
9	410	4	18	412	4
	3177	36		3608	36

Total 6785 yards, par 72
Course record • 63,
Gordon Manson, 1981

The 1st green, protected by a burn that rivals in menace the Swilcan Burn at St Andrews.

the sort of hole to win approving nods from today's tournament professionals who like everything visible and conventionally above board, but such sterile attitudes destroy the fun and make golf only half a game.

A lofty perch for the 4th tee, exposing players to the slightest puff of wind, is a fine introduction to the first of three short holes that make a distinguished set. Sandy Parlour's principal problem is a green wider than it is deep but the path to the distant turn is irrevocably set by now along the sea wall. The long 5th graduates from an undulating start to a flatter finish, the 6th is a quaint drive and pitch to an elevated green and the 7th a much longer 4 to a diagonally sloping target. The

8th, the second par 3, is a welcome variation in providing one of only two or three shots in the round that head due east. However the next three holes, all excellent, continue a directional variety all the more important for the fact that the last seven head straight back to the clubhouse, not that there is any sense of monotony about them.

Sidewalls on the 12th green can assist the second shot if it is long and powerful enough, an ingredient essential on the 14th where the tee shot must also be fired straight in order not to topple off the green into bunkers on the right or grassy hollow to the left. The 15th is a shade harder than the 13th primarily because the second shot has to have a measure of accuracy to

judge the slope beyond the ridge. It is rare that the green can be pitched but, if shots are played a little too hard or a little too far right, thoughts of a 4 vanish.

Placement of the drive is vital on the 16th, an old wartime gun turret representing the long, brave line to a fairway which drops into a low trough before ascending to a green reminiscent of Mount Olympus. It is a green of strange slopes and quirks. The 17th green has a quaintness, too. If the second shot here, which can be partly blind, is a bit of a lottery on account of the approach and the dangers of being too bold, the green can collect with its sloping sides.

The 18th is a noble finishing hole with no deceit or trickery. Ambitions vary, some venturing no more than to clear the stream from a good drive and others devising ways of pitching and holding a green raised three or four feet above the approach. Without a strong drive from a tee on the skyline to a fairway running away, horizons are limited but occasionally conditions catch you by surprise. In one final of the Halford Hewitt, three pairs in one team drove into the stream within minutes of each other, more used to days when the green is out of range in two. However, such extremes are one of the charms of seaside golf.

The punchbowl green of the par-5 3rd.

LITTLESTONE

Littlestone is a prime example of a course where only a relatively small elevation in the height of a fairway is needed to turn it from a flat, featureless plain into land with life and interest. At first appearance, it lacks appeal. Only twice in the first seven holes, in fact, is that impression relieved. The first occasion is when the shot to the 2nd green has to be threaded between a gap in the sandhills and the second at the short 7th which runs along an isolated plateau with a sharp drop on either side of the green. For the rest, it is largely a matter of bunkers providing the hazards although the design of the greens, notably the inviting target at the 4th, shows admirable skill in creating something out of nothing.

However, things change as the 8th turns parallel with the main road and hills on the right look thoroughly in place as the ground develops pleasant rolls. The stretch from the 8th to the 17th offers the best of Littlestone: as much variation as could be expected is experienced as demands on driving grow.

After another good short hole, the 9th, the next six run to and fro on a gentle diagonal, changing direction just enough to make the golfer think. The 10th green is tucked behind a dune that, if modest by the standards of Rye or Birkdale, is mountainous at Littlestone, while the drive at the 11th poses the vexed question of how much of the canal, flanking along the left, to cut off. The closer you run the gauntlet of risk, the greater the reward – exactly as things should be.

Another difficult green is the 15th but the 16th and 17th are the key to the round, two first-rate holes against which the others inevitably suffer by comparison. Apart from being the mightiest of the par 4s at 468 yards, the 16th doglegs left round a bunker set into a small hill with a limit to the freedom on the right. From the tee, the first real sight of the sea is obtained but it is very much a second-shot hole as the fairway, rising several

LITTLESTONE
Card of the course

Hole	Yds	Par	Hole	Yds	Par
1	297	4	10	413	4
2	410	4	11	372	4
3	392	4	12	393	4
4	370	4	13	411	4
5	491	5	14	183	3
6	157	3	15	359	4
7	507	5	16	468	4
8	385	4	17	179	3
9	175	3	18	498	5
	3184	36		3276	35

Total 6460 yards, par 71
Course record • 67,
Graham Godmon (A), 1984; Terry Gale, 1985; Simon Wood (A), 1988

yards to a delightful looking green, assumes the extravagant folds, slopes and hollows that the other holes lack. The long approach makes it quite a problem to find a landing area that won't divert shots aimed on the water tower, an old landmark somewhat reminiscent of that at Woodhall Spa.

It was the beguiling trademark of the Spanish architect, Xavier Arana, that the 17th on all his courses was always a short hole and he would therefore have looked with envy on Littlestone's. It is a gem. From a high tee, the angle of attack as well as the flight of the shot is all-important to hold a green whose width gives a wide range of pin positions. The green itself, well but not oppressively bunkered, nestles against a hill on the left but the fall of the ground deals harshly with shots not stoutly enough struck although the green is not that deep and penalties abound for overshooting.

The 18th is long and plentifully bunkered but hardly seems to belong to the same course. Nevertheless, in spite of its flattish nature, it constitutes a tough finish to a round on a Sussex coastline whose treasures are confined more to the east of the county. It hardly compares with the delights of Rye but it is a popular holiday spot and its advocates are loud in their praise.

Its championship qualities were confirmed by the staging of the 1961 English Ladies' and its emergency staging of the President's Putter two years later. The return of the Open Championship to Sandwich has brought Littlestone back into competitive vogue on account of its value as a qualifying course. A record as high these days as 67 shows how well Littlestone can look after itself but it is probably better as a matchplay test, allowing greater freedom to the mental approach and the chance of richer enjoyment.

The short 17th, played from the left, the hole by which Littlestone is principally remembered.

R Y E

My golfing daydreams revolve most frequently around Rye. There is a gentle breeze from the sea, the small boats with their coloured sails glide down past the harbour as the sun highlights the little town on its hill like a scene from fairyland.

There is about the journey out across the marsh a sense of expectation I feel nowhere else, a feeling heightened by a heavy tinge of relief that Rye's future was salvaged when wartime disaster stared it full in the face. The last of the flying bombs virtually demolished the clubhouse, while barbed wire, mines and concrete fortifications were strewn across the course. Its restoration was in serious doubt through lack of funds but happily a faithful few came to the rescue. Rye was reborn to rise to even greater heights.

No other course can stand comparison with it in terms of character, setting and atmosphere. Rye is Rye and that is the end of it.

The same goes for the town itself with its tiny, cobbled streets, picture postcard houses and the ancient landgate by which you enter. The attention of golfers, however, inevitably focuses on the links that, at a glimpse, offers a look that is unmistakably seaside. Even the make-up of its holes is unusual, proof that courses come in all shapes and sizes, and what a joy that they do.

It has only one par 5, the 1st; five short holes and the rest 4s but anyone achieving the par of 68 will reflect how much thought and skill punctuated the process. A conventional, stereotyped approach is as much use as a motorcar in Venice.

It is hard to know which makes the more strenuous demands, the classic collection of par 3s or the rich variety of 4s. In general, it is probably the former because an ardent admirer once contended that the hardest aspect of Rye is the second shots at the short holes.

It was a graphic way of stressing the penalties for missing greens that are smaller and narrower than most. The raised 2nd has deep bunkers to the right and an even more difficult pitch for those finishing wider than the smaller bunker on the left. At the exposed 5th, there are severe drops on both sides and on the 7th, nestling in the sandhills, trouble lurks all around. A row of low vertical sleepers is a merciless feature of the 14th, encouraging players to over-compensate and become entangled with the high dune on the left. Many consider the 17th a weak hole by comparison, one where luck may overplay its hand, but it is a gratifying green to hit and not all the bounces are bad.

It is said with obvious truth that good play and the short holes hold the key to a good score although Rye is a club where there are relatively few medal competitions. They set rightful store on preserving the foursome, a worthy cause, but

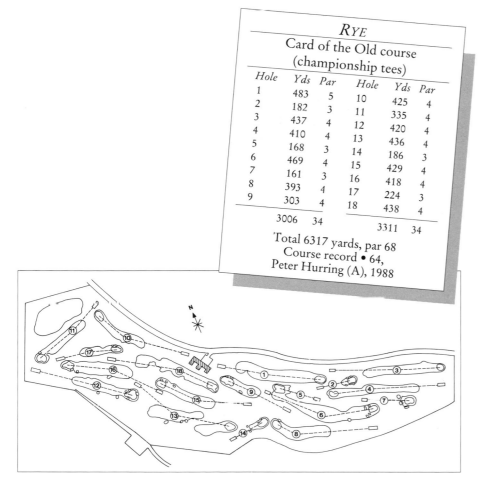

RYE
Card of the Old course (championship tees)

Hole	Yds	Par	Hole	Yds	Par
1	483	5	10	425	4
2	182	3	11	335	4
3	437	4	12	420	4
4	410	4	13	436	4
5	168	3	14	186	3
6	469	4	15	429	4
7	161	3	16	418	4
8	393	4	17	224	3
9	303	4	18	438	4
	3006	34		3311	34

Total 6317 yards, par 68
Course record • 64,
Peter Hurring (A), 1988

nowhere is it easier for the 4s to turn into 5s without, what is more, doing anything much wrong.

The 1st, the only true 5, is not perhaps a tough hole except for those for whom the blind carry from the tee is a hurdle. There is plenty of freedom on the second shot and no bunkers on the hole at all. In contrast, the second shot to the 3rd green, set against the terrace of the old coastguards cottages, has to be pitched to perfection in order to scale the rise and not to overshoot. Calculating the degree of run, and controlling it, is half the secret of Rye.

One of the finest and fiercest 4s on any links is the 4th, a demanding prospect if ever there was one. From a high tee that commands the best of all views, a thin shelf of fairway is the essential target if the ball is not to plunge down chasms left and right. There is more often than not a feeling of impossibility about the task but hitting the fairway is only half the story. In a cross wind or head wind, a long iron or wood must be flighted and struck truly enough to hold its line to a green so much simpler to miss than to hit. On the other hand, Ted Dexter, in preparation for the 1958 University Match, came close to driving the green.

From the 6th tee, no clue is given of the delights that lie over the ridge marked by a guide-post. The fairway below runs the length of the central spine of dunes that divides the outward half and there is a tight entrance between bunkers, or a long carry over them, if sights are fixed on reaching the green in two. From the peak of the ridge over which the drive flies, the eye also catches sight of the neighbouring Jubilee course, nine holes built and designed for next to nothing in the 1970s. To

The 5th, a reminder of the adage that the hardest part of Rye is the second shots to the short holes.

The 14th, one of a quintet of short holes, showing the band of sleepers on the right of the green that foils attempts to play pitch-and-run recovery shots.

Frank Pennink is owed the credit for the design, along with Dick Parton, his cohort from Rye Club, and Frank Arnold, the club's celebrated head greenkeeper for 44 years, who shaped the greens. They are worthy of the finest professional contractor and are an absolute joy to play.

Back on the Old course, the 8th and 9th are a splendid foil for each other, the 8th favouring a drive down the left and the 9th, a superb short par 4, demanding a precise pitch from a tight lie. Then it is off down the 10th, curving right between the gorse before turning at right angles onto the 11th flanked by a flooded gravel pit, often the only hole on the course either into or downwind. The rest are dominated by a crosswind that accentuates the excellence of the last seven. The 12th and 13th are very difficult, the 12th straight away and visible, the 13th, the Sea Hole, bending left and hidden.

Whatever criticism may be laid at the door of the 13th on that count, it is, nevertheless, thoroughly at home in a modern test as, indeed, are the 15th, 16th and 18th. The 15th, down a rumpled valley, can be two mighty hits; the 16th fairway rises several feet before angling left on higher ground round a cavernous bunker, while the 18th is another hole where the fairway is definitely the place to be. A deep pit awaits the hook, a sea of gorse and thorn the slice. The clubhouse is the perfect line from the tee and it can be very much in play later, its white walls forming the narrowest part of the hole thirty or forty yards from a green defended far better by slopes, mounds and hollows than it would be by bunkers.

It is in the world's top 10 of finishing holes, a suitable climax to a round worthy of the traditionalist and the connoisseur.

HAYLING

England's south coast, from Dover to Penzance, is pretty well devoid of seaside links. However, Hayling is an exception worthy of any of the regions.

Tom Simpson thought so highly of it that he classed it as 'the best links land in Britain' except, he added, 'for some near Bournemouth which is not yet a golf course'. Sadly, it never became one. Hayling Island's beauty lies along its shores and the golf links at the west end has no distinguishing features visible from afar. There is no hint of what lies ahead as the long, low bridge is crossed from the mainland. Even the holes close to the clubhouse enjoy none of the rolling terrain so full of characteristic folds and undulations but the challenge of Hayling builds up intriguingly, reaching its peak in lovely country at the far end with a nautical flavour about its setting.

There is only one really dramatic part where the hills form massive proportions, the high plateau of fairway at the 13th leading to a sharpish descent to the green. The drive reminds me of the 4th at Rye in the sense that there is a fall to destruction on either side although Rye's 4th has no bunkers, the Widow at Hayling being of a scale to rival the biggest in the land.

It is a hole which illustrates the art of the bulldozer driver, the course having undergone substantial revision under Simpson's orchestration in post-war years. Simpson's hand is also apparent in some of the half-blind shots that make judgment of length so tricky. It is a fallacy that you should always be able to see the bottom of the flag.

HAYLING					
Card of the course					
Hole		Yds	Par	Hole	Yds	Par
1	Trap	181	3	10 Pan-Ko Chai	270	4
2	Sea	497	5	11 Woulseners	152	3
3	Broom	397	4	12 The Desert	444	4
4	Butts	405	4	13 Widow	341	4
5	Narrows	162	3	14 Farm	534	5
6	Cutting	433	4	15 Jacobs Ladder	423	4
7	Death or Glory	492	5	16 Wharram	179	3
8	Crater	352	4	17 Sailors Grave	425	4
9	Plain	418	4	18 Sinah	384	4
		3337	36		3152	35

Total 6489 yards, par 71

Course record • 66, D.J. Harrison (A), 1970; Frank Gilbride, 1971; Kevin Weeks (A), 1979

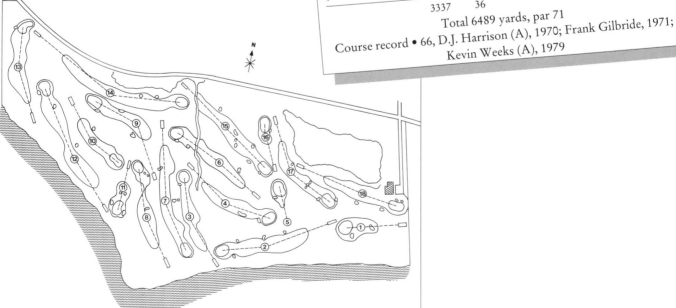

It is an accepted principle of architecture that brave lines from the tee should find greater reward than the more cautious or conservative approach and Simpson was a decided disciple of the creed, as seen on the 8th. Here you must place the drive on the extreme left of the fairway if the green is to be seen for the second shot, and a fine hole it is, too, in spite of the green being relatively unguarded. Not so the opening hole which is a par 3 with a central bunker 20 yards short of the putting surface to catch the bumble.

The first few holes take some playing although there is an impatience to look ahead. The layout is designed to play three holes out to the edge of the 7th before turning back with the 4th. A wide water channel has to be carried with the second to the 6th while the tee shot at the short 5th must be unerringly straight but the real heart of the matter lies in the first five or six holes on the inward nine.

This stretch starts with a short par 4 of high quality, gorse right and scrubland left divided by a bunker on the almost perfect line. A well bunkered shelf in the dunes describes the short 11th, a further line of dunes behind signalling the edge of the Solent, Langstone Harbour and Spithead. There is a nice confinement about the 12th, the longest of the 4s and the hardest, with a raised green nestling against the hills. Then comes the thrill of the 13th and the might of the long 14th where a ridge straddles the fairway and a pit forms an elbow jutting inwards for the second shot. A difficult, sloping green presents its headaches and the drive at the 15th, Jacobs Ladder, is beset with gorse and a two-level fairway – left higher than right.

By now, the ground has levelled out again, making the 17th and 18th a trifle plain but they catch off guard those players tempted to relax before their task is complete.

Looking down on the 13th green, a hole that houses the famous Widow bunker.

CHAPTER SIX

SOUTH WEST ENGLAND

Most chroniclers, in writing about golf in the south-west, think first of Westward Ho!, the oldest seaside course in England, an honoured name with so many historical connections. To say it is past its prime may seem something of an indictment. It is not intended as such. No golfer with a grain of romance in his or her make-up should forego the chance of a game and none could fail to be aware that a visit is a reverent pilgrimage. It is, for one thing, where J.H. Taylor was raised and died which, if nothing else, is a mark of distinction. Any subsequent lessening in importance is explained by the need to consider other courses.

Fashions inevitably change but Harry Vardon, Taylor's great contemporary, was a Jerseyman, and, out of deference to him, and by way of a change, it is fitting to begin in the Channel Islands. It also maintains better geographical order.

Royal Jersey, the older of the island's two 18-hole courses, is at Grouville, a mixture of links and common in contrast to La Moye on its western headland which is a mixture of links and flatter terrain which is harder to define. Vardon came from Grouville, the son of a gardener, and was 21 before taking up the game seriously. He was Open champion within five years. It is an amazing fact that Ted Ray, participant with Vardon in the celebrated play-off with Francis Ouimet for the US Open in 1913, was also a Jerseyman. He and Vardon were born within a mile of each other.

If Royal Jersey has the eminence of seniority, La Moye has figured more in recent times as a home for the Jersey Open and other professional tournaments. The inclusion of some of the turbulent duneland has certainly given a proud new dimension to its stature. Royal Guernsey, the first course Henry Cotton ever set eyes on as a babe in arms, is in part true links, the other part consisting of a few holes in which gorse is the main problem.

Both Jersey and Guernsey satisfy the needs each year of a host of locals and hundreds of holiday golfers but the volume of traffic on Cornwall's courses fairly depicts its popularity in summer although the autumn is sometimes a better bet for more genuine players. The Cornish coast, which can be so stormy, has many peaceful retreats with plenty of variation according to taste and ability. Whether all meet the definition of links is another matter. What does matter is that the sea is everywhere apparent and all are influenced by it.

Mullion, for all its relative shortness, is a quaint starting-point on the southern coast but West Cornwall at Lelant is the first to note as the north shoreline beckons, a list that takes in Newquay, Perranporth – of which I have hazy childhood memories – Trevose, St Enodoc and finally Bude and North Cornwall.

St Enodoc and Trevose are the best known, St Enodoc for its Himalaya bunker and magnificent

The 6th hole at Royal North Devon, where sheep act as co-tenants with the golfers.

views, and Trevose for its appeal as a centre for families in which friendly, enjoyable golf is high on the agenda. They are many who wouldn't go anywhere else.

From Bude, the coast road heads for Westward Ho!, home of the Royal North Devon Club, and Saunton, unquestionably the principal delights of a county which are so much more accessible than they once were. Taunton to Barnstaple via Tiverton is now a comfortable drive and the approach to Bideford over a new bridge can save half an hour. Although this same bridge has helped the journey from Westward Ho! to Saunton, Barnstaple and Braunton are still frustrating obstacles but journey's end at either makes it amply worthwhile.

The recent improvements to the West course at Saunton contribute to 36-holes which cannot be bettered anywhere. Saunton is one of the few of our ancient links which was laid out for the rubber-cored ball, very much a reason for its freshness. For all that, the dominant sandhills are a feature of most holes on both courses and, with small greens, there is a premium on control and accuracy with the second shots.

Its proximity to Westward Ho! resembles the situation in Ireland where Portmarnock and Sutton are separated by a narrow channel of water but Westward Ho! is the more lonely and desolate, more vulnerable to wind and tide: flooding, too, has become more prevalent as the Pebble Ridge has been breached.

The courses on Devon's south coast do not have the same problem because nearly all occupy exposed perches on cliff-tops. Of these, the best is East Devon at Budleigh Salterton though it is more heathland. Axe Cliff and Bigbury are other contenders but from Somerset and Dorset, there are even less candidates. The only one, in fact, is Burnham & Berrow – but it tests the superlatives.

Within sight of the Bristol Channel, the South Wales and North Devon coasts, it is a sea of wild buckthorn, dune-lined valleys, sporting dells and a stretch more akin to marsh – an indication of its nearness to sea-level. In addition, there is the more tranquil scene of the church which used to overlook the 12th green until a redesign of the course took the 12th to the right up into the hills. As the only true links for miles around, Burnham & Berrow is a notable outpost.

St Enedoc, source of inspiration for Sir John Betjeman who lies buried in the little church adjoining the 10th hole.

ROYAL JERSEY

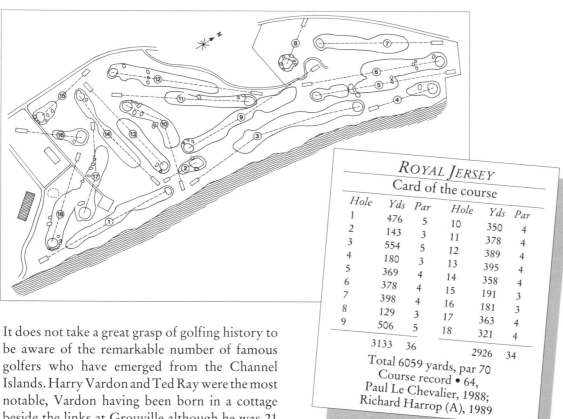

Hole	Yds	Par	Hole	Yds	Par
			ROYAL JERSEY		
			Card of the course		
1	476	5	10	350	4
2	143	3	11	378	4
3	554	5	12	389	4
4	180	3	13	395	4
5	369	4	14	358	4
6	378	4	15	191	3
7	398	4	16	181	3
8	129	3	17	363	4
9	506	5	18	321	4
	3133	36		2926	34

Total 6059 yards, par 70
Course record • 64,
Paul Le Chevalier, 1988;
Richard Harrop (A), 1989

It does not take a great grasp of golfing history to be aware of the remarkable number of famous golfers who have emerged from the Channel Islands. Harry Vardon and Ted Ray were the most notable, Vardon having been born in a cottage beside the links at Grouville although he was 21 before he took up the game seriously. The fact that he was Open champion within five years bears out the prediction of his father in comparing him with his brother, Tom. He considered Tom the better player but he added, 'Harry will win, he has no passions.'

Harry was only eight at the time of the founding of Royal Jersey which lies on quietly undulating ground on the edge of Grouville Bay, the pleasant harbour looked down upon by the giant castle of Mont Orgeuil. The settings of Royal Jersey and La Moye could not be more contrasting within the confines of a small island. Royal Jersey is the more sheltered, an observation that is strictly relative.

The first four holes follow the shoreline, the 1st hole itself acting as a dramatic opener between the walls of Fort Henry and the concrete gun positions built by the Germans during their occupation. Its adoption as the first hole came in a recent revision of the course designed to alleviate one or two danger spots, the compact nature of the layout indicating the scarcity of land on the island and the difficulty of expanding to meet the need for longer courses than a century ago.

None of Royal Jersey's par 4s, for example, is over 400 yards but there are two par 5s in the first three holes and five good short holes – two of them in succession, the 15th and 16th. Vardon had a fond regard for the short 2nd to a plateau green resembling an upturned soup-plate, but the best of the par 5s is the 3rd, a hole without bunkers which has a valleyed fairway of humps and hollows and a slightly hidden green.

The outward nine consists of three 3s, three 4s and three 5s, the 4s coming consecutively from the 5th running back and forth across the common.

Most highly rated is the 7th where the threat of gorse is real and a green on a raised shelf is not easy to hit.

A new short 8th is tucked up in a wooded corner, the 9th, alongside and in the opposite direction to the 3rd, returning to more open territory with a green on the side of the hill. Five enjoyable 4s then go to and fro, the 10th and 12th perhaps the best on account of having well bunkered greens surrounded by gorse.

The 13th and 14th have been much improved by new greens, the 13th on two levels; and the same applies to the 15th and 16th, the 16th now crossing back over the entrance road with a little gully on the approach to fox the tee shots.

About half of Royal Jersey's greens pose shots to elevated targets, the best being the 17th (the old 18th) which stands on what was an old German bunker. The drive features the Grouville Bay Hotel on the right, the new 18th passing the clubhouse on its way to a second shot on which you can see the top but not the bottom of the flag. However, the view from the green is stupendous, a definite feather in the cap of Royal Jersey which, a few modern buildings apart, is still ostensibly the same as in Vardon's illustrious day.

Although the course has seen changes, the view towards Mont Orgeuil along Grouville Bay is the same as in the days of Vardon and Ray.

`L A   M O Y E

In the last 25 years, La Moye, which stands proudly on an exposed headland at the western end of Jersey, has added mightily to its stature by the acquisition of new land. This has enabled it to graduate from the realms of holiday golf in which eccentricity and blind shots played too big a part to a links fit to examine the finest.

If actions speak louder than words, let the winning scores from professional tournaments complete the story. In 1964, Bernard Hunt won the Redifusion tournament with a total of 264, 17 strokes fewer than Christy O'Connor's winning score in the 1989 Jersey Open, the changes to the course accounting for an increase in length of over 650 yards.

On days when the wind sees planes from the neighbouring airport struggling into the sky, its challenge is full-blown – one or two of the shots adopting formidable proportions. The drive to the 15th across a hazardous hollow to a ledge-like fairway with a severe drop to the right is a case in point. Another takes the form of the 4th and 6th holes which wend their way out to a point on the cliff looking out on the golden miles of St Ouen's Bay and the loneliness of the lighthouse at Corbière after which a Grand National winner was named.

There are few lovelier or more dramatic settings for golf than La Moye or few where the scale of the golf matches its beauty. Several greens are set against the grey or blue of the sea with some of the other Channel Islands, large and small, adding to the scene when the sun shines.

The card reveals the outward half, which has two par 3s in the first three holes, to be the longer but the inward half is more interesting, particularly now that the superb dune country has been added for the 11th, 12th and 13th holes. Hitherto, the course embraced only fringes of it with one or two holes over deep valleys.

A big dogleg, moving through almost 90 degrees, follows an opening short hole but, after a somewhat pedestrian start, the course blossoms quickly with the 4th and 6th raising the tempo and the 7th adding attractive variety. It is full of seaside character close to the gorge that plunges down to the beach although central fairway hummocks mean that the tee shot is more of a lay-up. It is a question of establishing position for a second that must scale an uphill approach to a raised green.

LA MOYE
Card of the course (championship tees)

Hole	Yds	Par	Hole	Yds	Par
1	165	3	10	370	4
2	522	5	11	502	5
3	185	3	12	163	3
4	437	4	13	425	4
5	449	4	14	190	3
6	482	5	15	380	4
7	379	4	16	482	5
8	415	4	17	419	4
9	435	4	18	397	4
	3469	36		3328	36

Total 6797 yards, par 72
Course record • 62,
Gordon Brand Jnr, 1986

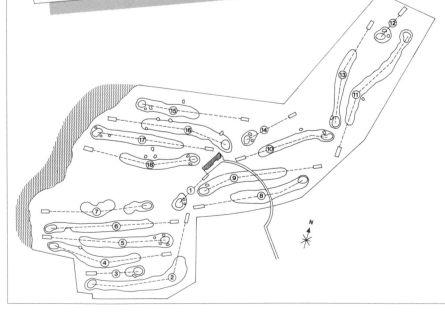

Assessing the angle of the second shot is also important at the 9th but already expectation is mounting on the exciting country ahead. The 10th whets the appetite with a drive between gentle dunes and a very pronounced two-tier green. Then the 11th and 12th, and part of the 13th, penetrate an area of sandhills and little else except for the stunted, wind-lashed pines that punish a pushed drive on the 11th. This is a fine par 5 that doglegs right before twisting back left to conform with the sweeping, angular slope of the green. It is the forerunner to a short 12th, whose green is the only remotely level piece of terrain in the midst of a seeming desert, and a bold drive onto a broad plateau at the 13th – the hole then swinging left and downhill to a green that, compared to the previous three, looks a little plain.

However, there is nothing plain about a stern finish, especially in a rousing westerly. The 15th and 17th match the 4th and 6th for strong shots to greens with superb views, the 17th guarded by a big dip on the approach. For a finale, the 18th is usually a fraction easier but the green is in full sight of a magnificent new clubhouse that emphasizes the extent of the transformation that La Moye has undergone.

Elevated splendour. The 11th green and the view across St Ouen's Bay.

ROYAL GUERNSEY

L'Ancresse, the part of the island which has been the home of Royal Guernsey for over a hundred years, is a popular place in summer. Golfers have to mingle with sunbathers, swimmers, picnickers and walkers, not to mention the tethered Guernsey cows which, under local law, have grazing rights. It calls to mind the tale related by *The Golfer's Handbook* of the young bullock in Yorkshire which was found on slaughter to have had 60-odd golf balls in its five stomachs. Certainly, on the more verdant common, a munching cow can receive some quizzical looks from those searching for a lost ball.

There is a nice contrast between the two halves, the first weaving a path through gorse and the second opening out to give far more of a sniff and sight of the sea. It was the first course Henry Cotton ever saw, his mother, a Guernsey woman, taking him for walks over the links although a move to London when he was 10 denied Royal Guernsey the claim of shaping the great man's

future. German occupation during the war meant certain changes, their ideas of bunkers affording little chance of recovery. However, the miracle of restoration was performed on much the same lines as on many of our links and the results have proved highly popular. The architect was Mackenzie

ROYAL GUERNSEY
Card of the course

Hole	Yds	Par	Hole	Yds	Par
1	336	4	10	381	4
2	401	4	11	426	4
3	189	3	12	189	3
4	438	4	13	322	4
5	392	4	14	526	5
6	476	5	15	406	4
7	173	3	16	297	4
8	339	4	17	304	4
9	460	4	18	151	3
	3204	35		3002	35

Total 6206 yards, par 70
Course record • 64,
Peter Cunningham, 1975;
Bobby Eggo (A), 1986

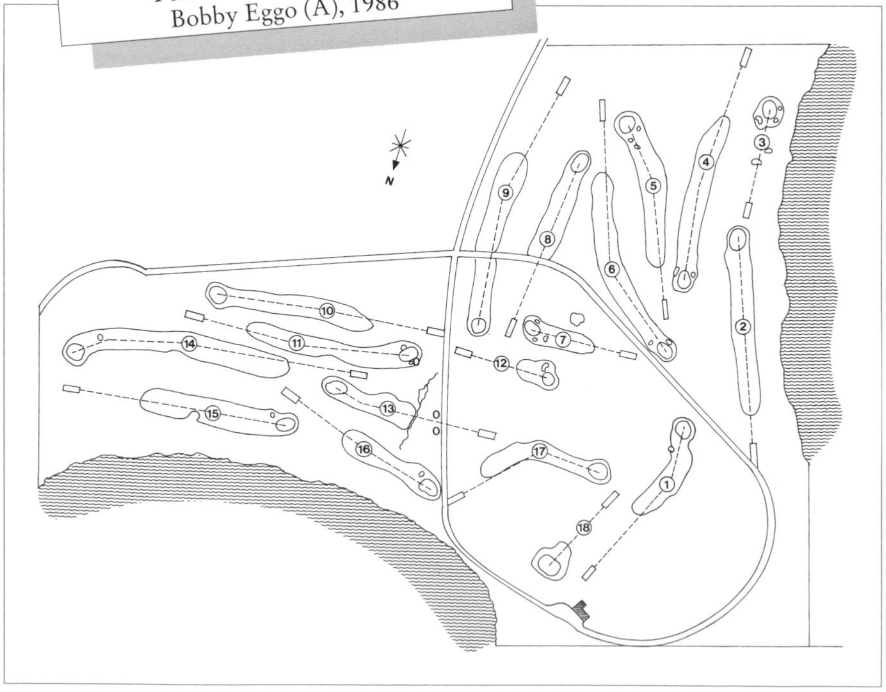

Ross, best known for his resurrection of Turnberry, further alterations being made some twenty years later by Fred Hawtree.

The 1st hole, curving round the hill in front of the clubhouse, makes a nice beginning with a shortish par 4 to a small green. Grand Havre on the right of the 2nd is an early introduction to the sea in the form of a more isolated bay but the aim from the back tee is on the distant Vale Church, an indication that the most pressing demand to the turn is a safe passage through the gorse. After the tightly bunkered short 3rd, the 4th, 5th, 6th and 8th, varying appealingly in length, present a wide range of shotmaking although the 9th, 460 yards, is much more a test of strength. It might have given rise to the old caddie's comment about needing three good shots to get home in two – or, more accurately perhaps, four good shots to get home in three.

The second nine, running more or less at right angles to the first, has more cunningly shaped greens – the essence of fine architecture. At the 10th, the target on a downhill approach is sunken in contrast to the raised 13th and the 14th which are neatly angled. From there, the eastern limit of the course, the 15th and 16th, a long and short par 4 running alongside the sandiest of beaches, head back towards the clubhouse as the prelude to an unusual finish.

A slight dogleg enables the 17th to scale the dominant hill, a bit of a slog on a hot day, but Royal Guernsey belongs to the band of clubs whose 18th is a short hole – in this case a fine, exciting short hole plunging down from a high tee, with resplendent views, to a green that is not the easiest to hold. The golf is in keeping with the holiday mood, enjoyable without being too serious, challenging without being overbearing.

WEST CORNWALL

One of the most remarkable facts about the development of golf is the number of great champions who hailed from remote outposts. Harry Vardon and Ted Ray were both raised on the island of Jersey; James Braid learned to play at Elie in Fife and George Duncan on the coastal courses of Aberdeenshire, but to Lelant in Cornwall belongs the credit for nurturing Jim Barnes, one of only five British-born golfers who have won the British and American Open Championships. Incidentally, Vardon and Ray are two others.

Barnes was born in the little village beside the links of West Cornwall, the most westerly course on the mainland of England, Wales or Scotland, which forms a noble trinity with Trevose and St Enodoc on the north Cornish coast. Its length is relatively modest although Atlantic winds can extend it alarmingly but its seaside character shines through in its guardian dunes and incomparable turf.

Cornwall's beauty is rugged and remote, the approach to Lelant by way of the tin mines and the towns of Redruth and Camborne being hardly prepossessing. However, the mood changes as signposts indicate St Ives, a place of charm beloved of artists, and the road leads on towards Lelant. When you find the church of St Uny, you have found the links which begins in the hardest manner imaginable with a par 3 of 229 yards. You take aim, what is more, on the church tower – an opening shot as demanding as those at Royal Mid-Surrey and the Blue course at the Berkshire.

Introduction to the sandhills follows in the delightful form of the difficult 2nd, bending right to a raised green that is tightly guarded. Lelant's is a tough beginning but, in favourable conditions, the challenge from there to the turn is more friendly than formidable, the 3rd returning close to the churchyard before the 4th descends towards the Saltings.

A single-track railway divides the 5th, 6th and 7th from the rest of the course. The short 5th is known locally as Calamity Corner and the 6th is a drive-and-pitch hole bolstered by the threat of out-of-bounds. From this part, Hayle looms large across the estuary but the 9th can be a jolt to the system, the hardest par 4 on the outward half. Nevertheless, matching the par of 33 is easier said than done.

A mounting sense of scenic expectation is by now apparent and enjoyed over the next three or four holes. The 11th is a superb hole dominated

WEST CORNWALL
Card of the course

Hole	Yds	Par	Hole	Yds	Par
1	229	3	10	331	4
2	382	4	11	362	4
3	342	4	12	494	5
4	352	4	13	264	4
5	179	3	14	446	4
6	337	4	15	135	3
7	191	3	16	521	5
8	325	4	17	194	3
9	406	4	18	394	4
	2743	33		3141	36

Total 5879 yards, par 69
Course record • 64,
Gary Emerson, 1989

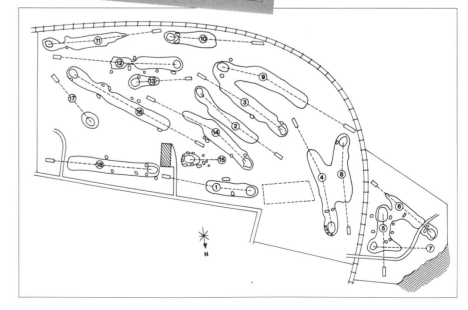

by another fine second over a ridge to a green in front of a hill adorned by gorse. The 12th, the first of two par 5s, reveals the full splendour of sea and sand while the 13th, though reachable from the tee, has the capacity to mar as well as make. Whatever the outcome, it is an inspiring tee shot. The last five holes constitute a finish full of good shots.

The 15th and 17th are short holes, of which there are five on the course, although only the 5th and 15th are under 190 yards. The 14th, in amongst the dunes, is the longest of the 4s, while the 16th, at 521 yards, is the longest of all.

There is the encouragement of a downhill 18th although the green is small and there is out-of-bounds along the right. However, Lelant is a charming course that induces contentment, a contentment that most golfers seek and find here more readily than on links of championship length which can be overbearing.

The elevated 2nd green.

TREVOSE

As the Cornish crow flies, Trevose and St Enodoc are just a mile or two distant from each other. By road, a more roundabout journey via Wadebridge is necessary but, in the character of their golf, they are worlds apart. Whereas St Enodoc's excursions in and out of mountainous dunes contrast with terrain that is almost downland, Trevose is a longer, more open course in a shallow bowl, less eccentric and less blind.

One thing the two courses do have in common is springy turf and an exposed setting that has no shelter from the wind but, in American parlance, Trevose is more of a resort course on which many golfing families descend year after year. For the purpose of enjoyable holiday play, there is none finer in Britain, although it is right to point out that Trevose is challenging enough as a testing-ground for more serious arguments – county matches, tournaments and championships.

In terms of par and length, the two nines are as well balanced as they could be. There is a fine start and a stern finish with plenty in the middle to hold the interest. The 1st and 2nd are attractive 4s that head straight for the sea, giving the impression of being slightly downhill to help golfers on their way; a helping hand is not to be spurned. The 1st, considerably the longer, is 443 yards while the 2nd has out-of-bounds on the left down its entire length. The 3rd is a fine one-shotter over a grassy valley and the 4th, the first of the three par 5s, a dogleg between dunes to a green overlooking Booby's Bay.

It is the moment to savour the Atlantic breakers that make the north Cornish coast a haven for surf-riders. It is a picturesque spot, the gold of the sand contrasting with the rocky coastline by Trevose Head which, in its darker moods, can be wild and desolate. The second shot can be quite fearsome on the 5th, a hole which, together with the 7th and 9th, contributes to a climax to the outward nine which was even tougher when, until recently, the 9th was a par 4. One of the most distinctive greens is the 7th with its lateral hog's-back, an example of the contrasting delights of seaside greens. The short 8th offers no comfort to the slicer.

Coming home, the 10th, so nearly a 5, has a distinctive, unguarded green while many view the 12th as the most difficult of all. As the short holes on the inward nine measure 199 and 225 yards from the back tee, there is no relief and there is

Opposite *Atlantic breakers pound the beach of Booby's Bay beyond the dogleg 4th.*

Below right *A fine impression of the approach to the 7th and its distinctive green.*

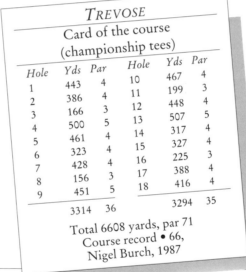

Hole	Yds	Par	Hole	Yds	Par
1	443	4	10	467	4
2	386	4	11	199	3
3	166	3	12	448	4
4	500	5	13	507	5
5	461	4	14	317	4
6	323	4	15	327	4
7	428	4	16	225	3
8	156	3	17	388	4
9	451	5	18	416	4
	3314	36		3294	35

TREVOSE
Card of the course
(championship tees)

Total 6608 yards, par 71
Course record • 66,
Nigel Burch, 1987

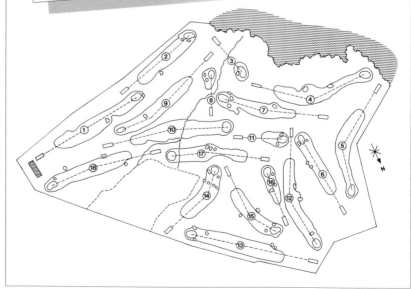

out-of-bounds to trouble the hooked stroke on the 13th. Then, after the 16th, the second par 3, two 4s to finish always represent satisfying work.

More control is necessary on the 17th than on many of the longer 4s. A clutch of three bunkers taunts the drive and the second shot is over a stream; then the 18th, up the hill, calls for another precise iron or, just as frequently, wood.

Nearer the tee, the ruined church bearing the name of the first Christian Emperor of Rome, St Constantine, acts as a reminder of the antiquity of Cornwall but, for golfers, the main priority is the next round. Such is Trevose's attraction that when one is finished, there is always an impatience to try again.

There is a definite charm about the remoteness of Trevose although its friendly air possesses a sense of captivation that is shared by the golf.

ST ENEDOC

St Enodoc is famous for a number of things, not least its Himalaya bunker on the 6th which many believe is the highest sandhill over which golf is played. The bunker at the 4th at Royal St George's must run it close but you are much nearer the target, or should be, at St Enodoc and, rather like viewing Niagara Falls from the gorge in a tiny boat instead of from afar, its dimensions appear more daunting. You need a more vertical take-off.

The size of St Enodoc's hills may, in fact, be something of a surprise. When Bernard Darwin first saw them, he commented that the golf had been described to him as 'eminently natural and amusing and yet, when I saw it, I was not prepared for such mighty hills nor for quite so many of them'. They dominate many of the holes but St Enodoc embodies three characters in one – true seaside, a few holes that straddle more marshy ground and some that are positively downland.

From the attractive new clubhouse that stands at the top of a narrow lane above the little village of Rock, the full splendour of its Cornish setting is somewhat obscured. All is not revealed until the peak of the high hummocks has been scaled at the 1st and you spy the green, the tiny, elusive target that the direction pole has indicated. Beyond, the widest part of the Camel Estuary merges with the Atlantic and, swinging left across the 16th fairway, you see the red rooftops overlooking the harbour of Padstow.

It needs a moment or two to assimilate one of golf's great sights, always assuming the wind and rain don't have you bent double, umbrella acting as inadequate shield. The 1st is one of only two par 5s but the course is so full of 4s that turn into

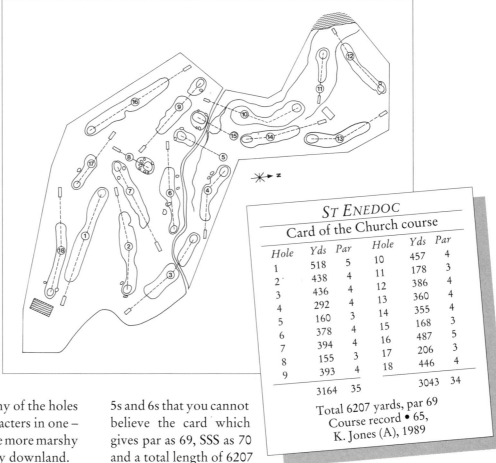

Hole	Yds	Par	Hole	Yds	Par
1	518	5	10	457	4
2	438	4	11	178	3
3	436	4	12	386	4
4	292	4	13	360	4
5	160	3	14	355	4
6	378	4	15	168	3
7	394	4	16	487	5
8	155	3	17	206	3
9	393	4	18	446	4
	3164	35		3043	34

St Enedoc
Card of the Church course

Total 6207 yards, par 69
Course record ● 65,
K. Jones (A), 1989

5s and 6s that you cannot believe the card which gives par as 69, SSS as 70 and a total length of 6207 yards.

Performing the 2nd and 3rd in eight shots is rare. The second to the elevated 2nd green is particularly hard to gauge although the downhill 3rd, with a road to cross and a wall to avoid, does give more encouragement. The 4th, which the maestros can drive, is a hole which, because you cannot go too far right, persuades you to go too far left. That destroys the angle for the pitch which then has to land on a sixpence.

A shallow valley, with a rushing stream in the bottom of it, is the feature of the short 5th but already the Himalaya bunker has cast a 'cloud' on the horizon. It can be skirted with the second shot if the drive can hold the left extreme of the fairway but negotiating the Himalaya is one hurdle cleared, and a big hurdle, too. However, hitting the shelf-like green is an accomplishment almost as severe.

After a blind drive over the dunes on the 7th, the course is more open for a hole or two, the 7th, and its view, quickly endorsing the feeling that the world isn't such a bad place and the 8th serving as a model of what a good seaside short hole should be. The inward half ends with another hole that does you good; an inviting drive to a tumbling fairway and an iron to a typical green that is pleasing to hit.

The 10th would not fit every course but it is right for St Enodoc, a long par-4 dogleg left between giant bank and fast-flowing brook. There is certainly no other way of linking the 9th and short 11th although one virtue of the 10th is its proximity to the tiny ancient church where John Betjeman, a staunch local, was laid to rest.

From the tee at the 12th, one of the best holes, Daymer Bay displays its sandy delights although the next two strike a change of note, more of pastureland. The 15th, with its dropping tee shot, contrasts to the regions of the 13th and 14th, a

birdie at the 13th once having prompted felicitous verse from Betjeman.

The finish is vintage. The 16th is a lovely par 5 showing off, at its best, the sunlit waters. The 17th, the last of five par 3s, is framed by giant sandhills and the 18th, a demanding 4, has an attractively contoured fairway and a green elevated as a symbol of defiance. The shot which will pitch the ball there and make it stop must be of supreme quality.

The club, having celebrated its centenary and bought the course from the Duchy of Cornwall, has been well served but never better than by Ned Burden, their former honorary secretary, whose memory is recalled in a poem by Betjeman. The first of several verses makes a fitting epitaph – an enticement to golfers to go and read the other verses on the clubhouse wall perhaps and indulge in a pleasant round or two:

The flag that hung half-mast today
Seemed animate with being
As if it knew for whom it flew
And would no more be seeing.

The target on the 6th if the giant Himalayas bunker has been successfully negotiated. On the other side of the road is the 4th tee to a green beside the wall in the distance.

ROYAL NORTH DEVON

ROYAL NORTH DEVON					
Card of the Championship course (championship tees)					
Hole	Yds	Par	Hole	Yds	Par
1 Burn	485	5	10 Rush	372	4
2 Baggy	424	4	11 Appledore	371	4
3 Sandymere	418	4	12 Hinde	425	4
4 Cape	354	4	13 Lundy	440	4
5 Table	137	3	14 Iron Hut	205	3
6 Crest	413	4	15 Church	431	4
7 Bar	400	4	16 Punch Bowl	145	3
8 Estuary	197	3	17 Road	548	5
9 Westward Ho!	481	5	18 Home	416	4
	3309	36		3353	35

Total 6662 yards, par 71

Course record • 66, Kel Nagle, Peter Dawson, Martin Foster, 1975; D.J. Boughey (A), 1982

Westward Ho!, a name once heard never forgotten, means different things to different people. To the holidaymaker, it may mean memories of traffic jams when it was very much more off the beaten track than it is today. To the literary world, it evokes the book written by Charles Kingsley in the house in Bideford belonging to Captain Molesworth. To evacuees from London in the last war, it represented a home from home but to golfers, and English golfers in particular, it is a bright echo of the days when it was on the tip of everybody's tongue. Of all the seaside links in England, it ranks first in seniority and, if Hoylake might claim its golfing sons to have been of greater eminence, Westward Ho! would dispute the matter fiercely.

J.H. Taylor, Horace Hutchinson and the Hon. Michael Scott would have had the devil of a battle with John Ball, Harold Hilton and Jack Graham. By winning the club medal in 1875 at the tender age of 16, Hutchinson enjoyed the unusual step of being automatically nominated as captain and taking the chair at the annual meeting. It was a rule that was later amended but it is a story that typified the great and glorious days.

If there is a sense of lingering in the past, it only serves to emphasize the problems that have since confronted the Royal North Devon Club. During the last war, the course suffered the ignominy of being used for bombing practice. The pot-wallopers of Northam and Appledore have maintained their ancient grazing rights to the detriment of the course's condition and, more recently, the sea has broken through the Pebble Ridge. No other club has endured quite such a succession of setbacks but Westward Ho! remains a haven for the connoisseur, a course of charm and a delightful place to play.

The feeling of excitement at the sight of the Burrows that first aroused J.H. Taylor's passion persists. The words of General Moncrieffe that 'Providence obviously designed this for a golf links' still rings true and, in an era when every-

body is tampering with courses, it is both comfort and compliment that the layout has changed hardly at all.

It spreads across a great panoply of linksland, flat and lonely. The landscape, though bold, is wild and barren. There are no avenues of dunes; instead, a sense of freedom abounds. It taught J.H. Taylor the need for a solid stance, the art of flight and the importance of control in winds that are

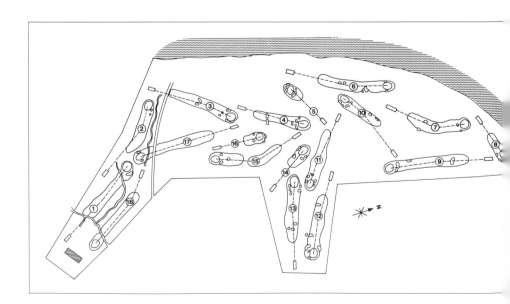

One of the most famous bunkers in golf, the Cape, on the 4th hole – not so formidable carry as in the days of hickory and gutty.

such a feature of the seaside. Such attributes are just as important today.

Westward Ho! begins slowly and breaks the golfer in gradually, the first two holes aiming straight for the Pebble Ridge and Bideford Bay beyond. There is no immediate sign of being on classic ground but the 3rd, another two-shotter, turns to the right with its narrow, well bunkered entrance to the green. Then, the true flavour is sampled.

The flatness left behind, the drive at the 4th must carry a huge black-boarded bunker, the Cape, a fearsome task (170 yards) with hickory and gutty. Nowadays, it is easier to sail over, leaving only a modest iron to a green in a bit of a hollow. The 5th is an appealing short hole played back towards the sandhills, a prelude to two of the best driving holes and the second short hole which, nevertheless, can be a wood.

The 9th, the second par 5, is a grand hole but

the golfer is now in the midst of the famous rushes, tall and spiky, with a good score depending on how well he can steer a straight path through, round or over them. The 10th and 11th are of medium length, the 12th substantially more, although the 12th takes us free of the rushes and back onto the flatter land.

The 13th is the longest 4 with a cluster of bunkers surrounding the green but the course gathers steam again with the 15th and 16th, the latter described by Bernard Darwin as 'perhaps the best short hole in the world'. It calls for a high shot over a bunker to a green that is inclined to shed the slightest error into one of a number of other attendant bunkers.

Thereafter, there is the long 17th, usually played into the wind and requiring a delicate pitch to negotiate the ditch in front of the green. Like all good 17th holes, it has turned the fortunes of many matches and medals as, indeed, has the 18th with its two burns and a raised green. The second of the burns is the more sinister and played a dramatic part in the outcome of the exhibition match played to mark the club's centenary in 1964.

As you might expect, it was no ordinary exhibition, a four-ball match between Peter Alliss and Brian Huggett, in modern dress and with modern equipment, against Christy O'Connor and Max Faulkner, wearing Norfolk jackets, knee breeches and starched collars, and using five clubs of the 1864 period – a wood, mid-iron, mashie, mashie-niblick and putter. They were carried in the traditional under-the-arm style by the local assistants. O'Connor and Faulkner also played with specially made gutty balls without the advantage of a tee.

In receipt of 12 shots each, O'Connor and Faulkner came to the 18th one-up after Faulkner had holed a long putt on the 16th and O'Connor had won the 17th. Alliss and Huggett were both on the 18th green in two, a feat beyond Faulkner and O'Connor, but O'Connor, trying for the green, finding the burn instead and having to pick out under penalty, followed by holing a mashie-niblick from about 40 yards to clinch victory.

It was a memorable moment to add to an illustrious past in which J.H. Taylor was a prominent figure. Having started his working life as a boot-boy in the home of Horace Hutchinson's father, he rose from caddie to being five times Open champion, captain of the PGA and finally club president. In his more active days, he was away from Westward Ho! more often than he can have wished but he died in his home on the hill above the links, a home which, in his own words, 'had the finest view in Christendom'.

A general view of the links at Westward Ho! The distant impression of lack of feature is dispelled on closer inspection.

SAUNTON

When Harry Vardon first saw Saunton, he said he should like to retire and live in a cottage there, and do nothing but play golf for pleasure. It is doubtful if any course received a greater compliment, for Vardon's idea of playing the game for pleasure undoubtedly included the fact that it must have the capacity to satisfy his incomparable talent as well.

Saunton has experienced a chequered history on account of its strategic importance in wartime. The lovely course on which Frank Pennink and Leonard Crawley contested the final of the English Championship in 1937 was a sad victim of the wartime Battle School although it has been restored as the East.

Saunton began life in 1893, with the local Post Office also being used as the clubhouse, on land at the northern end of Braunton Burrows leased from John Christie (whose family founded

Glyndebourne). It was the start of a long and happy association with the Christies but the strength of the old course – now the East – is that the modern version was laid out in the 1920s, twenty years or so after the introduction of the Haskell or rubber-cored ball. This gave it, and still does, a big advantage over older links, the design work of Herbert Fowler reflecting the fact that the Haskell ball went so much further. Ken Cotton undertook changes to the first two and last two holes in 1951 but Saunton offers majestic golf on some of the finest natural land you could find anywhere.

North Devon's charm lies in its remoteness, although it has become far more accessible in the last few years. From the M5 west of Taunton, a new road skirting Tiverton makes a comfortable journey to Barnstaple which is not the bottleneck of old. However, nobody would want the last part through Braunton any other way, the characteristic high West Country hedges gradually allowing the magnificent Burrows to come into

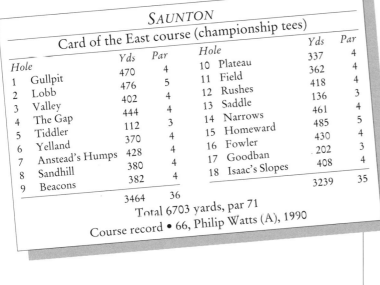

SAUNTON
Card of the East course (championship tees)

Hole		Yds	Par	Hole		Yds	Par
1	Gullpit	470	4	10	Plateau	337	4
2	Lobb	476	5	11	Field	362	4
3	Valley	402	4	12	Rushes	418	4
4	The Gap	444	4	13	Saddle	136	3
5	Tiddler	112	3	14	Narrows	461	4
6	Yelland	370	4	15	Homeward	485	5
7	Anstead's Humps	428	4	16	Fowler	430	4
8	Sandhill	380	4	17	Goodban	202	3
9	Beacons	382	4	18	Isaac's Slopes	408	4
		3464	36			3239	35

Total 6703 yards, par 71

Course record • 66, Philip Watts (A), 1990

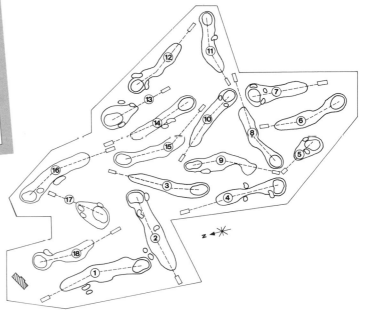

view. Of all the duneland that surrounds the British coast these must qualify as the Himalayan range, the finest impression of their breadth coming from the terrace of Saunton Sands Hotel.

The Burrows are a veritable treasure chest for botanists, rare specimens abounding in the dune grasses. It acts as an object lesson of how well golf courses preserve wildlife of all kinds and how common interests can co-exist to the benefit of all parties. In a period when applications are turned down for new golf courses for fear they will upset special habitats, it is a message that should be sounded loud and clear.

The dunes extend further from the shore than they do elsewhere, most parts of both courses enjoying their dramatic influence to spearhead their challenge.

Reaction from players to important events has always been a mixture of respect for the severity of the task in hand yet enjoyment that the rewards are utterly fair in spite of a par on the East course of 71. Although the 1st tee occupies a fine high platform, the start is immense – three par 4s in the first four holes between 402 and 470 yards that are inclined to sap the hopes straight away.

Problems on the opening hole surround the elbow of dune containing a bunker that juts out on the right into the fairway and two bunkers on either side of a green whose pinched waist makes control and accuracy essential when the pin is placed at the rear. As a par 5, one of only two in the round, the 2nd is less formidable than most although the plateau green can be difficult to hold. The 3rd, against the distant background of vast sandhills, curves elegantly through a shallow valley, the task of hitting the fairway being very much more demanding than on the 2nd. Nor is the second straightforward. Even without bunkers, the green, slightly raised like a crown, rewards only the truest shot.

On the 4th, the fairway tapers in such a way that only drives down the left claim a sight of the target marked by a guide-post, but on a course where mighty hitting is an obvious advantage the short 5th falls within the scope of all. However, an innocent appearance hides a devilment that is apparent as soon as you have played it. The raised green is not small but it falls away on all sides and the penalties for missing it are many.

By now, the scene changes with a move to flatter, more marshy ground with an open ditch running down the right of the 6th. This, together

The 18th green and 1st tee of the East course. The 1st tee of the West course is to the right.

way tapers to a narrow gap through which the green appears. The 2nd is apparently longer and the 3rd a dogleg par 4 with the green in a dell. Driving down to the 4th fairway which swings away right, parallel with the shore, the full coastal picture is opened up.

Lundy Island, in the middle of the Bristol Channel, lies between more distant glimpses of Somerset and South Wales although it provides no break to south-westerly winds that can so exercise and test the strength and control of golfers. It is easy to allow the second at the 4th, and the pitch up to the green, to drift towards the high bank of dunes but, after the pleasant short 5th, the dunes hide the view.

Moving the 6th green was another change necessitated by the amendments elsewhere although a very definite change for the better has been the drainage of the marsh and the demise of the wind-driven pump which often worked overtime.

The 7th and 8th, more flat and open, are formidable holes that highlight a different side to Burnham, a welcome variation that includes as fine a shot as any – the second to the par-5 8th. The

short 9th on the edge of the hills signals the end of the marsh, the 10th offering a blind drive over dunes to a lower-lying fairway. The 11th and the drive to the 12th follow the line of the road but, instead of a narrow second to a green in front of the church, the 12th fairway 'lifts up its eyes unto the hills' and a green against a background of sky.

Difficulty is the keyword to the new 13th and 14th but Burnham's old finish is very much alive and intact, a stirring climax to any occasion. A popular home for English championships, the last four holes have played a significant part in shaping their destiny. Straightness is essential on the 15th but options exist on the 16th, a low run-up to a two-tier green from the left or a higher, fuller pitch from the right.

On the short 17th, a stout carry is necessary to bridge the tee and green. On the 18th, there is a lovely drive to a fairway breaking left round a large grassy hollow. From the perfect position, there is a long flat approach to a green, well bunkered on the right – a hole to do rich justice to a course that more than lives up to its promise and reputation.

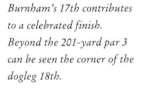

Burnham's 17th contributes to a celebrated finish. Beyond the 201-yard par 3 can be seen the corner of the dogleg 18th.

CHAPTER SEVEN

WALES

In a commentary about Welsh golf courses, Bernard Darwin expressed his determination to put Aberdovey first not because he made any claim about it being the best but because it was, in effect, his spiritual golfing home. My choice for mentioning it first is justified more by its alphabetical pre-eminence but it is undoubtedly one of the finest in Wales, epitomizing the ideal balance between challenge and enjoyment – a requirement of all great courses.

For our purposes, golf in Wales can be divided into north and south although the south must also include west Wales, a region that boasts Tenby, the oldest constituted club in the Principality, and a sheer delight. However, in terms of the recognition it has received in housing championships and big events, Royal Porthcawl must take precedence: a fine sprawling links with the sea visible from every hole.

There is more climbing to be done at Porthcawl than on any other links but the holes are first-rate, the first three following the line of the glorious, sandy beach and the 18th descending a long, gradual slope to a green set at three levels against the ocean. In sight of Porthcawl, although a circuitous drive by road, is Southerndown but, in spite of its resplendent views, it could never be classed as seaside.

Even closer on the other side of Porthcawl is Pyle & Kenfig with its definite contrast between the two nines, one meandering through giant dunes and the other more open and inland in character. Unfortunately, efforts to introduce more holes in the dunes failed but it is a lovely place to play and so easily combined with a visit to Porthcawl.

From there, it is on to Swansea, taking the road round Swansea Bay past the famous St Helen's rugby and cricket ground, eventually taking a slightly winding road up across the moor at Clyne to the village of Pennard. Pennard's links was described by James Braid as one of the finest natural courses he knew yet nowadays it is often overlooked. It has all the ingredients of a worthy links, undulating fairways with rarely a level lie or stance, inviting green positions in attractive settings and inspiring coastal views that take a lot of beating. The turf is springy underfoot and the wind invariably makes up for what today may seem a modest yardage.

Ashburnham, to the west of Llanelli, is one of Wales's oldest courses and certainly one of the best, the furthest holes from the clubhouse typifying all the finest features of seaside golf. The club has frequently played host to championships and professional events, presenting itself as a fair, demanding course, perhaps without the beauty of Tenby, but by no means unattractive.

Tenby, on the other side of Carmarthen Bay, has enormous charm, the course running out to the edge of more mountainous country and wending its way back with some holes close to the shore.

The historical grandeur of Harlech Castle which overlooks the Morfa.

The 3rd hole, Cader, at Aberdovey was one of Bernard Darwin's favourites: a blind tee shot on a hole where it used to be said that 'only a fool or a millionaire took a new ball'.

For years it suffered from the loss of three original holes, one solution being replacements on the other side of the little railway line. However, land reclaimed from the Ministry of Defence offers a further alternative that is more in keeping with traditional linksland.

To get from south to north Wales is no easy matter and there is little outstanding golf on the way except for Borth & Ynyslas, a few miles north of Aberystwyth. Redesigned by Harry Colt, it can be recommended on every count not least the joy of many fine individual holes and a variety of shots to be played.

Aberdovey is the next stop, a course to which Colt, Harry Fowler and Braid all lent an architectural hand, but, for the majesty of the setting and the distinction of the golf, nothing can quite compare with Royal St David's at Harlech. The scene is dominated by the castle, brooding massively over the links, with the dunes protecting them from the sea and the distant hills keeping further watch.

For many, Harlech bears the crown of north Wales golf but there are more delights along the stretch of coast running east from Anglesey to the Cheshire border. The North Wales Golf Club at Llandudno is more seaside in its terrain than Maesdu, once popular with professional tournaments. North Wales, on the curve of Conwy Bay, has some fine holes on its narrow strip of genuine links but the pick in the area is Conwy (Caernarvonshire). On the Morfa Peninsula, it has a highly respected name with long traditions, the early course depicted in a series of paintings that adorn the walls of many clubhouses. Recently, the building of a tunnel to bypass the ancient town of Conwy has resulted in the redesign of the course but the staging of the Home Internationals in 1990 is an indication of the esteem in which it is held.

Compared to the scenic delights of Conwy, the setting of Rhyl and Prestatyn is a shade more prosaic but both have their merits. Rhyl is only nine holes but Prestatyn has held Welsh championships, blossoming from a flat, meadowy beginning into a splendid links with much subtlety and strategy.

ROYAL PORTHCAWL

Some seaside courses, hidden behind houses or dunes, might be thought guilty of a breach of the Trades Descriptions Act. It is a nice point whether sight of the sea is implied by definition but at Royal Porthcawl there are no possible doubts. It is unique in that the sea is in full view from every single hole.

What is more, it is one of the few courses where the beach is in play, the first three holes following the line of the coast with Atlantic rollers breaking on the rocks and, it is hoped, the sun shining from a clear sky. In reality, the scene is often less tranquil, one of my abiding memories centring on the worst day I have ever spent on a golf course. Horizontal sleet and hail, carried on a storm force wind, numbed the brain, the senses and the swing, a state of affairs made worse by Porthcawl's total lack of protection.

It can represent the best and the worst, heaven and hell. However, few courses reward the good, old-fashioned virtues of control and flight better than Porthcawl, a happier memory being that of Peter Thomson winning the Dunlop Masters in 1961 with some marvellous golf in a strong wind. It is the only time that I have seen a major professional event held there, its somewhat remote setting not being exactly enticing to modern sponsors although motorways, and the Severn Bridge, make it far more accessible than it used to be now that London can be not much more than a couple of hours away.

The amateurs and ladies find it a most agreeable battleground, the latest compliment to its undoubted qualities being the 1995 Walker Cup. It might be thought that a links devoid of trees would be guaranteed to make Americans feel far from home but two of its Amateur champions have been Americans, Dick Siderowf and Dick Chapman, Chapman putting together an unbelievable run of figures to beat Charlie Coe in the 1951 final.

There is the unusual feature at the 1st of the opening drive crossing the 18th fairway on a hole

that strong men come near to driving although a sharp slope up to the green and its fairly heavily contoured surface can make the pitch awkward to judge. The 2nd and 3rd are altogether more severe,

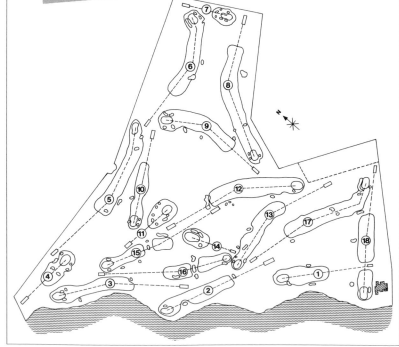

ROYAL PORTHCAWL
Card of the course
(championship tees)

Hole	Yds	Par	Hole	Yds	Par
1	326	4	10	337	4
2	447	4	11	187	3
3	420	4	12	476	5
4	197	3	13	443	4
5	513	5	14	152	3
6	394	4	15	467	4
7	116	3	16	434	4
8	490	5	17	508	5
9	371	4	18	413	4
	3274	36		3417	36

Total 6691 yards, par 72
Course record • 65,
Brian Barnes, 1980

A glorious par 4, the 2nd follows the line of the shore.

Overleaf A clear impression of the long, gradual slope down to the 18th green, which itself falls away from front to back.

longish carries from the tee leading to fairways of rolling character and two substantial second shots to greens hard by the shore.

Some relief is at hand as the first short hole appears, turning inland but not always so easy to clear the bunkers and hold the green if the wind is helping. Then follows a links hole unique in my experience, a par 5, the second part of which scales a steep hill to a long narrow green hard by an out-of-bounds wall. Such a full frontal attack is a test of wind and limb but the next few holes occupy the high ground.

This extreme change of levels is something else which makes Porthcawl unique among seaside links, its gorsy character giving more the flavour of heathland. The 7th, a rival to Troon's Postage Stamp for shortness, is a hole worthy of close study. The waist of its long green tapered between bunkers and mounds, and scarcely a straight holing-out putt, it is a satisfying target to hit even with a wedge, an outstanding rebuff to those who maintain that it is the woods and long irons that separate the men from the boys. There are many short holes around the world of over 200 yards less satisfying to hit.

Gorse catches many a faded drive at the 8th.

On the other hand, it is more of a second-shot hole as cross bunkers mark the rise to higher ground on the approach at a point where a stone wall juts in. Positioning down the right is essential with the drive on the 9th in order to obtain the best angle for the second to an eccentrically sloping green and there is another inviting drive as the 10th plunges back to the lower land, but it is only a temporary lull.

The short 11th does a smart about-turn before the hill at the 12th is tackled by the drive, only the longest getting anywhere near the crest. At the 13th, a long drive allows the considerable benefit of a sight of the green at the bottom of another slope. The tee also serves as an elevated look-out post to the coast of Somerset and Devon and to the splendour of Swansea Bay.

Although rarely little more than a short or mid-iron, the short 14th is a vital green to hit with disaster lurking all round but some of the toughest golf is contained in the finish. The 15th and 16th, in opposite directions, can vary considerably in the length they play, both nevertheless involving drives down into shallow valleys followed by stout, uphill seconds. Bunkers are more of a plague on the 16th where the green cannot be seen from the first half of the fairway.

There is greater contrast in the 17th and 18th. There is the very real fear of gorse on the 508-yard 17th, another slightly uphill drive tending to have the sting taken out of it unless it scales the peak. Then comes the decision whether to go right in order to open up the green and play for a safe 5 or to shape a long second to negotiate the change of angle on the approach and apron.

Porthcawl's 18th is a classic in every way, downhill and more often than not into the wind, the second having to cross a deep grassy dell and, if well enough struck, having to contend finally with a green sloping away on three levels. Even more alluring is the background of the sea, the sand and the anxiety that an overboisterous shot may topple over the edge. There is a nice balance in the strategies: whether to attack at all costs, whether to adopt a more gingerly stance and risk the embarrassment of taking three and, sometimes, four putts or whether to cut your losses and go for safety all the way. Because of the doubts it casts, it is a memorable hole, a fitting end to an examination of enjoyable demands.

PYLE & KENFIG

PYLE & KENFIG
Card of the course
(championship tees)

Hole	Yds	Par	Hole	Yds	Par
1	382	4	10	411	4
2	434	4	11	524	5
3	359	4	12	186	3
4	169	3	13	369	4
5	503	5	14	378	4
6	167	3	15	203	3
7	350	4	16	431	4
8	379	4	17	443	4
9	526	5	18	436	4
	3269	36		3381	35

Total 6650 yards, par 71
Course record • 68,
David Matthew, 1981;
Chris Gray, 1982; Mike Steadman, 1982

A mile or two along the coast from Royal Porthcawl, tucked in behind the shelter of the dunes, lies Pyle & Kenfig, a delightful course divided in half by a road. The road also marks a clear division of character in the terrain, the tract to the west displaying all the grandeur of true seaside golf and that to the east, while full of fun and challenge, suffering a bit by comparison.

There have been frequent pleas to add to the duneland holes by taking in the land which

Two of the holes that capture the true seaside character of Pyle & Kenfig, the 13th and (opposite) the 14th, both of them par-4 doglegs.

abounds in the region of the 13th and 14th and the club devised a plan for the idea. It would have been quite superb but there were objections from the conservationists who failed to acknowledge the part golf courses play up and down the country in this vital role and the opportunity was lost.

It was a thousand pities but Pyle & Kenfig remains both a delightful place to play, more protected than Porthcawl, and a demanding test at 6650 yards that can have everyone at full stretch. The two halves also have a contrast of levels, the first two holes moving up onto the higher ground in a far more compact arrangement than the second nine.

The 4th and 6th are fine short holes, while the par-5 5th has a well guarded green and approach, the bunkers posing a variety of strategic options. The even longer 9th leads to a spectacular descent to the clubhouse, the crossing of the road and the pleasures of the second nine which have a more enclosed look.

The 11th is a majestic hole to a green in the foothills of the dunes and the 12th, a par 3, penetrates the heart of them and introduces us to the dogleg 13th. Its charm and character gives another identity to Pyle & Kenfig, a fairway swinging right surrounded by hills and sandy hollows, with a distinctive green setting that resembles no other.

Another par 4 follows, curving right up a lower valley, but the sting of Pyle & Kenfig is undoubtedly in its tail, a long par 3 and three par 4s – the shortest of which is 431 yards. There is a little downhill help on the 15th which remains faithful to the dunes but the last three see a change of character to more open ground, although the 16th has to contend more with bracken and gorse.

The 17th is probably the toughest of the three 4s with the emphasis very much on the second shot. The 18th takes some beating as a finishing hole and completes a course that is a wonderful foil to Royal Porthcawl and deserves to be considered entirely on its own considerable merits.

PENNARD

The road along Swansea Bay eventually forks right up the hill across the moors until it reaches Pennard, a small hamlet with an idyllic seaside links. There are superb views along the coast of the Gower Peninsula, castle ruins, sandy coves, turbulent dunes and undulations that give an unmistakable flavour of seaside golf.

James Braid, who laid out the course, declared that he had never seen a better piece of natural land for golf and the modern version, which owed much to Ken Cotton, preserves the character to perfection. At 6289 yards, it is not overlong but the winds from the Bristol Channel can magnify the problems so significantly that scores under 80 are no mean achievement. Nevertheless, it has proved itself a worthy training ground by forging champion's qualities in Vicki Thomas, the Curtis Cup golfer, after she moved from Bargoed. The main benefit of golf at Pennard is in learning the art of flight and the need to make up a shot to fit any situation.

There is a demanding start with a hole of 447 yards, gorse to the right and a green on higher land contributing to its sternness. The 2nd is a short hole and the 3rd a left-hand dogleg but, after the drive at the par-5 4th, the air of hills, humps and hollows grows stronger. Out-of-bounds marks the right of the 4th, a hole on which change has recently

been carried out to relieve any danger to the general public. A new green site has been added and a new short 5th designed to replace what was a good and picturesque hole. The new tee is near the old 4th green with an engaging shot to be played to an interesting plateau green.

PENNARD Card of the course						
Hole		Yds	Par	Hole	Yds	Par
1	Founder	447	4	10 Three Cliffs	488	5
2	Cefn Bryn	145	3	11 Tower	184	3
3	President	371	4	12 Pennard Pill	296	4
4	Ilston	521	5	13 Colonel	195	3
5	Penmaen	171	3	14 Braids	340	4
6	Admiral	407	4	15 Boscos Den	174	3
7	Castle	350	4	16 Great Tor	489	5
8	Church	362	4	17 Helwicks	508	5
9	Southgate	441	4	18 Highway	400	4
		3215	35		3074	36

Total 6289 yards, par 71
Course record • 66, George Ryall, 1987

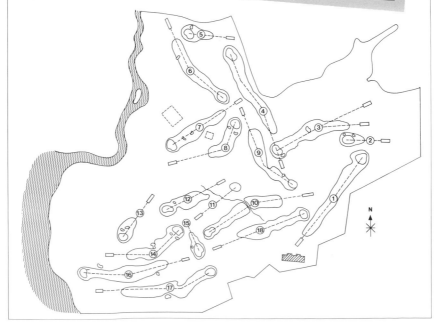

The 1st (foreground) and 3rd greens. The latter is rated the hardest hole on the course and is named after Dai Rees.

A feature of many ancient seaside links is a blind shot to a green in a dell, with a bell to sound when the green is clear. Predictably, perhaps, the 4th is known as the Bell.

Under the new arrangement, the lovely old short 9th becomes the 12th, the 14th and 15th later revealing more aesthetic splendours, the line from the tee on the 14th being on Giltar Point. The 13th, on which you should take aim on the railway cottage, commemorates the original architect, James Braid, whose handiwork is still readily evident in the shaping of many greens.

Another nice short hole comes at the 15th where two hollows are to be avoided, while the 16th is a drive-and-pitch hole which has you in two minds – whether to attack the dogleg or play more circumspectly. What we should do is not always what we actually do at golf, for temptation is hard to resist.

The 17th is the only par 5 and has a long, narrow green in front of the Black Rock that falls away on either side. There then remains a strong finishing hole from a high tee over a house immediately below, the threat of out-of-bounds to the left combining with a long second to complete an experience to be cherished.

ABERDOVEY

As Patric Dickinson wrote in his book, *A Round of Golf Courses*, 'If one dare write about Aberdovey at all, one must begin by letting Bernard Darwin through on the way to the first tee.' Darwin once wrote, 'About this one course in the world, I am a hopeless and shameful sentimentalist and I glory in my shame.'

There is no doubt that Darwin's writing about Aberdovey has given it great eminence, writing that had its roots in his family's connections with a place where he spent his annual holiday. It was one of his uncles, Colonel Ruck, who is said to have borrowed nine flower pots from a woman in the village and cut nine holes on the marsh in which to put them.

From such simple beginnings, golf at Aberdovey started over a century ago but its reputation is based on the genuine grounds of being an admirable stage for championships and for the more modest aspirations of legions of holidaymakers. Situated at the mouth of the Dovey Estuary and against the backdrop of mountains, there is the feeling of escape that means so much to golfers. In high summer, it can be hard to get a game but it is a course for all seasons, a links where the walking is easy and its recovery powers after rain great.

It lies on a long narrow strip of land close to the sandhills which are protective rather than having any strategic influence on the play. The holes go more or less straight out and straight home but there are humps and hollows everywhere and more variety in the characteristics of the holes than might be expected. One added characteristic is that the greens are relatively small, placing emphasis on the virtues of control and accuracy.

Memories of the game long ago are revived by the 2nd and 3rd, the 2nd involving a daunting drive along a gorge between the hills and the 3rd, Cader, a blind tee shot. This short hole may not be as frightening as in the days when 'only a fool or a millionaire took a new ball' but golf is duller for the absence of such holes and Cader was a favourite of Darwin's – as, indeed, was the old Maiden at Sandwich.

From a high tee at the 4th, a fine view and a demanding hole unfold, the drive to the fairway below followed by a longish second to a green which can be expensive to miss. The short 5th

ABERDOVEY
Card of the course

Hole	Yds	Par	Hole	Yds	Par
1	441	4	10	415	4
2	332	4	11	407	4
3	173	3	12	149	3
4	401	4	13	530	5
5	193	3	14	389	4
6	402	4	15	477	5
7	482	5	16	288	4
8	335	4	17	428	4
9	160	3	18	443	4
	2919	34		3526	37

Total 6445 yards, par 71
Course record • 67,
J. Smith; Bruce Macfarlane (A), 1985

turns inland, the considerably shorter outward nine ending with three par 4s with the railway on the right and the third of the four short holes across a large bunker.

As intimated, Aberdovey's small greens accentuate the difficulties of scoring, particularly on the homeward holes where the demands stiffen noticeably. The 10th, a long two-shotter, crosses a marshy area, the next three skirting the foot of the sandhills. A dogleg is the feature of the 11th; the 12th has a raised green in the dunes with a welcome glimpse of the sea while the 13th is the longest hole of all. The drive at the 14th poses a teasing question of whether to attack or play safe but for those who maintain that every course should have a challenging short par 4, the 16th, in

A fine short par 4, the 16th follows the railway fence.

the wake of the 15th which many believe is the best hole, is the answer to their prayers.

From the 15th green bordered on the left by the railway and a sandy track, there is another tempting tee shot round the curve of the railway fence, the success or failure of the shot having a direct bearing on the ease or difficulty of the pitch. Then it is back home via two more testing 4s over flat territory skirted by rushes and ditches.

The clubhouse is close to the station from where there is a service to Harlech via Barmouth. The trains never seem to be in much of a hurry but at least Aberdovey still has its railway line. The loss on courses elsewhere has been as sad as the demise of the romance that accompanied them.

ROYAL ST DAVID'S

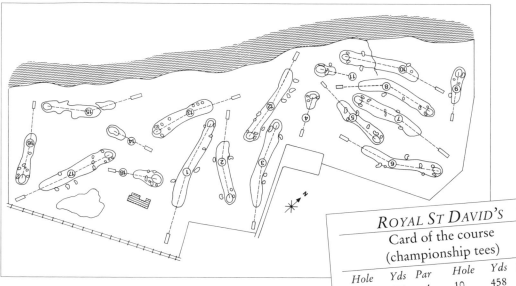

ROYAL ST DAVID'S					
Card of the course (championship tees)					
Hole	Yds	Par	Hole	Yds	Par
1	436	4	10	458	4
2	373	4	11	144	3
3	463	4	12	437	4
4	188	3	13	451	4
5	393	4	14	218	3
6	371	4	15	427	4
7	481	5	16	354	4
8	499	5	17	427	4
9	173	3	18	202	3
	3377	36		3118	33

Total 6495 yards, par 69
Course record • 64,
Kevin Stables, 1988

Harlech, a name that symbolizes Wales, is a small town with a large castle that forms a resplendent backdrop to the links of Royal St David's. The area of the links is known as the Morfa, an old sheep-grazing plain on which, almost a hundred years ago, a party of locals decided to try their hand at the Scottish game of golf.

It was an obvious choice, for the land was ready-made for the purpose and, with the castle standing on a sheer precipice of rock looking down on it, they had a guarantee of success from the start. In addition to an imposing foreground, however, is the distant framework of the mountains of Snowdonia, a combination that gives the golf here a more dramatic edge.

Such beauty can be a distraction from the play on holes which meander more than on most seaside links. From the ramparts of the castle, a bird's-eye view is possible of the flat part protected from the sea by a rugged range of dunes. This adds a sweet flavour to the finish of a round that begins from a point close to Harlech station, the line on which Cambrian trains run down at a pleasant, leisurely pace to Barmouth and Aberdovey.

If the setting has an unchanging air, there have been many changes to a course that is a particular favourite of golfers from Birmingham and Cheshire. Its most famous competition at the height of the holiday season is the Harlech Town Bowl, which Harold Hilton won long ago off a handicap of plus eight, but the club has housed many Welsh championships, the Home Internationals and several Ladies' British Open Amateur Championships. The list of British champions is impressive, starting with the fourth victory of Cecil Leitch in 1926 and followed by the first victories of Frances Stephens (1949) and Barbara McIntire (1960), the second of Elizabeth

An avenue of fairway between hummocks and hills on the 15th.

Chadwick (1967) and the first of Janet Collingham (1987).

The challenge is sound and demanding although much of it is more meadowland than seaside in character. The greens are large and the driving, if important, is not claustrophobic. Like Hoylake, it has its share of out-of-bounds over walls and fences and four fine short holes, the most famous of which is the 14th. It is a welcome fact that, for the first thirteen holes or so, no two consecutive holes run in the same direction except for the 3rd and 4th but the 14th plunges into the heart of the hills for undoubtedly the best part of all.

Even with modern equipment, the 14th involves quite a carry from a tee near the clubhouse to a green surrounded by dunes with a far more predictable landing area now that you get a sight of the target from the tee. Hitherto, there was a large hill to surmount in front of the tee. The 15th is a tough two-shotter with a nice, rolling fairway that runs obliquely to the line of the drive. Here, the green is slightly obscured and, at the 16th, it needs a long drive to bring that green into view. The 16th is notable for the only sight of the sea in the round from the tee, the fact that the hole runs at right angles to the 15th and 17th and for having its green down below the hotel. But the decision at the 17th is whether to attempt to carry the cross bunker in front of the green.

Then, in the mould of Lindrick, Killarney and St Pierre, there is a short hole to end. Harlech's is as often as not a wood with bunkers to miss but there is a last glimpse of the castle to act as the fount of inspiration.

159

CONWY
(CAERNARVONSHIRE)

Some of the most scenic road journeys quickly lose their charm when susceptible to traffic jams. One of the worst holiday bottlenecks used to be centred on the ancient streets of Conwy on the road between Chester and Anglesey, but the building of a tunnel across the estuary has relieved the congestion and, though a number of holes at Conwy (Caernarvonshire) had to be altered as a result, the upheaval was generally reckoned to be to the common good.

In any event, things might have been worse and, more important, no doubts have been cast about the quality of the golf or the course's considerable reputation. Without perhaps knowing it, golfers have seen more of the links of Conwy, which lies on the Morfa Peninsula, than they may think, for the walls of many clubhouses carry old paintings of the course without, for some reason, identifying the subject.

The ground is a little flat but there is no mistaking a natural look and there is sufficient variety in the make-up of the holes to erase any suggestion of monotony. Gorse also plays its part near the clubhouse and there are splendid views both inland and out to sea. The course lies under the shadow of hills which strike an air of timelessness but the links, even before its latest revision, has undergone its share of change.

The Morfa suffered in two World Wars, almost going out of existence in 1918, while sand-blow on what are now the 7th, 8th and 9th necessitated the planting of huge areas of marram grass to provide stabilization. Apart from changes to the holes, the biggest debate has surrounded their

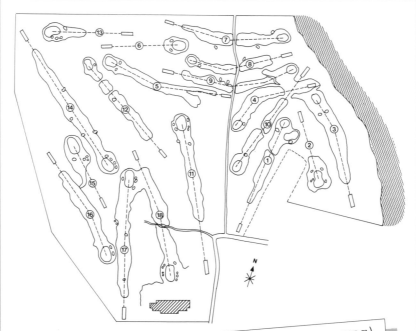

CONWY (CAERNARVONSHIRE)
Card of the course

Hole	Yds	Par	Hole	Yds	Par
1	370	4	10	540	5
2	152	3	11	384	4
3	368	4	12	512	5
4	408	4	13	180	3
5	454	4	14	513	5
6	191	3	15	161	3
7	459	4	16	428	4
8	451	4	17	415	4
9	542	5	18	373	4
	3395	35		3506	37

Total 6901 yards, par 72
Course record • 71,
David Young (A), 1988

numbering but the club has hosted many Welsh championships, the Home Internationals, the 1983 Ladies' British Open Amateur Championship – won at last by Belle Robertson – and the Martini Tournament of 1970 in which Peter Thomson and Doug Sewell tied.

Their winning score of 268, however, does less than justice to the demanding nature of Conwy for the tournament was held during a long, dry spell with little or no wind to add to the usual difficulties. However, it was no surprise that Thomson and Sewell, two players known for their skill at controlling and manoeuvring the ball, should prevail. Conwy responds to the virtues of positional play although it certainly does not lack length. Off the championship tees, it measures 6901 yards. In a big wind, it can be awesome.

The latest changes involved a new 13th, the extension of the 14th to a par 5, the renumbering of the short 14th to become the 15th and a brand new 17th utilizing part of the old 16th, including the green. The old 17th was scrapped but the new version highlights the threat of the gorse.

The 7th green, perched above the shore.

This is the part furthest from the sea, but the seaside character is soon apparent with the short 2nd, turning back towards the town, and the 3rd which curves along the line of the shore to a plateau green. From there until the turn, the holes run up and back more or less parallel, the 7th and 9th greens closest to the beach. The 10th is a par 5 towards the clubhouse, the second of four in the space of six holes, but the 11th brings a contrast of direction that is pretty well maintained by the remainder of the inward half with the exception of the 13th.

Aesthetically, the finish has lost a little of its charm but beauty still abounds in the broad sweep of the bay, the low form of Anglesey, the mountains and the Great Orme above Llandudno. A course once nestled on its slopes but, metaphorically speaking at least, Conwy is a course to which you look up. It holds a high place in the annals of Welsh golf.

CHAPTER EIGHT

NORTH WEST ENGLAND

Whatever new names have been thought up for regions of England – like Merseyside, Greater Manchester and Cumbria – golf in north-west England means Cheshire, Lancashire, the Isle of Man, Cumberland and Westmoreland. What is more, it is a land flowing with milk and honey. From the Wirral Peninsula to the southern shores of the Solway Firth, there is a succession of marvellous golf on noble duneland with historical attachments by the score.

The biggest problem is where to start. However, Hoylake, the home of Royal Liverpool, is convenient for a number of reasons. We can begin in the south and make our way north. We can salute the eminence of its golfing sons and pay our tribute to a course which, if now in a sort of Open Championship wilderness, is still as fine a test as ever it was.

Certainly, there is a wonderful 'feel' about the place, an unmistakable air of reverence that so many great deeds have graced land that, at first sight, may appear unremarkable. A vast expanse is divided up into cops or banks and lined by houses. Only along the coastal strip from the 9th to the 12th is the sea apparent but beneath this deceptive mantle lies a course whose challenge is rivalled only by the pleasure of trying to meet it.

There is always an urge to linger at Hoylake and look at all the photographs, portraits and trophies adorning the clubhouse walls, but it is time to move on to neighbouring Wallasey and its pic-turesque spectacular dunes on the edge of the Mersey.

Coastal erosion has caused a headache or two, resulting in the loss of some of the original land although without diminishing the fun and enjoyment to be had. Wallasey can hold its own in even the most exalted company and is doubly renowned for its connection with Dr Frank Stableford who devised the scoring system associated with his name.

There is only one means of continuing the journey beyond Liverpool and that is by the electric train which runs past almost all the famous clubs in the area: West Lancashire, Formby, Southport & Ainsdale, Hillside and, if you crane your neck and know where to look, Royal Birkdale.

West Lancashire, oldest of these clubs, can stand comparison with any of them although Formby's protagonists claim that the others lack its profusion of trees to complement the more rugged look of mighty hills. Formby enjoys more seclusion and shelter as a result but it is enchanting and as difficult to make a score there as anywhere.

The far end of S & A, as Southport & Ainsdale is affectionately known, overlaps Hillside on the other side of the railway, a course that has gained eminence in the last 25 years as it gained extra length from its new holes. Its formidable test has become much in demand for championship events, a test beginning with a hole alongside the

The clubhouse of the Royal Liverpool Golf Club, the 16th green in the foreground.

railway in the manner of Prestwick except that, at Hillside, the hook is the shot to be plagued.

Hillside also borders Birkdale, a convenient alliance when championships are held at either. Since it first housed the Open in 1954, Birkdale has shot to prominence with a reputation for handling large crowds and presenting a severe examination for the world's leading players who have all played there in the last 30 years. The thing they like is that the fairways down avenues of dunes are more or less devoid of the more eccentric slopes and levels elsewhere, but one must not leave Southport without mention of another fine course, Hesketh, famous as the home of the Bentley brothers, Harry and Arnold.

The Ribble Estuary is a handy division between what can be called the courses of Southport and the courses of the Fylde coast – most notably Royal Lytham & St Annes, St Annes Old Links and Fairhaven – all of which feature when the Open Championship is held at Lytham.

None enjoys the beauty of the settings further south. Lytham's look is positively confined. Bordered by railway and suburbia, out-of-

bounds is a constant threat for 12 holes but Lytham, St Annes Old and Fairhaven need much hard-hitting golf if they are to be conquered. They most emphatically want playing.

It is only a short hop by air from Blackpool Airport, close to St Annes Old, to the Isle of Man and then only a short taxi ride to the Castletown links which is greatly to be praised. Surrounded by three separate bays or stretches of sea, it represents a gap in the golfing education of many. It was redesigned after the Second World War by Mackenzie Ross and captivated me on my first visit in spite of inclement weather.

The Cumbrian hills are in full view on a bright day and you might swear you could spot Seascale on the coast below St Bees Head. It needs a bit of a detour by road when heading for Scotland but it is well worth it; the same goes for Silloth-on-Solway, the home of Cecil Leitch, a suitable advertisement for Cumberland turf, heather, hummocks and superb golf. It is the northernmost of a string of courses from Hoylake in the south that comprises more jewels than any comparable stretch anywhere.

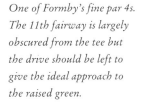

One of Formby's fine par 4s. The 11th fairway is largely obscured from the tee but the drive should be left to give the ideal approach to the raised green.

ROYAL LIVERPOOL

If Royal Liverpool really has staged its last of 10 Open Championships, there should be no wailing or lament for what is past and gone. Its misfortune is merely that, in the modern world, it can no longer accommodate the thousands who would flood there daily and whose demands are so consuming in terms of space. In that, it keeps good company.

There is a danger nowadays that eminence is judged by the ability to house great events but that misses the point. What matters far more, where Hoylake is concerned, is that it has adapted naturally to all the changes the game has seen, retained its freshness and preserved its challenge – not to mention its place in history.

John Ball and Harold Hilton, two amateurs who could, and did, beat the professionals, were Hoylake men, honing their skills on a seaside links that is the second oldest in England. It concedes seniority only to Royal North Devon but Hoylake's influence is second to none. The club started the Amateur Championship, housed the first International Match, witnessed the first Open victory with the rubber-cored ball and held the inaugural English Amateur Championship, having donated the Warwick Vase for presentation to the winner.

Perhaps because of Hilton and Ball, the club's roots are closer to amateur golf and the decision to take the 1983 Walker Cup to Hoylake was a matter of particular pride. However, memories of Open Championships lend a touch of adventure and romance no other event can. Four stand out: J.H. Taylor's sweeping victory in 1913 in one of the great bad-weather Opens; Bobby Jones's triumph in the second leg of his Grand Slam in 1930; Peter Thomson's third successive victory in 1956, the first person to achieve the feat since Bob Ferguson in the 1880s; finally, the sentimental crowning of Roberto de Vicenzo in 1967.

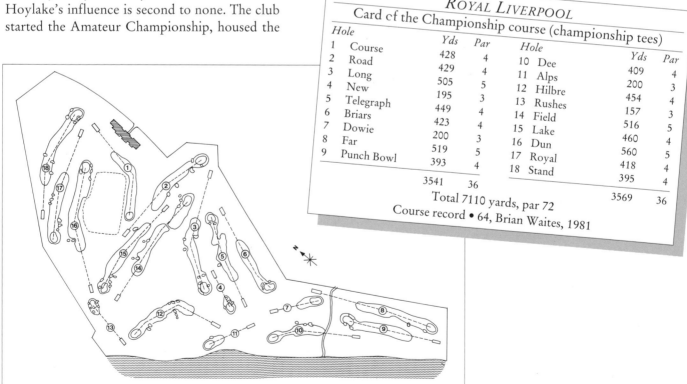

ROYAL LIVERPOOL
Card of the Championship course (championship tees)

Hole		Yds	Par	Hole		Yds	Par
1	Course	428	4	10	Dee	409	4
2	Road	429	4	11	Alps	200	3
3	Long	505	5	12	Hilbre	454	4
4	New	195	3	13	Rushes	157	3
5	Telegraph	449	4	14	Field	516	5
6	Briars	423	4	15	Lake	460	4
7	Dowie	200	3	16	Dun	560	5
8	Far	519	5	17	Royal	418	4
9	Punch Bowl	393	4	18	Stand	395	4
		3541	36			3569	36

Total 7110 yards, par 72
Course record • 64, Brian Waites, 1981

Hoylake's notorious 1st hole, with its green set hard by the artificial bank, or cop, which separates it from the out-of-bounds of the practice ground.

All typified the courage and skill needed to master a course relentless in its demands and consistent in its punishment. There is no let-up in the task of solid striking but, at first glance, Hoylake appears a trifle flat and dull. Even the approach to the club along Meols Drive hardly suggests that hallowed ground lies behind the line of suburban houses.

The fact that, in its early days, it was racecourse first and golf course second says something about the terrain. The 1st and 18th holes, Course and Stand, are reminders of those days but, as the gaze broadens, the course, without any appreciable change of level, assumes a character that is more interesting, varied and beautiful, although the truly seaside stretch is limited to the four holes from the 9th to the 12th.

The rest find feature in cops and banks, copious rough, the odd bush and in the quantity of out-of-bounds unmatched almost anywhere in the world. It was possible, and there was evidence to prove it, to go out-of-bounds on something like 13 holes, the most controversial being those inside

the course on the 1st, 16th, 7th and old 3rd. The 1st plays round two sides of the practice ground and the 16th round the other two, the right-angled nature of the doglegs leading to cutting corners, particularly on the 16th, a par 5 of 560 yards.

In the 1967 Open, the 1st gave rise to an amusing interchange at a press interview between Jack Nicklaus and a writer who opened by saying, 'You said yesterday, Jack, that the 1st is not a particularly good opening hole.' This brought an immediate and comprehensive denial from Jack that he had ever said such a thing and led to a friendly and protracted ticking-off.

'Well,' said the writer, not wishing to admit defeat, 'what do you think of the 1st?'

Came Jack's reply after due pause for thought, 'It is not a particularly good opening hole.'

Personally, I beg to differ but, whatever its golfing or architectural merits, two facts are beyond doubt. It instils fear both with the drive and second shot, and, without out-of-bounds, it would be no hole at all. However, as with the 1st at Prestwick, it is an even better 19th.

The 2nd, with a difficult angle for the second shot no matter what the club, is followed by a dog-leg par 5 swinging left and a short hole up onto an elevated perch. Changes to the 3rd and 4th came in readiness for the 1967 Open.

A cross-belt of sandy scrub influences the second on the 5th although the 6th, Briars or Orchard hole, is far more terrifying, the drive being probably the most demanding from the championship tee. The Orchard juts out to constitute a formidable carry.

No hole anywhere has aroused more debate than the short 7th, Dowie, out-of-bounds in the form of a low bank once running along the left of the green. Nowadays, the out-of-bounds has been abolished but not so on the 8th, a dangerous par 5 that builds up to a lovely green position at the furthest point of the course.

Now begins the best section, four holes following the curve of the sands of the Dee Estuary with views of the Welsh hills and the island of Hilbre after which the 12th hole takes its name. All is revealed from the 9th tee whence the fairway dips down into a low valley culminating in an old-fashioned punchbowl green flanked by sandhills. The 10th and 12th have a common general shape although the 12th is longer and much better. In between, comes a superlative short hole, the Alps, set in among the dunes which, if not as formidable as the Alps at Prestwick, are mountainous by Hoylake's standards.

Three bunkers in the hill on the left and three on the flatter plain to the right pose questions on the 12th, the answer lying in firing as close to the left as possible to gain advantage of the best line to a green which breaks away sharply on the right.

The holes that follow the range of sandhills along the shore of the Dee Estuary add welcome variety to Hoylake's generally flat appearance. The Alps (above) is a superb short hole played across a valley from a pulpit tee, while the 12th (opposite) is a curving par 4 with cunningly placed bunkers to trap those tempted to cut the corner with their drive and a narrow entrance to a raised green.

166

The short 13th is usually only a short iron but the last five holes, averaging about 470 yards, are all woods and long irons, some of the mightiest hitting on any finish. It has brought grief to many a bright hope.

A lengthened 14th has also been toughened to make it a genuine par 5 even downwind and much the same applies to the 16th. It was on the 16th that de Vicenzo settled matters in 1967 with a superb spoon shot across the corner of the field to the heart of the green. The 15th and 17th are treacherous 4s: the 15th is strategically bunkered, and on the 17th the road behind the angled green erodes positive thought.

It was in the old Royal Hotel, the first clubhouse, on the other side of the avenue, that John Ball, son of the owner, was born; it was no wonder therefore that he grew up with golf and helped shape the illustrious name of Hoylake. Study of the 17th will have taught him that the drive must flirt with the bunkers guarding the right-hand side of the fairway if the flag is to be attacked with any confidence, particularly when the second was a jigger or a spoon. The more conservative the drive, the more you stare at the out-of-bounds and the smaller the landing area.

The last word belongs to Tom Simpson and the obituary which, by mutual agreement, Henry Longhurst wrote before Simpson's death. In discussing some of his philosophies about golf course architecture, Simpson declared that, to be any good, a golf course must have out-of-bounds. 'In that case,' asked Longhurst rhetorically, 'I take it you regard Hoylake as the finest in England.'

'Without any doubt,' came the unhesitating reply.

WALLASEY

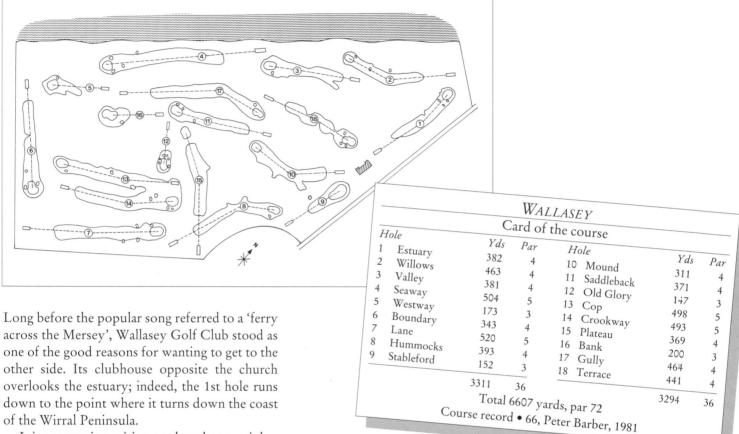

WALLASEY Card of the course						
Hole		*Yds*	*Par*	**Hole**	*Yds*	*Par*
1	Estuary	382	4	10 Mound	311	4
2	Willows	463	4	11 Saddleback	371	4
3	Valley	381	4	12 Old Glory	147	3
4	Seaway	504	5	13 Cop	498	5
5	Westway	173	3	14 Crookway	493	5
6	Boundary	343	4	15 Plateau	369	4
7	Lane	520	5	16 Bank	200	3
8	Hummocks	393	4	17 Gully	464	4
9	Stableford	152	3	18 Terrace	441	4
		3311	36		3294	36

Total 6607 yards, par 72
Course record • 66, Peter Barber, 1981

Long before the popular song referred to a 'ferry across the Mersey', Wallasey Golf Club stood as one of the good reasons for wanting to get to the other side. Its clubhouse opposite the church overlooks the estuary; indeed, the 1st hole runs down to the point where it turns down the coast of the Wirral Peninsula.

It is a strategic position not least because it has mighty sandhills that are fascinating, picturesque and exciting, lending a thrill to the golf on some holes that would be difficult to better. Sadly, there are not quite enough of them because the more inland holes, although only a few yards distant from the dunes, are flatter and inevitably less interesting.

In common with many of our seaside links, Wallasey has had its share of change. The abandonment long ago of three typical seaside holes owing to coastal erosion led to the adoption of the flatter land but the modern Wallasey is full of so many fine things that the fateful hand of nature is almost forgotten, if not quite forgiven.

Wallasey's other famous connection is with Dr Frank Stableford, the author of the scoring system that bears his name. A fine player who was a long serving member of Wallasey, it may have been his experience of golfing and the hazards of keeping a score at Wallasey that persuaded him to seek an alternative, for there is plenty of punishment to be found. There is a premium on controlled driving into the correct spot, and several greens are elevated and therefore difficult to hit when the wind decrees that iron shots should be held low.

Some of the best holes come in the opening five. The 1st occupies the spare land down to the estuary before the formidable 2nd turns in the opposite direction, a slight dogleg between willow scrub and some of the lower hills which, nevertheless, hide the fairway from the clubhouse. True seaside flavour is struck at the 3rd, a valleyed fairway rising up to a raised green, a change of

A fine view of the 3rd fairway which rises to an elevated green position.

level that reveals the glories of the view from the tee at the 4th, a par 5. It is the most magnificent from any of the courses along the Cheshire or Lancashire coasts, but it must not distract from the task in hand, a drive that must steer clear of out-of-bounds on the right. There are no bunkers to plague the drive on a fairway divided by a bank and shared with the 17th although four bunkers

A marvellous tee shot at the par-3 16th, a shot that must be straight and truly struck.

near the green influence the strategy thereafter.

A lofted shot over low mounds with the sea beyond at the short 5th is the last of the seaside holes for the time being, the 6th changing course along the boundary fringing part of the old links. A nice green at the 8th is the best feature of the remainder of the outward half which culminates in a hole entitled Stableford, one that would not be my choice for naming after the good doctor.

The 10th and 11th plunge us back into the lovely dune country, the 10th a sharp dogleg to the most elevated green of all and the 11th a delightful example of a good par 4 – attainable by most with two good shots. The short 12th drops down over five bunkers in horseshoe formation, the lower level occupying the thoughts until the second to the 15th hoists us back up again.

It is like ascending from everyday life into something infinitely more romantic and inspiring. The 16th is a beautiful long par 3 to a green on a ledge, a sentinel dune on the right and a fall-away to the left. The 17th, 464 yards, is very definitely a second-shot hole, the green in a sheltered dell marked by a direction pole, while the 18th completes a stern finish, returning to hills left and right with clubhouse always beckoning.

WEST LANCASHIRE

There is no stretch of golfing ground in Britain more noble than that seen on the railway journey from Liverpool to Southport – not even that of East Lothian or Ayrshire. To be sure, the Scottish links are more scenic but that is because the courses of the Lancashire coast have their views largely hidden by the protective screen of dunes that give them their character.

West Lancashire is a fine example with the added distinction of being the oldest club in continuous existence in a county that can boast three courses that have housed the Ryder Cup. West Lancashire has never managed to squeeze into the highest league of staging major championships or top international matches but that has more to do with the quality of its neighbours than a criticism of itself. Nevertheless, it owes its founding to the influence of Scottish businessmen who, during the shipping industry boom on the Mersey, catered for their golfing needs by building the course at Hall Road, Blundellsands.

Like Formby, the position of its clubhouse – on the seaward side of the railway line beside a level crossing – is not ideal for handling crowds, but the first clubhouse in 1873 was on the other side of the railway line which divided the course more or less in half. It was a clear-cut division with the flat holes on the inland side lacking the dash and excitement of those on the other.

There were some who may have welcomed the contrast but the resiting of the clubhouse nearer the sea, allied to fairly recent alterations to the course by Ken Cotton, has given West Lancashire a consistency and merit deserving of close attention. What is more, it now has two loops of nine

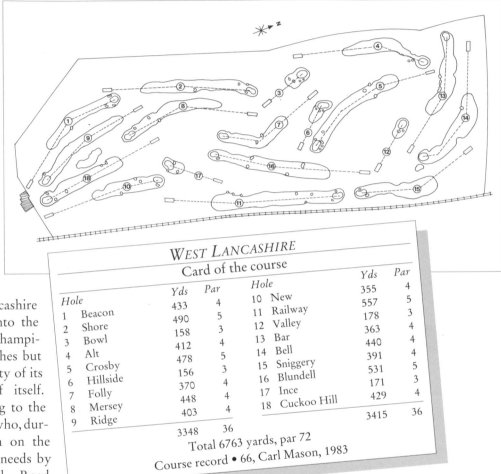

Hole		Yds	Par	Hole		Yds	Par
1	Beacon	433	4	10	New	355	4
2	Shore	490	5	11	Railway	557	5
3	Bowl	158	3	12	Valley	178	3
4	Alt	412	4	13	Bar	363	4
5	Crosby	478	5	14	Bell	440	4
6	Hillside	156	3	15	Sniggery	391	4
7	Folly	370	4	16	Blundell	531	5
8	Mersey	448	4	17	Ince	171	3
9	Ridge	403	4	18	Cuckoo Hill	429	4
		3348	36			3415	36

WEST LANCASHIRE
Card of the course

Total 6763 yards, par 72

Course record • 66, Carl Mason, 1983

radiating from the clubhouse with a nice balance between them.

The opening is along the edge of the Irish Sea, close to the shipping channel out of the port of Liverpool, the 1st, a long par 4, and the 2nd, a par 5, doglegging slightly to the right to produce an angle for the second shot that makes the longer players think. Much the same shape as pertains at the first two holes exists at the 4th but the 3rd is the first of four good and pleasant short holes, a recently added swale on the left of the green making it a harder target.

Added bunkers around the 5th green have also provided extra difficulty and the dogleg theme

Approached from the left, West Lancashire's 3rd hole is one of four challenging par 3s on linksland that has been played over since 1873. Bunkers guard the green front and right, a swale has been introduced on the left and the green falls away at the back, making it a hard target.

continues at the 7th (which assistant pro Peter Parkinson holed-in-one in 1972) and 8th before the 9th straightens out for home. The 10th is the shortest of the 4s while the 11th is the longest hole on the course, bringing the constant threat of out-of-bounds from the railway on the right.

The relative seclusion of the short 12th is followed by a drive from a high tee on the 13th that has to avoid three bunkers that mark a change of direction to the left. On the 14th, the features are a drive over a ridge and a second to a green tucked under the lee of a wooded hill. Another dogleg

greets players on the 15th, a sharp right-hander with the aim from the tee on one of several white circles on the stone railway wall.

The finish consists of three fine holes, a 5, a 3 and a 4, the 16th having a new green in the dell to the right of the old one, an arrangement which now provides more room to expand the scope of the tee shot on the short 17th. There is much to admire in the variety of West Lancashire and, as competitors in the Open Championship qualifying rounds can testify, it possesses a formidable edge.

FORMBY

One big difference between Formby and other seaside links is that it is bordered on at least three sides by trees – stately green firs or pines. These confer an air of seclusion or privacy although there is no sense of masking the traditional character of the golf which is full-blooded and challenging.

There are many who prefer Formby for a day's golf to any of the other courses on the Lancashire coast largely because of its setting, encircling the separately run Ladies' course which is a gem. Charm and elegance are not words always associated with the barren land of the seaside, certainly not if the wind is howling, but they are right for Formby. It has many delightful holes and a pleasant contrast between the more open land around the clubhouse and the holes in the middle enclosed by dunes and woodland.

The woodland area was enlisted some years ago when the threat of coastal erosion caused the club to give up the old 8th, 9th and 10th holes and, in a knock-on effect, the old 7th as well. Change at established clubs is invariably regarded as an interloper and many mourned the passing of attractive holes, but players who never knew them are just as adamant in their approval of the revision in country at which many had previously cast covetous glances.

Formby is part of the rich seam of golf that permeates the country north of Liverpool, originating in the prosperous Victorian era and blossoming as the game took hold throughout England. At first, Formby was content to be a stronghold for its members and it is as such that one still principally looks upon it. So saying, it just as unmistakably developed championship pretensions and it was only right and proper that these should win recognition.

English Amateur Championships became regular occurrences and then, in 1957, the Royal and Ancient Golf Club chose it for the Amateur, an honour they have since bestowed a couple more times, the last winner being Jose-Maria Olazabal, the only player to have won the Boys', Youths'

and Amateur Championships. It is a club whose connections are very much more in the amateur world than the professional. For one thing, it is the way they want it and, for another, the railway and limited access would pose problems in handling large crowds.

Hole	Yds	Par	Hole	Yds	Par
1	415	4	10	182	3
2	381	4	11	384	4
3	518	5	12	405	4
4	312	4	13	380	4
5	162	3	14	420	4
6	402	4	15	403	4
7	377	4	16	127	3
8	493	5	17	494	5
9	450	4	18	390	4
	3510	37		3185	35

FORMBY
Card of the course
(championship tees)

Total 6695 yards, par 72
Course record • 65,
Neil Coles, 1961

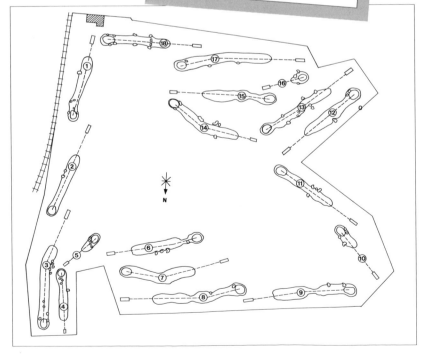

Formby's new holes lend it a more enclosed look, a feeling confirmed by the view from behind the raised 7th green.

Overleaf The delightful setting of Formby, where access to the 15th green is between sentinel dunes. The 16th can be seen in the distance, by the woods.

The club is conveniently served by Freshfield Station and it is the railway line that occupies the mind as players try to guard against a slice off the 1st tee. A bunker, as well as the railway, inclines you to the left which is the side to be but the green is menacingly bunkered and hard to hit. Heather is a definite feature of the 2nd which, like the 3rd, heads north, a long iron often needed to reach and mount the slope to a raised green.

A network of bunkers dominates the drive on the par-5 3rd and two more, centrally positioned, have to be carried or skirted with the second shot. The green is in a slight depression. The 4th is a puzzle for all its modest length, positional play being more important than raw power. Short par 4s have a place on every ideal course and the 4th is a fine example of tempting with the prospect of a birdie and teasing, not to say tormenting, if temptation overspills.

Formby is also well served by its three short holes, the 5th being one to envy. The green, slightly higher than the tee, is a beautiful target though jealously protected and easy to miss.

By now, the proper duneland is reached and the 6th has an altogether more enclosed look, the dune character extending to an admirable cross section having to be negotiated if the green is to be hit in two. It is a typical seaside hole but encroachment of the new land puts a high premium on straightness. At the 7th and 8th, trees give a directional guide that must be obeyed. There is an uphill second to the 7th and incentive at the 8th for a bold drive, punishment lying in wait on both sides for anything less. There is a definite chance of a birdie in a long second over an undulating fairway but safety play can be a wise option.

A high tee on the 9th is an inviting platform

from which to attack and a long drive is an undoubted requisite to leave the green within range. After that, a walk through the pine wood is the herald to the 10th, a short hole to the old 10th green which was designed for a par 5 from a different direction. A certain tightening has been necessary to adapt it to a change of role and the hole is settling down to become an accepted part of the revised Formby.

Then it is back on old familiar territory, a lovely stretch full of variety and satisfying strokes. The 11th drops down from the tee and rises up to the green, the intervening part forming a pleasant fairway – bunkered on the right. It is the last hole heavily influenced by the sandhills on both sides although the 15th is a marvellous hole in which there is a drive onto a high plateau and a thrilling second between substantial mounds to a two-level green.

The 12th and 14th are excellent 4s and the short 16th a pillar of virtue. Often little more than an 8-iron, often less, it proves a small target with deep bunkers all around – the perfect reminder of the strength of short holes that are not all muscle.

The 17th turns back alongside a wood on the right, a shortish par 5 which curves left round a fairway bunker. Land to the left is sandy scrub and there is an imaginatively shaped green ideal for the purpose it presents.

Formby's 18th is fine without being formidable. It falls within the compass of most players, the chief difficulty being a long thin green somewhat unusually bunkered for which judgment of the second shot is all important.

HILLSIDE

No course in the last twenty to thirty years has undergone such a transformation as Hillside. From being a pleasant test lacking the devilment of its august neighbours on the coastal chain of Lancashire, it has graduated to be an honourable member of their company – in some eyes, the hardest of all. Change came about in 1967 by the sale of some of the old land for housing development and the acquisition of some infinitely more formidable dune country that rubs shoulders with Royal Birkdale. Mastermind of the operation was Fred Hawtree whose father had shaped the modern Birkdale.

My own first memories of Hillside are of the first appearance in Britain as a professional of Jack Nicklaus in 1962. It was a cold, bleak May day and I can see him now standing by the clubhouse, fair hair bleached by a Palm Springs sun, wondering perhaps what on earth induced him to come. In spite of finishing well down the field, he was US Open champion within a month although he would almost certainly feel more at home on the new version of Hillside than the old. It is not one of aesthetic delight except towards the end but it is relentless in the challenge it sets and unforgiving if its standards aren't met. To have staged the PGA, Amateur and British Ladies' Open Amateur Championships within a few years of each other is proof of how highly regarded it is as a meeting-ground for the finest players.

It is within walking distance of Hillside Station and, in keeping with West Lancashire, Formby and Southport & Ainsdale, the railway bursts in on the act straightaway. It can best be described as the first hole at Prestwick in reverse, which is to say with out-of-bounds running left not right and wire fence

opposed to stone wall. It is classed as a great railway hole, not giving any leeway on the right either and setting the nerves on edge from the start.

It inclines you to steer rather than strike out but the 2nd is the first of four par 5s, all over 500 yards, and, without some measure of attack, the course can be overwhelming. There is a belt of fir trees running through the course that is a feature of the short 7th although the 10th, through a different glade, is more spectacular and picturesque. Two good par 4s end the outward nine, the 9th

Hole	*Yds*	*Par*	*Hole*	*Yds*	*Par*
1	399	4	10	147	3
2	525	5	11	514	5
3	402	4	12	398	4
4	195	3	13	398	4
5	504	5	14	400	4
6	413	4	15	419	4
7	176	3	16	222	3
8	405	4	17	548	5
9	425	4	18	440	4
	3444	36		3486	36

HILLSIDE
Card of the course
(championship tees)

Total 6930 yards, par 72
Course record • 66,
Paul Way, 1982

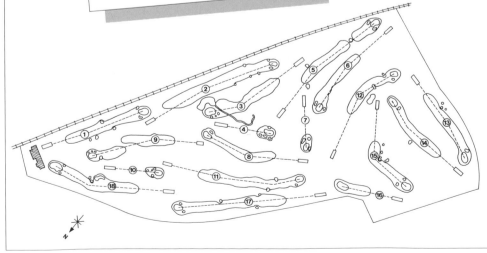

Pine trees form a distinctive feature on parts of Hillside, as on the attractive short 10th.

The roller-coaster 17th, with views overlooking Birkdale.

breaking left to a green that appears slightly raised, but it is the inward nine which is the better and more appealing – much of it taking in the newer territory which has more of the character of the best seaside links.

The 13th, 14th and 15th are more or less parallel holes but with none of the monotony that such an arrangement suggests elsewhere. An uphill second to the 13th that sealed Tony Jacklin's last major victory in 1982 is followed by a chance to open the shoulders on the 14th and a sharp dogleg to the left on the 15th. A green on a low plateau can be an elusive target on the 16th, a long short hole, but the scenic pick of the bunch is the 17th, an uphill and down dale sort of par 5 showing off turbulent undulations on the fairway.

The green occupies virtually the highest point but that means that the 18th descends slowly from a peak, the drive held fractionally left to obtain the most obvious angle for a second shot to a green close to out-of-bounds. With Hillside, there is no room to relax.

SOUTHPORT & AINSDALE

Southport & Ainsdale has been somewhat over-shadowed in terms of a home for championships, and particularly professional events of eminence, by Royal Birkdale and Hillside. Both lie just the other side of the railway line which provides such a regular service between Southport and Liverpool. However, it shares with Moortown, Lindrick and the Belfry the distinction of having witnessed the only British and Irish Ryder Cup victories on home soil. In 1933, Syd Easterbrook holed the putt that claimed victory, S & A hosting the match again in 1937 perhaps in the belief, and certainly the hope, that lightning might strike twice.

Sadly, the Americans, under Walter Hagen's captaincy, prevailed but S & A continued to hold professional tournaments, notably the old Dunlop-Southport. Beyond more regional events, its most regular use now is as a qualifying course for the Open Championship but it retains an undoubted freshness that owes much to the quality of the lay-out planned by James Braid in 1923. Hitherto, the club existed under the title of the Southport Grosvenor GC on a little nine-hole course in Birkdale – later absorbed by a housing estate.

Housing surrounds at least two sides of the pre-sent course, the part at the far end which has been most recently changed being the least meritorious. However, the first half is first class in its variety and challenge and there is a fine finish beginning with the 16th, the Gumbleys.

The 1st and 18th holes occupy something of a spur, resulting in the 1st being a short hole in a class for difficulty with those at Royal Mid-Surrey and on the Blue at the Berkshire. Only from the right is there a clear approach to the green in a shallow dell but, on the par-5 2nd, the focal point from the tee is an elevated terraced green which is the culmination of a hole much admired by Archie Compston.

It is assumed from the name given to the 3rd, Braid's, that it was perhaps the great man's favourite, an understandable choice since a strong, bold drive is necessary from a high tee to carry over the sandhills. Braid was said to have driven with 'divine fury', a quality that would have helped him at S & A which continues with a much shorter par 4, the 4th.

The next three raise the tenor an octave or two. The 5th is a very good hole through a gap in the hills, and the next two are doglegs, the 6th to the right and the 7th to the left. The drive at the 6th calls for proper control but not so much as on the 7th where the green, with the cemetery behind, is hidden from view unless the drive is immensely long. It brings to mind the story of James Braid

SOUTHPORT & AINSDALE
Card of the course

Hole		Yds	Par	Hole		Yds	Par
1	Trial	200	3	10	Chair	160	3
2	Terrace	520	5	11	Regent	447	4
3	Braid's	418	4	12	Warren	401	4
4	Ridge	316	4	13	Firs	154	3
5	Hen Pen	447	4	14	Gorse	383	4
6	Gap	386	4	15	Railway	353	4
7	Steeple	480	5	16	Gumbleys	510	5
8	Plateau	157	3	17	Heather	443	4
9	Old Dogleg	482	5	18	Home	355	4
		3406	37			3206	35

Total 6612 yards, par 72

Course record • 62, Chris Moody, 1991

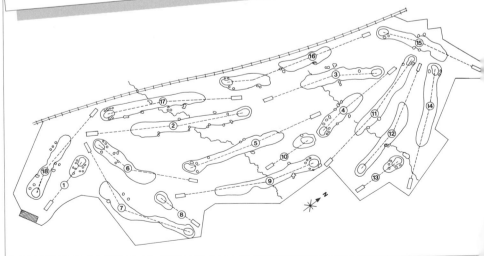

After an opening short hole, the 2nd takes players on a gradual climb to a green that is ideal for a par 5.

playing one foggy morning with a first-time visitor to Walton Heath, Braid's home club. Trying to be helpful on one tee, Braid said, 'You aim on yon' church spire. You cannot see it this morning,' he added, 'but that's the line.'

There is no doubting that the only place to be on the short 8th is the green on a plateau with drops all around. It is a most individual hole, and a most attractive one, but after the turn some of Braid's original design has been altered, some think to advantage and others to the detriment of the course.

We must leave that argument to those more qualified to take part, moving onto Gumbleys, one of the famous holes of golf very much in the old-fashioned mould, with a spectacular second over a massive sandhill into which is set a sleepered bunker. The unseen part on the other side is more plain but on the 17th a big slice will land on the railway and an even bigger on Hillside, while the 18th, a stiffened finishing hole, involves a drive over a low crest before the fairway swings left to finish beside the clubhouse.

A close-up of the Gumbleys, the name by which the 16th is known.

ROYAL BIRKDALE

Royal Birkdale came late to the ranks of Open Championship courses although it soon made up for lost time. In the last 30 years, no club has hosted more major events, a clear mark of recognition, particularly among the professionals, that its lack of the eccentricities of some other seaside links is more to their liking. It accords with the modern belief that drives landing on the fairway should not be deflected by freak bounces and that greens should be visible targets receptive to the best shots.

Birkdale's fairways are flat but they form valleys between mighty dunes, providing a sturdy frame to a landscape embellished by a profusion of tenacious buckthorn and willow scrub. For country so close to Southport, there is surprise at the size of the mountain range of sandhills, wild and wind-blown. There always appears land enough for two or three golf course architects to let themselves loose for a year or two and come up with more authentic masterpieces. The scene portrays the best that seaside golf can offer but Birkdale's excellence as a meeting-ground for modern giants is equally due to its ability to handle and accommodate the crowds, cars and commercial trappings that are part and parcel of great championships. It is this combination that makes it so formidable.

The Open Championship in 1991 was its sixth in exactly 30 years, its roll of winners reading like a page from a golfing Debrett. For Peter Thomson (1965) and Tom Watson (1983) victory marked the climax to two outstanding careers, and for Lee Trevino (1971) and Johnny Miller (1976) it was proof that they never played any better. For Ian Baker-Finch (1991), who turned the last round upside down by going out in 29, it was confirmation of a rising talent, a day when the course and the occasion summoned his finest. However, it was Arnold Palmer's triumph in 1961 that had the true story-book element. In a week of bad weather, he rode the storm and tamed the whirlwind. In the postponed second round that saw conditions at their worst, he strode like a Colossus across a scene that was mostly black and sombre. His play provided virtually the only light.

For six holes, his golf was well-nigh perfect but the thought occurs many years later that his miracles would have been impossible anywhere else than Birkdale. With less even stances and lies, he

ROYAL BIRKDALE
Card of the course
(Open Championship tees)

Hole	Yds	Par	Hole	Yds	Par
1	448	4	10	395	4
2	417	4	11	409	4
3	409	4	12	184	3
4	203	3	13	475	4
5	346	4	14	199	3
6	473	4	15	543	5
7	156	3	16	414	4
8	458	4	17	525	5
9	414	4	18	472	4
	3324	34		3616	36

Total 6940 yards, par 70
Course record • 63,
Jodie Mudd, 1991 Open Championship

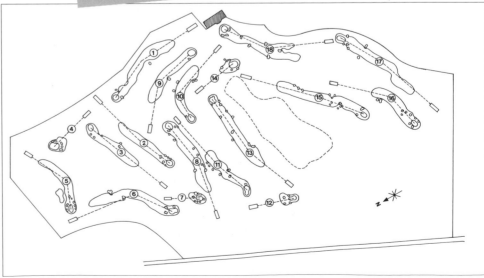

A view of the drive at the 8th, which curves left round a shoulder of dunes. The 7th green is seen to the left.

might not have been able to hit with the force necessary to give his fairway shots the flight of tracer bullets or to hold his pitches under the wind.

It would also have been more difficult to putt as consistently as he did on greens more exposed than Birkdale's. The dunes and low lying fairways offer just the hint of shelter denied some other links but his deeds were quite literally recorded on tablets of stone. His second at the old 15th (now 16th), clawed onto the green from seemingly impenetrable undergrowth, has a plaque erected in its memory. In contrast, 15 years later, Johnny Miller found Birkdale infinitely more benign. His problems on fairways parched by drought were of a different sort of control although, again, life was easier in that respect than it would have been elsewhere.

The start at Birkdale is invariably the key to the round, the first three holes constituting an opening that is as difficult as on any championship course. Unusually, they all follow a different direction, a fact that keeps everyone on their guard. The drive at the 1st must hug the bunker set into the hill on the left if a proper sight is to be had of the green but the 2nd and 3rd are more

straightforward in the sense that position from the tee is not quite so important.

A reshaping of the short 4th has made the green far less open although changes at the 6th have presented greater options from the tee, opening up a route to the left of the big central bunker and a view of the raised green for those driving far enough. Meanwhile, the 5th, the shortest of the par 4s, has menace in its gentle dogleg. In 1961, Palmer stumbled on the 7th and 8th, bunkering a 7-iron on the short 7th and pulling his drive onto the low hills at a point where the 8th bears left.

By now, the white clubhouse is in sight again, Birkdale sharing with Muirfield, of the Open courses, the luxury of two loops of nine. The 9th is a fine 4, the plateau fairway obscured as well if the drive is pushed too far.

A sharp dogleg left, and a drive from a high tee, are the features of the 10th and 11th but a clearer reminder of the dunes is forthcoming on the picturesque 12th, the short hole designed to replace the 17th which was sacrificed when found to be a barrier for crowd control.

In the old days, there used to be (or could be) four par 5s in the last six holes; nowadays, for the

Homeward bound . . . an ideal appreciation of the drive and how the 18th hole bears to the right.

Left A par 3 that replaced the old 17th, the 12th represents target golf at its best to a green surrounded by dunes.

Open, the 13th and 18th have become long par 4s but statistics stress the length and toughness of a finish to match those at the other pillars of the north-west, Lytham and Hoylake.

The 15th is the best of the par 5s, the drive having to avoid bunkers down the left and the second shot a cluster of bunkers that appear almost haphazard in their placement. There is one to tease the landing area of most second shots, the number actually reaching the green being few and far between, particularly as the hazard of bunkers is reinforced most effectively by vast banks of willow scrub with trunks as thick as cricket bats.

Memories of the 16th are centred not so much on Palmer as the time two years later in the PGA Championship and Brabazon Trophy when a terrible winter had left its scars. Only prodigious second shots found the windswept green, and these could easily be putted off it. Regular lengthening of the hole has made it quite an achievement to reach the hidden fairway in unhelpful winds but there is no doubt about the main task on the 17th: the tee shot must bisect, skirt or clear the large sentinel dunes, known as Scylla and Charybdis, that devour anything wayward.

Revisions to the 17th hole for the 1991 Open have lent a more sheltered appearance to the approach but it is still not as forbidding as that on the 18th, a hole at which half of Birkdale's Open champions – Thomson (twice), Palmer, and Watson – could afford no slip-up.

Watson's closing 4 is the one that remains most indelibly in the mind, a huge drive perfectly placed to stay clear of the bunkers and a 2-iron aimed at the dining-room window packed with onlookers who were suitably impressed. He made it look so simple.

It was the green on which Jack Nicklaus and Tony Jacklin ended their epic single that resulted in the 1969 Ryder Cup being tied; the green on which Peter Thomson joined the elite ranks of those who have won the Open twice on the same course; and the green to which Severiano Ballesteros, joint runner-up to Miller, played an incredible pitch in 1976 to confirm the major championship launching of a precocious talent.

Adjectives such as fair, honest, rugged and stern are all applicable to Birkdale, a course that, because of its many virtues, will remain in heavy demand to decide golf's weightiest issues.

ROYAL LYTHAM & ST ANNES

Bernard Darwin once wrote of Royal Lytham & St Annes, 'It has beautiful turf, but not much else of beauty. It is a beast but a just beast.' There is neither sight nor sound of the sea. It is the only links encircled on all sides by suburbia but it remains a first-class examination of seaside golf even if its look is not entirely natural.

In Tony Nickson's wonderfully comprehensive history of the club, *The Lytham Century*, he refers to a report by Horace Hutchinson in which he mentioned that 'Some wonderfully ingenious vast sandhills, that stretch across the course at the 7th and 11th, have also been constructed.' He then observed that 'The bent grass thereon looks a little bit artificial and regular, but no doubt in time it will look as wild and terrible as need be.'

It is thought that Herbert Fowler was probably the designer, a tribute to the skill of those architects who can make the artificial appear real. Lytham relies on a variety of hazards to weave its torment. There are bunkers galore, grassy hollows and dells to tease and divert shots that are not truly enough struck and several elevated greens to pose questions of judgment.

There is also the railway that runs the length of the course, intimidating the drives on the 2nd, 3rd and 8th with the scare of out-of-bounds, an added problem lying in the fact that there is little freedom on the left either. Fine driving is essential because there is a punishment for every blemish. Hit your ball to the right position all the time and all things are possible but stray by as little as a few

yards in places and you may be consumed by sand, bushes, mounds and rough that really is rough.

The wind can, on occasions, unbalance the course rather as it does Royal Troon. In the prevailing north-westerly at Lytham, seven holes may be downwind and many in the Open Championship have stormed to the turn in 32 or less, particularly as there are three par 3s. However, the journey home is a different story. Only one par 3, the difficult 12th, and the sheer length of some of the par 4s contribute to situations in which 38 or 39 represents fine play. Lytham is impossible to force. Patience is an undoubted virtue.

One unique part of Lytham is that it is the only Open Championship course beginning with a short hole although, until the 1920s, Muirfield could have said the same. Quite why Lytham was

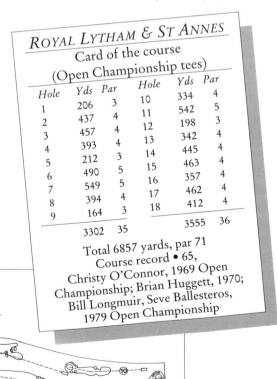

ROYAL LYTHAM & ST ANNES
Card of the course
(Open Championship tees)

Hole	Yds	Par	Hole	Yds	Par
1	206	3	10	334	4
2	437	4	11	542	5
3	457	4	12	198	3
4	393	4	13	342	4
5	212	3	14	445	4
6	490	5	15	463	4
7	549	5	16	357	4
8	394	4	17	462	4
9	164	3	18	412	4
	3302	35		3555	36

Total 6857 yards, par 71
Course record • 65,
Christy O'Connor, 1969 Open Championship; Brian Huggett, 1970; Bill Longmuir, Seve Ballesteros, 1979 Open Championship

Lytham is the only Open Championship course to begin with a short hole. The red flag in front of the clubhouse belongs to the 18th.

designed that way is less easy to explain, unless it was the presence of the hill at the 2nd or a pond on the right of the green in the early days which dictated the plan.

There is a pleasant walk to the 1st tee past the putting green, under the windows of the Dormy House and the professional's shop, the tee itself enclosed by trees and the railway. It is not the best of the short holes, a longish iron having to find the entrance to the green between bunkers, but the 2nd and 3rd can be the very devil. On both holes, there is merit and reward in taking the tight line from the tee, on the 2nd over the hill and down the right, and on the 3rd as close to the bunkers on the left as you dare.

Exceptions to the pattern of holes running straight out are the 4th and 5th, the 4th turning about and serving as a timely reminder of what to expect later on. It is a notable example of the severity of Lytham's 4s, the correct side to be from the tee being the right in order to negotiate the stern pin position on the left. The short 5th is heavily bunkered, then two par 5s follow in succession, the 7th better and more difficult. The 7th green, hidden from view by mountainous dunes, is most attractive.

The 8th is a classic hole, rather more daunting and demanding in the era of the hickory shaft although still a good one to get behind you. Apart from the definite fear of driving out of bounds or of overcompensating and losing a ball in the hills, the green, on an exposed plateau, can be a tantalizing target. In certain winds, the shot needs elevation to clear bunkers and scale the crest while, at the same time, it must possess piercing flight to hold its course.

A third short hole, overlooking Ansdell Station, ends the outward nine and then it is a question of bracing oneself for the long run home, starting with a hole with one of the most attractive fairways and greens on the entire links. Huge bunkers are a feature of the drive at the 11th, a long hole that is a trifle dull apart from the green.

The 12th, the last short hole and one made infinitely more demanding in the 1960s, involves a long iron or wood in a substantial carry to a raised green with out-of-bounds close on the right. Some relief to the hard-hitting golf is found on the 13th, little more than a drive and pitch, but the finish is immense.

The 14th is straight and a shade flat but it requires two big shots to get home to a green beside a quiet avenue. Even more demanding is the 15th where the rising fairway, running diagonally to the right, demands a clear decision on the tee as to how much to bite off. Unless the drive

favours the most daring line, the green will still be out of sight but not out of mind. The second shot, dropping down a little from the dunes, has bunkers and rough to avoid, the length of the apron and approach being particularly deceiving. 'God, it is a hard hole,' lamented Jack Nicklaus in the 1974 Open, a sentiment freely echoed in a championship in which the weather was tough throughout and only Gary Player broke par over four rounds.

A blind drive and another raised green surrounded by bunkers are the features of the 16th, a hole on which Severiano Ballesteros plotted his own unconventional path in 1979. He ended with

A superb aerial view of the 8th (right), the short 9th and the 10th (left), showing how the course has become enclosed by the railway line and suburbia.

Part of the challenging finish, the 15th is perhaps the hardest of the five par 4s on the back nine.

a birdie all the same but birdies are rarer on a 17th hole that matches the Old Course at St Andrews for the drama it unfolds.

A minefield of bunkers line the left side of the fairway, pushing you to the right, the only place where the green can be seen between a gap in the sandhills. The left is wild country but execution does not always match intention even when the name is Bobby Jones. With one of the most famous single shots ever played, he hit the green on the 71st hole of Lytham's first Open in 1926 from a clearing in the sandy tract of land on the left. His mashie, which hangs in the clubhouse like an ancient spear on a castle wall, had to carry all kinds of rough and scrub, the merest error spelling disaster. With Al Watrous already on the green, it was death or glory.

Jones remains the only American winner of the Open at Lytham. On seven subsequent occasions,

no American professional has managed to conquer there.

The 17th is not the end of the worry. Lytham's finishing hole is as good as any, certainly one that has seen more despair than delight. Heading straight for the Victorian clubhouse, the fairway is the only safe place, a statement easier made than followed. A perfect drive threads its way over and between a formidable array of bunkers veering neither left nor right. Bushes adorn the right and rough the left. That is the major part of the task but the green is well protected, too.

Open champions (Peter Thomson and Tony Jacklin) have played the hole as if bunkers did not exist, the very reason why they were champion. Under the gaze of the clubhouse windows, less convincing acts can be embarrassingly public but somehow the 18th is the epitome of Lytham, a severe test of accuracy and courage.

CASTLETOWN

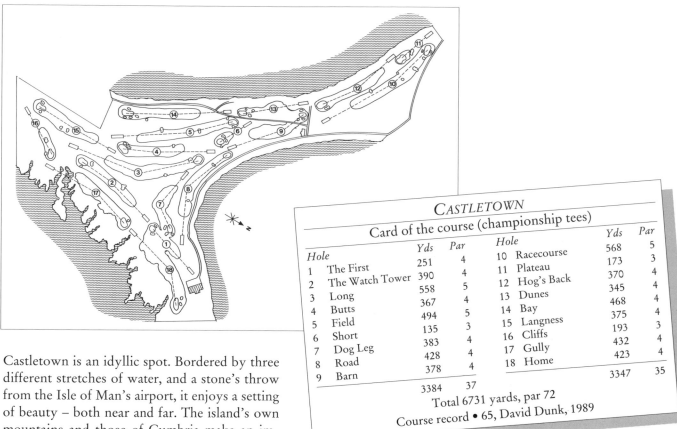

CASTLETOWN					
Card of the course (championship tees)					
Hole	*Yds*	*Par*	*Hole*	*Yds*	*Par*
1 The First	251	4	10 Racecourse	568	5
2 The Watch Tower	390	4	11 Plateau	173	3
3 Long	558	5	12 Hog's Back	370	4
4 Butts	367	4	13 Dunes	345	4
5 Field	494	5	14 Bay	468	4
6 Short	135	3	15 Langness	375	4
7 Dog Leg	383	4	16 Cliffs	193	3
8 Road	428	4	17 Gully	432	4
9 Barn	378	4	18 Home	423	4
	3384	37		3347	35

Total 6731 yards, par 72

Course record • 65, David Dunk, 1989

Castletown is an idyllic spot. Bordered by three different stretches of water, and a stone's throw from the Isle of Man's airport, it enjoys a setting of beauty – both near and far. The island's own mountains and those of Cumbria make an imposing backcloth but the two giant sweeps of bay and the little boats paint an unmistakable seascape into which the noble links blend naturally and impressively.

In friendly weather, the golf is none too taxing, testing without being formidable, subtle without being harsh. The splendour of the setting brings out the best in golfers but it doesn't need much of a wind to stir for skill, control and strength to be instantly required. There are no dunes or trees to provide succour or shelter, errant shots being washed up on the rocks or disappearing over a cliff.

There is a remoteness, almost a loneliness on the peninsula when the clouds descend and the rain becomes relentless. It is a flavour with which all links are familiar. Some say it needs wild conditions to show their true teeth but a walk across

Dartmoor is very much more pleasurable when the sun magnifies the colours and, while part of the fun of golf is in taking what comes, Castletown needs the sun to help it sparkle.

Like Gleneagles and Turnberry, it is a hotel course, the Castletown Golf Links Hotel making a magnificent base camp, the 1st tee no more than a few yards from its front door. The 1st, though uphill, is, in fact, a gentle opener, the sort of hole that good players can drive but, if the 2nd is altogether sterner, the course really steps up a notch with the long 3rd.

A well positioned drive to the left is the secret of the 4th while the first of three marvellous short holes at the 6th puts an even greater premium on accuracy. An enclosed green makes an attractive looking target amid the gorse but there is no let-up on the 7th. The fairway, turning left, is difficult to hit and the green, near the clubhouse, is quite a puzzle.

Mackenzie Ross, saviour of Turnberry and designer of Southerness, did a great job of restoration at Castletown after the Second World War, his imaginative attention to detail being apparent in the contouring of greens that are full of interest. The 8th, after a good drive to a fairway that is punitive to miss, is a case in point but, by now, the 9th has turned away towards historic ground, the ground on which the first Derby was run – the drive itself aimed on the square stone frame of King William's College.

Castletown was the residence of the Earl of Derby who, as Lord of Man, founded the race bearing his name before taking it to Epsom where it has remained. The 10th, not surprisingly named Racecourse, occupies part of the site of the old racecourse – or almost three furlongs to be more precise. It is somewhat plainer in character than many of the other holes but the 11th is a cracking par 3 by the shore and here, and at the next three holes, it is advisable not to drift to the right.

There is less risk in this regard on the 14th but, at 468 yards, it yields few 4s. Out-of-bounds enters the reckoning again on the uphill 15th but Castletown saves the best until last. Rocks, cliffs and gorges feature large particularly on the 17th. There is an alarming carry from the tee and a dramatic drop to the right. It is the last reminder of the variety encompassed in the 18 holes, a round that ends with a splendid 4 back to the welcome and comfort of the hotel.

The 17th, the hole where everything can be washed up on the rocks.

SEASCALE

Visitors to Cumbria are usually climbers, fell-walkers or those attracted by the lakes. On account of so much unsuitable terrain, it is not noted for its golf although Seascale and Silloth-on-Solway are notable exceptions.

Seascale is roughly in the middle of the coastal section, a few miles south of Whitehaven, but the approach from the south is full of examples of the beauty of the hills and dales that inspired so much of Wordsworth's verse. In places, it is winding and rugged but suddenly the sea beckons as the road turns down to the small town of Seascale whose links provides a convenient focal point that conveys a mark of excellence.

It is an area that has become better known for the proximity of the Sellafield Power Station but, in spite of its brooding presence, the setting of the links is dominated by incomparable views of the Isle of Man and the Lakeland hills. It is a course of pleasant contrast with a hint of downland to supplement the holes nearer the sea where the fairways ripple and undulate appealingly.

The 16th runs under the shadow of one long sandhill with steep banks while the 7th takes advantage of the flatter expanse on the top. It is a course, in fact, of constantly changing levels, a feature that compensates for the relative lack of length by modern standards.

The start is modest, three of the first four holes being par 4s of under 340 yards, but the 1st involves quite a climb and the 2nd continues along the out-of-bounds to the right, the best line, nevertheless, to counter the bunkers to the left of the green being as close to the wall as possible. The 3rd raises the challenge a gear, a right-hand dogleg marked by a grassy bank and a barbed wire fence.

At the 4th, a marker post

signals the line of the drive over low dunes to a hole that the longest can almost reach, but the 6th, 483 yards, is very definitely out of reach unless the wind is helping, its rather more open character making it more a test of strength than accuracy. The par-5 7th turns in the opposite direction, leading on to a nice, downhill short hole at the 8th before the outward half ends with a lovely par 4, the fairway tumbling away to a green that makes an inviting target. The 9th also offers the only hole that plays towards the sea, a hole, like many, that offers the chance of a birdie but with pitfalls as well.

Above right *Looking down on the mighty 16th.*

Below right *The 6th green and, beyond it, the brooding presence of Sellafield.*

SEASCALE
Card of the course

Hole		Yds	Par	Hole		Yds	Par
1	Wasdale View	325	4	10	Beck	143	3
2	Sherwin's	339	4	11	Calder	470	4
3	Corner Dyke	407	4	12	Independence	392	4
4	Ridges	326	4	13	Railway	216	3
5	Over the Dyke	187	3	14	Rabbits	499	5
6	Bank Side	483	5	15	Punch Bowl	312	4
7	Long	561	5	16	Links	473	4
8	Stone Circle	199	3	17	Manx View	344	4
9	Newmill	387	4	18	Home	353	4
		3214	36			3202	35

Total 6416 yards, par 71

Course record • 67, Glen Shuttleworth (A), 1987; Steven Holden, 1991

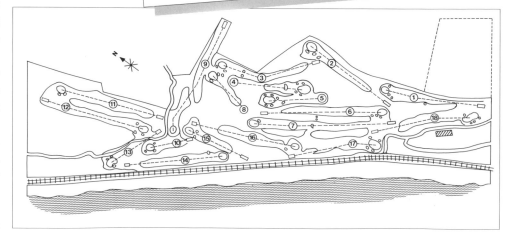

The 10th is a delightful short hole over a stone wall with a stream providing obvious menace, as it does again on the very much longer, short 13th. In between come the 11th, a very long par 4, and the 12th which comes straight back. A good par 5, the 14th, follows the line of the railway but, after the short par-4 15th, with an approach sloping down to a green between hills, the finish is highly testing.

Foremost is the mighty 16th which has more of the character of a par 5. The fairway rises onto a large crest guarding a green in a slight dell with a gully on the right acting as further defence. The 17th tee beside the railway and overlooking the beach signals a formidable drive over a high hill, the brave line shortening the length of the second shot. Finally, the drive at the 18th passes in front of the clubhouse leaving a second shot over a sharp slope to a fairly wide green.

SILLOTH ON SOLWAY

In much the same way that the Honourable Company of Edinburgh Golfers found a new home on the broad reaches of the Firth of Forth, the Carlisle and Silloth Golf Club owed its formation to a band of Carlisle businessmen seeking a golfing retreat. Theirs was an inspired choice. In 1892, the same year that the Honourable Company moved to Muirfield, they developed an area of fine, natural blessings into one of our outstanding seaside links.

If the surroundings were bleak and sombre, the golfing challenge would still be supreme but what lifts Silloth onto a pinnacle of excellence is a setting of remote splendour and beauty. Across the Solway lie the links of Southerness fringed by miles of golden sand while, guarding the southern aspect, are the Cumbrian mountains.

Silloth also has the proud historical connection with Cecil Leitch, one of three daughters of the local doctor, who became one of the most celebrated of all British lady golfers. It is easy to see how her full range of shotmaking powers was forged on fairways of crisp Cumberland turf that are full of the ripples and characteristic crests and ridges so beloved on seaside courses.

There is a high premium on good driving, the valleyed fairways, lined with heather and gorse, needing no bunkers from the tee except on the 10th. There is such consistency in the punishment for missing fairways that you undoubtedly get what you hit. It is a feature that you cannot always see the drives finish but you always know where they have gone and whether or not they have found a safe haven.

The clubhouse stands proudly on the edge of the town close to the old harbour and flour mill. It is quite a landmark from several tees notably the 4th which turns back after the first two holes have made a pleasant start and the 3rd has dog-legged left to a raised, plateau green. All the ingredients of heather, gorse and undulations are immediately apparent. The second to the 1st has to scale a ridge to a hidden green while the drive

at the 2nd involves a substantial carry, the green, high at the front, dropping away towards the back.

The 5th is a fine par 5 along the Solway and the second to the 7th is reminiscent of the 1st except that there is a bigger drop to a picturesque green. By now, the golfer is well acquainted with the all-embracing beauty of Silloth, the 8th tee providing one of the best reminders. The outward half ends with a short hole to a small green that is the last to rub shoulders with the shore.

SILLOTH ON SOLWAY
Card of the course

Hole		Yds	Par	Hole		Yds	Par
1	Horse Shoe	380	4	10	Blooming Heather	308	4
2	The Close	319	4	11	Spire	403	4
3	Criffel	358	4	12	Heather Bank	200	3
4	The Mill	372	4	13	Hogs Back	468	5
5	Solway	482	5	14	Milecastle	477	5
6	Natterjack	187	3	15	Heather Blooming	417	4
7	Battery	403	4	16	The Mount	182	3
8	Valley	371	4	17	Duffers	495	5
9	The Manx	134	3	18	Home	401	4
		3006	35			3351	37

Total 6357 yards, par 72

Course record • 66, Chris Wallace (A), 1966; Ian Little (A), 1987; Donald Watson (A), 1989

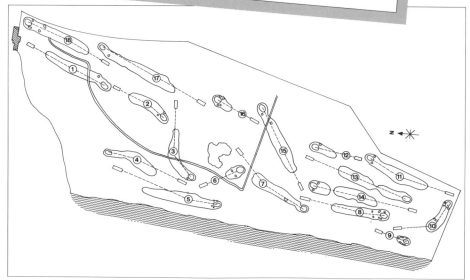

The dogleg 10th, around a heathery knoll at the furthest point of the course, moves inland. It is a hole that can be driven under certain circumstances in spite of two bunkers set into the corner. A straight drive is advisable on the 11th where the fairway falls away left and right but the 13th is perhaps the most memorable hole coming home. The green stands defiantly on the skyline as the second shot must mount dramatically higher ground – a task that is easier said than done when against the wind. However, if the 13th faces a headwind, there is decided help on the 14th, another par 5, which is the reverse of the 13th in many ways. A plunging second leads onto the 15th which, like the 3rd, runs diagonally to the rest of the holes. A stout finish follows.

The Mount is an apt description of the short 16th although that of Duffers for the 17th is not. It is a par 5 to a sunken green by a short row of terraced houses. The 18th then rewards two fine shots although severe on anything less. It is a comment that applies generally at Silloth, host to the Ladies' Amateur in 1976 and 1983 and worthy of the best. In a more accessible spot, it might have staged a national men's championship but it is as a remote jewel that it shines most brightly.

The 5th, following the shoreline and looking across to Southerness on the other side of the Solway Firth.

193

CHAPTER NINE

IRELAND

One of the many paradoxes about Ireland is that its sleepy tempo and timeless beauty are in danger of being eroded by the healthy tourist industry it encourages and needs in order to survive. Donkey carts, for instance, may be preserved to attract the coach parties but, if the latter really are a necessary evil, there is one ample consolation. Golf courses maintain the peace and tranquillity of the countryside more effectively than anything; in Ireland, peace and tranquillity abound.

There is about golf in Ireland a spaciousness and grandeur unmatched anywhere. Cecil Ewing, one of the most famous of Irish golfers, used to express his dislike of those courses which run alongside the backs of people's gardens, out-of-bounds fences rearing their 'ugly heads'. To a man born free in Sligo, it was a natural sentiment. Irish courses are a vision of wild sandhills, lonely, golden beaches, teasing winds and seas embracing many moods.

In the remoter regions of the west coast, you can drive for miles without seeing a living soul. For many who live there, a journey to Limerick or Galway is a continental safari, a fact all too apparent if you stop and ask for directions. They can be as bewildering as the Irish caddie who described a putt as 'slightly straight' or the other with the beguiling revelation that, 'You've a strong crosswind against you'. However, it is an approach perfectly attuned to golf.

The game is leisurely and friendly. Everyone is delighted to see everyone else. There is a charm and generosity about hospitality that insists nobody can start 18 holes of golf without sampling one of the many local brews; certainly none can be deemed complete until you have joined the assembled company in a rendering of every Irish ballad ever written.

All Irishmen see themselves as Count John McCormack, pillars of uninhibited gusto, and it is a characteristic that spills over into their golf – or maybe it is the other way round. The Irish do not take kindly to regimentation. They adopt an individual style that pays no heed to the coaching manual meaning that, while they may not allow conventional technique to be instilled into them, they do permit natural ability to leak out.

Their instinctiveness is a response to their good fortune in having so many great courses from which to choose. The problem confronting the visitor is in knowing where to start, particularly as North and South are united as one country where golf is concerned. The pearls of the North are Royal Portrush and Royal County Down, Portrush beside the Giant's Causeway and County Down where the Mountains of Mourne really do roll down to the sea.

Both are superb, each with its own fond admirers willing to talk persuasively about why it is better than the other, and the Irish are nothing if not persuasive. A little to the north of Portrush

The breathtaking setting of the 5th green at Royal Portrush.

are Ballycastle and Portstewart which typify the links tradition but the more popular destination is the Dublin area where Portmarnock and Royal Dublin await.

However, there is an important stopping-place on the journey south from Newcastle at Baltray, home of the County Louth Club. A mile or two from Drogheda, near the border, it is not quite as well known as it deserves to be although it is the setting for the annual East of Ireland Championship and is famous for having produced two of the most famous women golfers in Ireland's history, Clarrie Tiernan and Philomena Garvey.

It was the handiwork of Tom Simpson and is another links on the grand scale, a description that fits all the courses mentioned here including Portmarnock. As host to so many championships, professional tournaments and international matches, it is the best known, a fame established by its closeness to Dublin and helped even more nowadays by its greater closeness to the airport.

You could be on the first tee within half an hour of landing, eager to tackle a test as honest as Muirfield although Portmarnock's dunes are not of the giant variety found out west. Royal Dublin is nearer the city with evidence of it all around but a seclusion is lent to it by being an island, connected to the mainland by means of a low wooden bridge.

Mention must also be made of the Island at Malahide but for those whose preference is to get right away from the cities and civilization, all roads lead south and west – first to Kerry and then north to Rosses Point via Ballybunion and Lahinch and several other quaint ports of call. Among the latter is Dooks which is as far off the beaten track as could be imagined.

Waterville is more publicized, the longest course in Britain or Ireland, and one embellished by the inclusion of much of the land near the sea. It is on the Ring of Kerry at whose head, so to speak, is the most recent creation at Tralee. Frank Pennink regarded it as the finest piece of terrain he had seen but Ballybunion is always spoken of in superlatives, Herbert Warren Wind rating it even higher than that. One must distinguish between the Old and New, the New the work of Robert Trent Jones Jnr. Lahinch, on the other side of the Shannon Estuary in County Clare, has some mountainous dunes as well as some magnificent holes – and some, like the Dell (the sole survivor from Old Tom Morris's original layout) and Klondyke, which are unique to this course.

Rosses Point, home of the County Sligo Club in the heart of country made famous by the poetry of W.B. Yeats, occupies the same Atlantic coastline that could accommodate many more links of quality and challenge. The blessings of nature are everywhere apparent at Rosses Point.

ROYAL PORTRUSH

Given only one day in Belfast, golfers face a major decision: whether to head north up the Antrim coast to Royal Portrush or south towards the Mountains of Mourne and Royal County Down at Newcastle. Those with more time should undoubtedly sample both for no other major city is surrounded by two championship courses of such supreme quality.

The Antrim coast road is one of the most beautiful in Britain and is therefore the favoured approach route. It sets the tone for the majesty of the golf as Dunluce Castle is passed and the links lie exposed in the distance: green fairways, guarded by dunes, running down to a shining sea with Benbane, Inishowen and the Skerries offshore and often the faint outline of Islay and Jura.

The Giant's Causeway is another local landmark, thought by some to represent stepping stones to Scotland, but whilst the frame to the picture, as it were, is breathtaking, the picture itself is the real centre of attraction. The Dunluce course, named after the ancestral home of the Lords of Antrim, housed the Open Championship in 1951 but there is a second course, the Valley, which is a fine foil.

When Bernard Darwin saw Harry Colt's work in remodelling the version of the Dunluce known today, he wrote that he had built himself a monument more enduring than brass. Darwin was writing during the Open, the only one ever held in Ireland, although the fact that it has never returned has nothing whatsoever to do with any fading qualities of the course which will always more than hold its own. It is remembered, too, for its connections with Fred Daly, the only Irishman to have won the Open. He spent his boyhood days as a caddie there.

It is a magnificent links on the grandest scale but two qualities set it apart: it is one of the most demanding tests of driving because the fairways are narrow and the rough is rough; and the relatively small greens are full of hidden subtleties and tricky slopes although they do not rely heavily on bunkering. Another dimension to the difficulty of the driving is the fact that so few of the holes are straight. Many curve and dogleg just enough to make calculations difficult regarding the correct line, particularly when the wind is strong.

ROYAL PORTRUSH
Card of the Dunluce course (championship tees)

Hole		Yds	Par	Hole		Yds	Par
1	Hughies	389	4	10	Dhu Varren	480	5
2	Giant's Grave	509	5	11	Feather Bed	166	3
3	Islay	159	3	12	Causeway	395	4
4	Fred Daly's	455	4	13	Skerries	371	4
5	White Rocks	384	4	14	Calamity	213	3
6	Harry Colt's	193	3	15	Purgatory	366	4
7	P.G. Stevenson's	432	4	16	Babington's	432	4
8	Himalayas	376	4	17	Glenarm	517	5
9	Tavern	478	5	18	Greenaway	479	4
		3375	36			3419	36

Total 6794 yards, par 72

Course record • 66, Jack Hargreaves, 1951 Open Championship

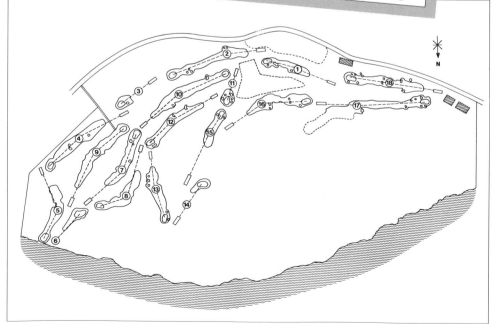

The undulating 13th, Skerries, a hole that doglegs to the left. The low islands, resembling a wrecked ship, after which the hole is named can be seen in the distance.

The opening holes work their way gradually towards the sea, the 1st with an uphill second. The 2nd is a downhill par 5 through dunes and the 4th a fine hole where there is a stream to drive over and out-of-bounds to the right. Out-of-bounds is a bigger threat than the stream. However, the course might be said to begin with the 5th, a sharp right-hand dogleg to a green perched high above the beach. When the sun is shining, the true glory of Portrush is revealed.

It was just such a day when Joe Carr, the greatest of all Irish amateurs, stood 10-up and 10 to play in the final of Portrush's only British Amateur Championship in 1960, the pinnacle of achievement in a career that knew many peaks. A similar sense of euphoria greeted the triumph of Catherine Lacoste in 1969 in the Ladies' British Open Amateur Championship, a year in which she captured the American title as well. In the final, Lacoste lost the first three holes against Ann Irvin but her recovery included winning the short 6th in spite of both players missing the green. It is a beautiful hole, turning back inland,

the perfect shape of shot being a long fade.

The next six holes swing to and fro in an unusual pattern for a seaside links, the 7th (which honours the long-serving father of Portrush's current professional, Dai Stevenson), 9th and 12th greens standing more or less side by side, the ideal position for the halfway refreshment hut. The 13th – Skerries, named after the offshore islands – heads back towards the sea, a left-hand dogleg well bunkered on the right of the fairway.

The two most famous names follow, Calamity and Purgatory, titles that speak volumes for the trouble they generate. Calamity is another short hole, frequently a wood, across a grassy chasm that threatens the direst punishment for the slice. The green can look a tiny target. At Purgatory, the hook is less to be recommended.

The last three holes are largely flat and not entirely in character with the rest, but the 16th is a hole that has decided more than one great issue. The 17th and 18th, running up and back on the other side of the clubhouse, until recently constituted the rarity of a finish comprising two par 5s.

ROYAL COUNTY DOWN

Reaction to a first sight of Royal County Down at Newcastle is one of open-mouthed wonderment. It is a reaction that never changes. For visual splendour and golf on a heroic scale, there is nothing better. Against the inspiring backdrop of the Mountains of Mourne and the shining sands of Dundrum Bay, the holes form avenues of green amidst turbulent dunes and, in summer, a sea of golden gorse.

You could go to Newcastle for the setting alone but aesthetic delights are merely an accompaniment to a challenge that has few, if any, peers. The Open Championship has been staged on courses that are not as good. Newcastle is a meeting-ground for giants who must have command of all the golfing virtues – power, control, patience, and

the competitive coolness to plot the correct strategy and the ability to think clearly under pressure.

Here altogether is a rich and varied feast of strokes and there is almost always a wind to make them more varied still, sometimes almost painfully so. It is essentially 'big' golf with great emphasis on sound driving – often involving sizable carries. Driving is an art that has been blunted by the miracles wrought by the 1-iron to which professionals resort at the drop of a hat but Newcastle, in demanding conditions, makes the driver a mandatory weapon.

The greens, too, are distinctive with subtle drops and slopes that magnify the merest blemish and the bunkers have an attractive look with wild grasses sprouting from their faces like wispy eyebrows although they are rather less attractive from the inside looking out. Long, long ago, Harry Vardon declared Newcastle to be the hardest course in Ireland. That is a compliment that can now be cast more extensively, golfers coming from far and wide to sample its charms and analyse its greatness.

Its devoted adherents include many advanced students who see a sequence for the first 13 holes that is close to perfection. The first three holes along the bay represent a fine start; the short 4th, 7th and 10th are a joyous foil for each other; the 5th and 8th are classic 4s and the 9th a photogra-

ROYAL COUNTY DOWN					
Card of the No 1 course (championship tees)					
Hole	Yds	Par	Hole	Yds	Par
1	506	5	10	200	3
2	424	4	11	440	4
3	473	4	12	501	5
4	217	3	13	445	4
5	440	4	14	213	3
6	396	4	15	445	4
7	145	3	16	265	4
8	427	4	17	400	4
9	486	5	18	545	5
	3514	36		3454	36

Total 6968 yards, par 72
Course record • 66,
James Bruen (A), 1939;
Mervyn Jamison (A), 1972

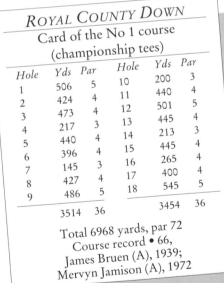

pher's dream. The drive is one of several shots at Newcastle that are blind but traditionalists regard that as a feather in its cap. In the case of the 9th, it is like the unveiling of a long-awaited painting as the heathery crest is scaled and the spotlight suddenly focused on one of golf's great sights.

There is a hint of what lies ahead on the elevated back tee on the 4th but the scene is magnified on the 9th as Slieve Donard, the highest of the Mourne Mountains, towers over the spires and roofs of the town and the slopes of its neighbours really do roll down to the sea.

The first three holes head north away from the peaks, each with its own identity and enclosed look. The 1st, a par 5, has a reasonably inviting drive although the long approach to the green has to be steered past a guardian hillock. The 2nd is more demanding from the tee with the first of sev-

eral carries followed by a shot between a gap in the dunes to a plateau green, the first indication that the greens are precise targets.

One of the legends of Newcastle is that Old Tom Morris laid out the course for a sum not exceeding four pounds, a figure that seems more likely to have been his fee. Whether that is true or not, the story proves the incredible raw material with which he had to work even if it was, in those days, bare of gorse. There have been a few variations of layout and there is little now recognizable of Morris's design but Morris was undoubtedly responsible for the birth of a legend that is the source of such pleasure and pride.

Another valley plots the course of the 3rd which heads for a marker post on a hill overlooking the green. The 4th then changes direction, the championship tee offering a challenging stroke

One of the toughest of the par 4s, the 5th doglegs to the right round a large dune. The whispy 'eyebrows' lining many of the bunkers are readily apparent in the foreground.

over gorse and bunkers – no place for the frail or timid. A dogleg at the 5th calls for a daring drive across a heathery outcrop if the green is to be in range in two against a breeze but, under such conditions, the 6th, the only par 4 on the course under 400 yards, is much less severe, the main problem being in holding one of the smaller greens.

With so much big hitting elsewhere, the 7th is a model for lovers of short, short holes, the tee shot involving a carry over a central bunker that has to counter the threat of a small hill on the right and a natural drop down a sharp slope on the left. One person for whom it presented no problem was Eric Fiddian in the final of the Irish Open Amateur Championship in 1933. He holed-in-one in the morning and repeated the feat at the 14th in the afternoon but neither bolt from the

blue saved him from defeat at the hands of Jack McLean, later professional at Gleneagles.

Bunkers and a long rise up to a green backed against sandhills dominate the 8th but it is the drive at the 9th, high over the crest before plunging to a fairway below, that epitomizes the dramatic dimension of Newcastle. Not that it is merely a driving hole. The second has to negotiate two bunkers that mark a change of level and lengthy approach to the green.

The turn is reached under the clubhouse window, a rarity on a links, a corner of the lounge bar looking directly down the 10th, a long short hole where bunkers abound. Thereafter, four holes follow almost the same line, the 12th, a par 5, offering the chance of a birdie. Birdies are less common at the 13th, a well channelled hole swinging right.

This is all you can see from the tee of the short 7th, a shot that is difficult to judge and must hold a distinctly shaped and contoured green.

An inspiring backdrop to an inspiring hole. The drive at the 9th must carry the high crest to a hidden fairway below.

Sandy waste, gorse and a marshy area to the left are the feature of the 14th, the last and second longest of the short holes, while the 15th is similar in shape and length to the 13th although it runs in the opposite direction. It leads on through the thickest of the gorse to a short par 4 where power is more of an advantage than usual. A shot carrying 200 yards will clear the ridge, leaving a gentle run down to a green plainer and less protected than any of the others.

A change of character is signalled as the 17th penetrates more open country particularly on the right and the 18th, the longest hole of all,

flanks still more gorse on the left, the shorter second course acting as a safe haven for those nursing a good score. If the last couple of holes suffer by comparison, it is a reflection of the magnificence of the rest rather more than any criticism of them.

One person who will hear not one note of criticism is Michael Bonallack, winner of Royal County Down's only Amateur Championship in 1970. His victory over Bill Hyndman, a repeat of the previous year's final, was his third in succession and his fifth in all. One down at lunch, he raced away to win by 8 and 7.

COUNTY LOUTH

One of the joys of golf in Britain and Ireland is finding treasures in spots where you least expect them. There is also the danger of nipping from one famous course to another and bypassing some of these out-of-the-way jewels. Don't make that mistake over County Louth at Baltray in heading to Portmarnock from Royal County Down. County Louth is great in its own right, a glittering example of the architectural genius of Tom Simpson.

From Drogheda, near the border of Ulster and the Republic, you take the road to Baltray, slipping unmistakably from the shadow of town to the open country so characteristic of great links. The man who defined life as a series of agonizing waits between one game of golf and the next could be imagined, as the clubhouse comes in sight, striving to control a mounting impatience. In fine conditions, distant ribbons of fairway convey a message of renewed hope that today might be our day and, though Baltray is a finer test than most, there is no harm in hoping.

In assessing the value of any course, it is tempting to put the clock back and try to visualize the state of things before its conversion and the resources that enabled founding fathers and architects to do what they did. The pioneers of Baltray were knowledgeable and tenacious enough to look beyond the Mornington end of Bettystown Burrows where they laid out a few holes initially and cross the River Boyne to the promised land. The club history called it 'one of the best pieces of golfing ground in the world' but it wasn't until Simpson wove his magic that it assumed championship proportions. James Bruen, at the height of his prodigious powers, opened the new course in July 1938 and it quickly made its mark. In spite of a repositioning of the clubhouse, necessitating renumbering of the holes, most of Simpson's work remains intact.

His best surrounds the holes in the dunes nearest the sea, the part Simpson would no doubt say offered the finest scope, but the most observant will see it everywhere from the shaping of the greens to the sympathetic use of original contours. Baltray is a magnificent test for the skilled without in any way intimidating the handicap golfer. Joe Carr found it much to his liking in winning the East of Ireland Championship 12 times although it obviously responds as much to the feminine touch. Clarrie Tiernan (Mrs Val Reddan) and Philomena Garvey were both products of the links.

COUNTY LOUTH Card of the course (championship tees)						
Hole		Yds	Par	Hole		Yds	Par
1	Drummond	433	4	10	Gannon's Way	398	4
2	Bather's Path	482	5	11	Long Bank	481	5
3	Punch Bowl	544	5	12	The Crater	410	4
4	Horse Shoe	344	4	13	Manx Mens Gap	421	4
5	Haven	158	3	14	The Cup	332	4
6	Inver Colpa	531	5	15	Jubilee Bank	152	3
7	Shepherds Bank	163	3	16	Water Hole	388	4
8	Beag Bearna	407	4	17	Jib	179	3
9	Cloc Stuca	419	4	18	Cowan Well	541	5
		3481	37			3302	36

Total 6783 yards, par 73

Course record • 65, Jimmy Hegarty, 1985

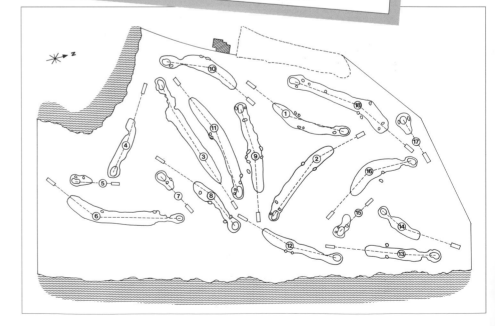

The short par-4 14th, Tom Simpson at his best.

The present course makes a stern beginning with the longest of the 4s and two of the five par 5s. The 3rd, without a bunker, is full of natural blessings including a high ridge which hides the tiny green from the second shot. It is a lesson to those deploring blind holes, showing instead how to lay down the gauntlet by creating no obstructions yet pinching the fairway into a narrow waist nearer the green to make life as demanding as possible.

A short 4, the old 1st, lends temporary respite at the 4th but two of the excellent short holes follow in the next three holes, the 5th to a green cut into the low hills and bunkered accordingly on the right. There is plenty to commend the holes around the turn, particularly the 10th green near the water's edge. The 6th has tigerish qualities but the four holes from the 12th come closer to vintage seaside than any. They can be traced by the rising outline of the dunes and the more exciting roll to the fairways.

As difficult a stroke as any is the second to the 13th through a narrow gap but, for its aesthetic merits and sporting nature, the 14th, 332 yards, is most appealing. An elevated tee looking over the beach with the Mountains of Mourne forming the horizon gives an inspiring launch to a drive that poses the age-old puzzle – whether to risk all in favour of a shorter second or whether to adopt a more conservative approach. However, the solution to the puzzle is the precision of the pitch to a green raised like a top hat.

As in the outward nine, two par 3s occupy the space of the next three holes before the 18th takes us home with the none-too-difficult prospect of a 5 to finish.

A year or two back, Joe Carr was playing at Baltray with a young caddie unaware of the name of Carr who, admittedly, was not giving much of a hint of the glories of the past. So much so that the caddie enquired: 'Ever played here before'?

'Yes,' replied Joe, 'as a matter of fact I have.'

'Did yer ever play in the East of Ireland Championship?'

'Yes,' said Joe.

'And did yer ever do any good?' insisted the boy.

'I won it twelve times,' came the answer from Carr with a modest nonchalance, thinking he might have the last word.

'Well,' concluded the boy, 'the standard must have been much worse in your day.'

PORTMARNOCK

In its earliest days, access to Portmarnock was by means of pony and trap across the estuary at low tide. It is ironic that it made a quicker progress than the long queue of traffic that builds up today on the approach road, taking crowds home at the end of a major tournament. It can also take longer to cover the mile or so to the end of the road than it does to fly to London but the story speaks volumes for the enormous demand on Portmarnock for important events and the peace and tranquillity of the setting when all have departed the lonely promontory.

In terms of a world stage, Portmarnock is Ireland's premier course although that owes much to its closeness to Dublin and the Irish passion for watching golf which, head for head, is second to none. Its choice for the 1991 Walker Cup was one of unbridled joy, the Irish displaying as much partiality for watching amateur golf as professional. They liked nothing better than the day when Joe Carr, born in the clubhouse, beat all except Christy O'Connor in the Dunlop Masters of 1959, and the gathering for the Home Internationals is a special favourite. They will die happy if Portmarnock can house the Ryder Cup, not that they are unused to American visitors. Several have been invited to the Carroll's Irish Open and it was at Portmarnock in 1960 that Arnold Palmer made his first appearance in Europe, partnering Sam Snead to win the Canada Cup.

Professionals' liking for Portmarnock is based on its fairness, its almost complete lack of blind shots, the flattish nature of the fairways and the greens which encourage a smooth stroke. There are none of the mountainous dunes to be found out in the West but the rough is fierce and tenacious and the bunkers deep. You pay in plenty for your indiscretions.

Apart from the 15th, it is not particularly scenic although the waters of the estuary can lap the 1st tee. The first four holes make their way in a gentle curve around the tip of the headland, gaining a glimpse of the Sutton Club as they go.

It was from somewhere there in 1893 that curiosity got the better of Messrs Pickerman and Ross who, believing some suitable land for golf existed on the other side, crossed by boat to see for themselves. What they discovered led to the founding of the Portmarnock Club, the early course having the added hazard of Maggie Leonard's cow which had a liking for golf balls – presumably the gutty which modern ruminants might think a lot less palatable than ones with a rubber centre. It is interesting how many other

PORTMARNOCK Card of the Championship course (championship tees)					
Hole	M	Par	Hole	M	Par
1	358	4	10	341	4
2	346	4	11	389	4
3	351	4	12	136	3
4	407	4	13	516	5
5	364	4	14	359	4
6	550	5	15	191	3
7	161	3	16	484	5
8	368	4	17	423	4
9	404	4	18	381	4
	3309	36		3220	36

Total 6529 metres, par 72
Course record • 64,
Sandy Lyle, 1989

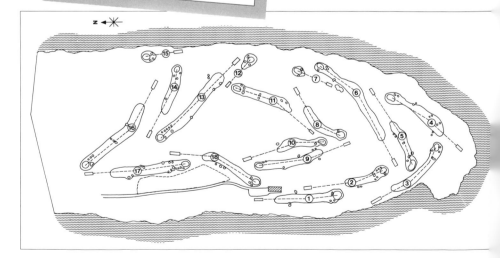

The opening tee shot along the estuary.

clubs came into being in the same arbitrary fashion and how remoteness has always appealed to golfers. Small townships have grown up locally but Portmarnock's opening quickly sets the mood.

The 1st is neither difficult nor straightforward, an ideal way to start. The 2nd and 3rd raise the challenge a notch the 2nd by means of a longish carry to the fairway and contoured green, and the 3rd with a well placed drive. The fairway, following the line of hills on the left, falls away to marshy ground on the right, a snare to the intentions of getting up in two. The rather enclosed 4th and the 5th, one of the best holes on the course, are stern 4s, then comes Portmarnock's only outward par 5. The 6th can be immense, particularly if the wind

is in the face. Nevertheless, in helpful summer conditions, such as those experienced during one or two recent Carroll's Irish Opens, the best players have found it little more than a drive and mid-iron, sobering proof of the miracles in the advance of equipment manufacture.

The valleyed 7th brings the first short hole, bunkers providing the main resistance to hopes of a 3. It needs two good shots to get home at each of the 8th and 9th, the 8th with a modified, raised green and the 9th where there is much character and interest on the approach to a green close to the clubhouse.

Arrangement of the course in two loops of nine is evidence of careful planning although most of the credit is largely anonymous. In common with

most links, Portmarnock has undergone its share of alteration but there is still much that Messrs Pickerman and Ross would recognize in broad outline, if not in detail. Certainly, they would approve the lofty heights to which their ambitions have risen and the esteem in which Portmarnock is held. There is a hardly a weak link and a nice balance between the halves, to which were added a further nine in 1971 (there are those who consider the latter harder than the original 18).

Another characteristically tough hole opens the inward half which continues with an even longer 4 and a short hole into the hills guarding the shore whose feature is a narrow entrance to an almost precipitously sloping green. Either by coincidence or design, all three short-hole greens are set into the dunes. A high tee at the 13th signals an inviting drive even if a varied network of bunkers is somewhat less inviting in haunting both the drive and the second shot.

Portmarnock's best and most famous holes are the 14th and 15th. The 14th doglegs slightly left round a deep bunker with two or more in front of a plateau green, a delightful prelude to the last of the par 3s along a ridge in the dunes with commanding views of the strand, Lambay and Ireland's Eye. There are perils for missing the green anywhere, recovery depending on a deft touch and a clear picture of the shot intended.

The finish calls for a girding of the loins and

The green of the 6th, the only outward par 5 and one which varies enormously according to the wind in the length it plays.

A picture postcard setting to the short 15th, along the strand. Severe drops on either side of the green contribute to its reputation for being perhaps the hardest hole on the course.

indulgence in a succession of stout-hearted shots to consolidate a promising score or to rescue one fading into insignificance. The 16th pursues a straight path to the course's northernmost point, a par 5 where 4s can be as hard to make as on the 17th, a very long par 4 that has brought its measure of despair and disappointment. There is no alternative to a sound drive and hefty second, one of the greatest of which was a 4-wood that won Christy O'Connor the 1959 Dunlop Masters.

It was a great Irish occasion in every sense because Joe Carr, the first Irish captain of the Royal and Ancient, was the other principal and, between them, they produced some of the best golf ever seen at Portmarnock. Although the course's defences were lowered on a glorious final day, O'Connor played the last 23 holes in 83 strokes and professional embarrassment was spared.

For the final lap, the 18th skirts a group of bunkers on the right with the drive followed by a stiff second to a green around which a natural grandstand is formed to accommodate the crowds that greet their heroes. More familiarly, the banks are deserted and recognition mute but pleasure and enjoyment are thankfully not dependent on a glittering performance. Modest practitioners by the hundred have made for the clubhouse happier and more fulfilled than those who play the game for their living. Portmarnock's appeal is full ranging.

ROYAL DUBLIN

Royal Dublin is one of the very few links courses which is situated inside a city boundary. Known by the pleasant name of Dollymount, it is set on Bull Island in Dublin Bay although it is connected to the mainland by a splendid wooden bridge to serve the clubhouse and by a causeway further out to provide access for crowds for major tournaments.

Bull Island is a sanctuary for hares which you are more than likely to disturb during the course of a round. If a little flat and compact, the terrain is ideal for golf and, in spite of the nearness of the city, there are fine views of Howth, Dublin Bay and the Wicklow hills.

Royal Dublin, the second oldest club in Ireland and the oldest in the Republic, had its first home in Phoenix Park and its second at Sutton but they have been on the North Bull at Dollymount since 1889. In its early days there, the landlord of the links was against the idea of Sunday golf. However, the locals were undeterred. While the front door of the clubhouse remained closed, golfers used the back door, and Bombardier Fletcher, the steward, and his wife would invariably have a pot of Irish stew on the boil to provide inner warmth. Members ate in the locker room with plates on their knees and a bottle of Guinness to help it down.

The course and clubhouse were used by the military during the First World War, after which Harry Colt was brought in to redesign the course. It quickly became recognized as a test fit for the best. It has been in regular use for Irish championships and, for many years, the club professional was Christy O'Connor who played the links better than anyone.

It has two slight disadvantages: in common with many seaside links, the layout goes out and back, and the two halves are somewhat unbalanced. The second half is some 500 yards longer than the first; with a par of 37 as opposed to the 34 going out. On the other hand, the outward half, which follows the line of the shore, can be more interesting.

What is more, the wind is more likely to be of assistance going out although the short 4th doubles back and the short 9th, at the far end, slants across. Unless the wind is in the face, the par-5 8th is easily reachable by the best players, as was the 2nd until it was recently reduced to a par 4. The 3rd and 7th are also good 4s. Its routing has similarities with Royal Troon and

Above right The 6th green, with the clubhouse and chimneys of Dublin forming the background.

Below right The sinister out-of-bounds ditch on the right of the 18th.

ROYAL DUBLIN
Card of the course (championship tees)

Hole		M	Par	Hole		M	Par
1	North Bull	361	4	10	Marne	378	4
2	Babington's	440	4	11	Colt's	479	5
3	Alps	363	4	12	Campbell's	188	3
4	Feather Bed	163	3	13	Dardanelles	425	4
5	Valley	423	4	14	Moran's	455	5
6	Pot	180	3	15	Hogan's	397	4
7	Ireland's Eye	338	4	16	Dolly	245	4
8	Ben Howth	465	5	17	Coastguard's	345	4
9	Davidson's	164	3	18	Garden	453	4
		2897	34			3365	37

Total 6262 metres, par 71

Course record • 64, Bernard Langer, 1984

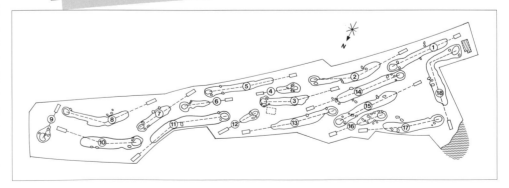

Royal Lytham, it being fairly imperative to have a score made by the time the turn is reached.

The long par-5 11th, with an out-of-bounds drain up the right, can be a fearsome hole and the next four hold the key to the round, the 13th, Dardanelles, with the same dell-like green as the 11th. Daring drives on the well bunkered 16th can get home, and O'Connor holed for a 2 in the 1966 Carroll's International in which he covered the last three holes in five under par to tie with Eric Brown.

Such mastery was nothing unusual but perhaps the best known hole at Royal Dublin is the 18th, the Garden, a long par 4 (it used to be a short par 5) in the form of a right-hand dogleg with out-of-bounds on the right. It is not a classic hole but it can be a daunting way to finish especially if the result of a match or a fine score hangs on it.

WATERVILLE

Sport in County Kerry is first and foremost an indulgence in Gaelic football which, to outsiders, is an amalgam of all the other versions of football – minus rules. One of my earliest journalistic assignments was to cover the All-Ireland final which, with fine Irish logic, took place at Wembley. This was either to conform with the national partiality for a trip to London (or anywhere) or as a convenient means of organizing a reunion with the thousands of their countrymen living and working in England. I should have understood more about a lecture on micro-electronics delivered in Russian but I remember well that the Men of Kerry won.

Golf and Gaelic football have little in common but not so golf and Kerry. Against a background of scenery that is divertingly stunning, a rich sense of escape is unmistakable in a number of their remote courses of which Waterville is one of the highlights.

The most symbolic spot at Waterville is the high tee on the 17th, Mulcahy's Peak, named after John Mulcahy, the man who, in the early 1970s, transformed Waterville into a place for world travellers to congregate.

There is a vastness about the scale of the west of Ireland's links that is rare and a grandeur about their mountainous dunes that is unrivalled. Waterville is not all dunes but the most fascinating part surrounds the holes that stream like green ribbons through the hills.

If the grandeur of the setting is immense, the length of the course is of similar proportions. Stretched to its last inch, it measures 7184 yards which, for the statistically minded, is the longest in Britain and Ireland. For most, it is a daunting thought, particularly bearing in mind the ferocity with which the wind blows, but fear not. There are alternative tees, reducing the length to 6599 (medal) or 6024 yards (society). Nevertheless, Waterville is not for the weak or faint-hearted.

The first nine embraces the flatter inland ground that would be more remarkable were it not for the comparisons that are inevitably made with the land nearer the sea. To my mind, the best of the outward half comprises the 4th, 7th, 8th and 9th. The 7th, a short hole played back towards the clubhouse, has a well protected green with a recently introduced water feature while the 8th and 9th are both stern 4s.

WATERVILLE Card of the course (championship tees)						
Hole		Yds	Par	Hole		Yds	Par
1	Last Easy	430	4	10	Bottleneck	475	4
2	Christy's Choice	469	4	11	Tranquillity	496	5
3	Innyside	417	4	12	The Mass Hole	200	3
4	The Dunes	179	3	13	The Twin	518	5
5	Tipperary	595	5	14	The Judge	456	4
6	Lost Palm	371	4	15	The Vale	392	4
7	The Island	178	3	16	Liam's Ace	350	4
8	Ponderous	435	4	17	Mulcahy's Peak	196	3
9	Prodigal	445	4	18	Broadway	582	5
		3519	35			3665	37

Total 7184 yards, par 72
Course record • 65, Liam Higgins, 1986

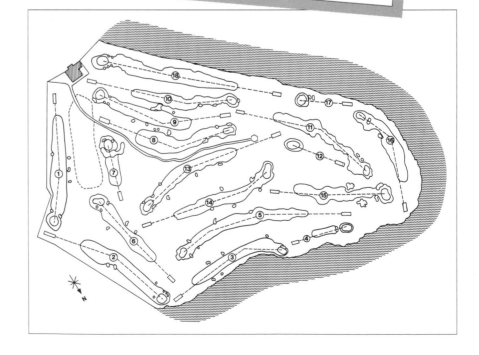

The 11th, felt by some to be the best par 5 in Ireland.

The tempo is raised as the 10th heads back towards a green set between a narrow entrance in the hills. Now comes the 11th which has been described as the best par 5 in Ireland. From a high tee, you aim at a thin channel of dune-lined fairway that later dips down in front of a green which, as a result, appears prominently raised.

There is a touch of history surrounding the short 12th, named Mass after the bad old days in Ireland when locals had to celebrate mass in unofficial places or risk prosecution. As the site of the existing 12th green was hidden, it was the ideal spot. The 13th is not so attractive but the 14th returns to the hill country and the finish is superb. It contributes to a half that is as stern as any.

Notoriety was lent to the 16th, a hole curving round the golden beach, by the feat of the local professional, Liam Higgins, a hitter of mighty repute, holing in one. Taking the direct route, he cleared the wilderness of hills and scrub with a prodigious stroke of around 330-340 yards.

Mulcahy's favourite hole begins on a high tee and ends with a remote target, completing four marvellous short holes. The 18th might be rather more mundane, but it is one of the longest closing holes in golf. However, if christened with the length of Broadway in mind, it is positively the only common factor that Waterville has with New York. In every sense, Waterville is a place of tranquillity and rare, natural beauty.

211

TRALEE

All the way out from the town of Tralee, there is little to suggest that advanced reports about the golf will live up to their extravagant billing. The lanes beyond Ardvert towards Barrow are narrow and, at times, uneven, but, as a final crest is mounted and the drive slips down towards the clubhouse, there is a dramatic transformation. It is as if the curtain in a theatre has risen to reveal a quite stunning set.

Comparisons with Turnberry or Pebble Beach are perfectly valid. Tralee is the most recent links in Britain or Ireland, opening its grand doors in 1984 with the name of Arnold Palmer to bolster its undoubted reputation. It is a course of distinct contrasts, the first nine one of flat lies and little undulation, the second an absorbing mix of mountainous dunes, carries over cavernous valleys and holes that remain etched in the memory.

For all the original pasture-like character of the outward half, there are three holes which stand out on account of their close proximity to the ocean and the part they play in wrecking a good score. The 2nd can do so before one has even taken shape, a par 5 round a long curve in the shore, over the road to the magnificent beach and on to a green on the edge of a slight cliff.

It is a reflection of the difficulty of maintaining good turf when the Atlantic breakers are forever depositing salt spray that a rather unnatural, protective collar of mounds has had to be built behind the green, but the 3rd green is even more exposed. Except in the raging gales that are commonplace in the west of Ireland, it is a lofted iron that can become washed up on the rocks if the range finder is faulty. Here is a heavenly spot to reflect upon a well played and well gauged shot but every hole has picture postcard qualities. Golf at Tralee combines stimulating lessons in geography and history that can be delightfully distracting.

The foreground is dominated by the sandy stretches of the Long Strand but the distant panorama embraces Kerry Head, Mount Brendan, Slieve Mish mountain and the coastline tracing the mouth of the Shannon. Saint Brendan was reputed to have been born at Barrow, a place that was known later as a port frequented by pirates and smugglers.

Randy Quay is identified nowadays more as the backcloth of the short 7th, the maritime influence preserved on the superb 8th which follows the shore to the left. Then, it is up the hill to the clubhouse and down the dogleg 10th to be introduced to the different challenge of the inward half.

TRALEE
Card of the course (championship tees)

Hole		M	Par	Hole		M	Par
1	Mucklough	367	4	10	The Warren	390	4
2	The Cuilin	537	5	11	Palmer's Peak	531	5
3	The Castle	175	3	12	Bracken	408	4
4	Cuchullian's Table	392	4	13	Brock's Hollow	146	3
5	Brandon	389	4	14	Crosty	370	4
6	Chough's Corner	380	4	15	Poulgorm	279	4
7	The Randy	142	3	16	Shipwreck	181	3
8	The Creek	356	4	17	Ryan's Daughter	321	4
9	Hare's Lane	451	5	18	The Goat's Hole	424	4
		3189	36			3050	35

Total 6239 metres, par 71
Course record • 66, Gerard O'Sullivan, 1987

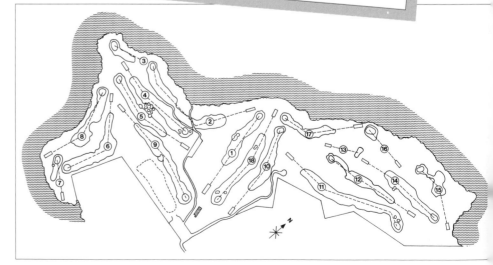

The 11th gives a stern baptism with a par 5, Palmer's Peak, which necessitates a second shot aimed on a white stone marking the line to a hidden green set into the slope on three levels. An about-turn for the 12th signals a downhill drive but it is essentially a second-shot hole, the small target of green on an isolated spur of dune headland posing great demands. All or nothing is the only description of the short 13th, a yawning chasm known as Brock's Hollow separating the tee from the green on its duneland perch. It strikes a note of defiance although the penalty for falling short can be incalculable.

A sloping fairway and a shoulder on the approach are the features of the 14th but the 15th, if modest in length, is an intriguing par 4. It involves a drive onto a sort of island fairway, only those hit to the right catching a glimpse of the green through a funnel of low hills. Against a frame of the ocean in the heart of the sandhills, the short 16th can be a mammoth shot in the prevailing wind while the 17th, with stunning views of the Long Strand featured in *Ryan's Daughter*, can assume similarly inflated problems in such conditions. It has another extremely undulating fairway that turns half-right round a hill to a green on a lofty pinnacle.

The 18th returns to the more open country, the longest of the 4s, but the happiest part of a round at Tralee lies in the afterglow of surveying the scene from the upstairs window of the clubhouse. On a fine day it can captivate you for hours.

The scenic splendour of Tralee, showing the distant 17th green from the 13th green.

BALLYBUNION

For well over half a century, the peaceful town of Ballybunion and the glories of its links remained largely uninvaded and unsung. Knowing voices in Ireland spoke with awe about it but its real elevation to select circles emanated from a visit made by Herbert Warren Wind in 1968. His subsequent assertion that 'Ballybunion revealed itself to be nothing less than the finest seaside course I have ever seen' was the publicity it needed to shoot up the rankings, cause an invasion of golfers from all over the world and bring hitherto undreamed of wealth to the club. In 1990, its income from green fees alone exceeded £600,000.

It attracted the illustrious as well as the curious, Tom Watson describing it as a course you will always enjoy and never tire of playing. Ballybunion became a fashionable word in the vocabulary just as Dornoch, another remote bastion, had a few years earlier. It featured in all the golfing tours of Ireland as travel was made easier and a thriving tourist industry built up. Personal preference for golf courses is as varied as opinions on art but for Ballybunion, on the southern entrance of the Shannon River, there is unanimity. Not a harsh word is said about it.

Ballybunion is a place of giant hills and deep valleys, the perfect structure for an authentic seaside links although, as the road approaches from the town, you see immediately how narrow is this strip of superlative country. The holes close to the boundary have none of the daunting identity of those dominated by dunes or ocean but the other striking fact is that, where the vastness, range and majesty of dunes on seaside courses is concerned, Ballybunion represents the Himalayas themselves.

It is fascinating to contemplate the task facing the founding fathers in 1896 of laying out nine holes on such inspiring land although it did not become 18 holes until 1926. There was little demand and, in keeping with the early trend of golf course design, a clubhouse position was chosen as near to the neighbouring community as possible with the holes arranged more or less up and down.

When the course was extended, it was obviously skillfully and knowledgeably done because, when Tom Simpson was invited to suggest subsequent improvements in time for the Irish Amateur Championship in 1937, his alterations were confined to amended greens on the old 2nd, 4th and 8th greens and a mid-fairway double bunker at the 14th (the new 1st) which was christened Mrs Simpson.

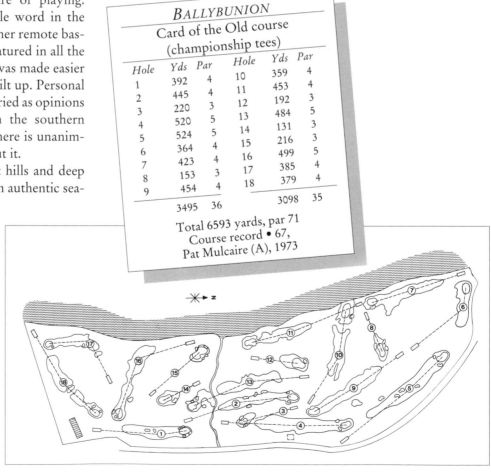

BALLYBUNION
Card of the Old course (championship tees)

Hole	Yds	Par	Hole	Yds	Par
1	392	4	10	359	4
2	445	4	11	453	4
3	220	3	12	192	3
4	520	5	13	484	5
5	524	5	14	131	3
6	364	4	15	216	3
7	423	4	16	499	5
8	153	3	17	385	4
9	454	4	18	379	4
	3495	36		3098	35

Total 6593 yards, par 71
Course record • 67,
Pat Mulcaire (A), 1973

A gap in the dunes provides a glimpse of the 11th green, one of the most photographed holes in the world.

The most significant change since then has been the resiting of the clubhouse in a position above the old 13th green. This means that the old 18th is now the 5th and the old 1st the 6th. One advantage of the rearrangement was that the old 17th and 18th, which used to be said to comprise a dull finish (if anything at Ballybunion can be dull), are absorbed into the earlier part of the round when the symphony is still warming up. However, the main reason for the change surrounded the decision to build a second course. The new clubhouse serves both equally.

Mrs Simpson is the first hazard to confront golfers although the town's graveyard on the right of the 1st gives rise to plenty of comment. The hole makes a pleasant opener, tough enough to make you think yet not so severe as to leave the impression of embarking on an impossible mission. Ballybunion is a lesson to those architects and clients who judge standards purely in terms of the length of a course. At its limit, it measures 6593 yards but the 2nd is as demanding a 4 as any and one which emphasizes a unique aspect for a links.

A high proportion of shots have either to carry across large sandy gullies to greens or be hoisted to elevated positions although some pitch-and-running is possible. The 2nd green, however, is very much of the target variety and a hole of 445 yards at which only a handful get home in two. This is partly because the second must bisect a V-shaped gap in the sandhills and partly because the final approach must overcome a sharp bank in front of the green.

A long short hole at the 3rd is the prelude to two par 5s mentioned earlier but the 6th, a left-handed dogleg, leads into vintage Ballybunion. The 7th tee is the spot to be made instantly aware both of the beautiful beach and of the fact that the links is perched on a sandy clifftop; more sadly, it makes apparent the threat of coastal erosion. The 7th is perhaps the most notable victim but the orig-inal green has survived to make it one of the most talked about holes. Yet that is a recurring theme on a course of inviting greens and strong hitting. The dangers are many but the rewards great.

A neat triangle is forged by the next three holes, the 8th, a short hole turning inland with a tightly guarded green, the 9th, a hole dominated by a cen-tral bunker short of the green, and the 10th, a drive

The second of consecutive short holes, the 15th provides a thrilling tee shot to a green on two levels.

The 16th, a dogleg whose fairway climbs between the dunes away from the sea.

and iron in calm conditions that twists back towards the Atlantic. This is another hole where the second must carry onto the green, a sandy, hummocky dell barring the way to any form of scuttle-and-run. In days before high pitches were rendered easier by the manufacture of modern equipment, it was no surprise that Ballybunion's first Irish Amateur Championship was won in 1937 by the 17-year-old James Bruen, a prodigious player of shots through the air.

Nearly all the publicity photographs of Ballybunion feature the 11th, a continuation of the 7th, as it were. There is a spectacular drive along the cliff edge to a fairway that falls away in shallow terraces towards a green reached by a penetrating shot between dunes. Against a backdrop of beach and ocean, it is a real eye-catcher.

The 13th, sandwiched between short holes that have greens above the level of the tees, is a par 5 across an unseen stream in front of an angled green protected by mounds. An unusual feature of Ballybunion is that the 14th and 15th are consecutive short holes, the 15th the best of the bunch. A glorious view, both near and far, can divert the gaze from a downhill shot to a two-tier green.

For its climax, Ballybunion sports three doglegs to the left that are as grand as any you will find, fairways plunging and climbing in the midst of the best of the dunes. Additionally, the 16th boasts the last opportunity to embrace the sea, the

big decision concerning the line from the tee. It is tempting and possible to cut the corner but, at the 16th, three fairway bunkers await the longest hitters while, at the 17th, the best side for the second is the right in order to counter three nice mounds to the left of the green. There is nothing prosaic about Ballybunion and, symbolically, the final drive, aimed on the clubhouse window, must be between dunes and the final second shot must split an awkward gap in front of the green.

The Old course's greens are not large but they are altogether bigger than many on the New course which lies to the south in the same wonderland of sandhills. In spite of a par of 71, it is more than 450 yards shorter than the Old. It is full of fine drives and the dunes lend an imposing, custodial look that, in conjunction with the superlative coastal stretch, makes it every bit as scenic as its neighbour. It is more a test of stout legs but some of the greens are far too small, particularly with the presence of so much wind.

The green on the 1st is no more than 200 square yards in area, its 7-yard width making the Dell at Lahinch seem conventional and wide open. Size of greens reflects the length and type of hole as well as the length and type of shot played at them. They are the focus of every hole on every course and must also blend well with the landscape but, in this vital respect, the New cannot compare with the Old.

LAHINCH

Alister MacKenzie, designer of Cypress Point, Royal Melbourne and Augusta, could be said to know good land when he saw it. So, when he said of Lahinch, 'It will make the finest and most popular course that I, or, I believe, anyone else has ever constructed,' you have to accept his word.

Described by Herbert Warren Wind as the St Andrews of Scotland, Lahinch is a small town on the Atlantic coast of County Clare which might be almost totally unknown were it not for the mountainous dune country lining the shore to provide the perfect medium for links golf. It is a spectacular example of the changing levels, hummocky dips and extravagant contours that architects strive in vain to introduce, and there is a whiff of whimsy about it which the Irish appreciate more than most.

Their love of the unconventional finds expression in Klondyke and Dell, successive holes that defy most principles of golf course architecture. The par-5 5th is less outrageous than the short 6th, a greenkeeper's nightmare. Klondyke's shortcoming is no more than a longish second over a hill to a hidden green with the 18th drive crossing in front of it but Dell is completely obscured by the precipitous sides of twin hills, the tee shot calling for the flight of a mortar and the soft landing of a bird. Elsewhere, it would have been condemned long ago; at Lahinch, it is as precious as yeast to beer.

Founded in 1892 by soldiers of the Black Watch as part of the Limerick Club, Lahinch is the permanent home of the South of Ireland Championship and housed the Home Internationals in 1987. Its pedigree is long and distinguished as both prime test and enjoyable place to play.

An uphill opening hole can be a rude awakener although the 2nd tumbles back down again to a green beside the clubhouse. A delightful short hole follows and then it is up over the first of the big hills with a hefty second to follow. However, the exciting holes on the front nine are the 7th, 8th and 9th – notably the 7th, involving an inviting drive onto a crest that leaves a second plunging down between the hills against a background of the ocean. It resembles a little the drive from the high tee on the 9th, a rousing shot that heralds the solid hitting that lies ahead.

The 10th quickly proves the point, while the 11th, something of a foil, is sheer joy. The shortest of the short holes, it snuggles neatly into the dunes with a green that is an artistic creation – just big enough to hold a well hit shot yet sloping enough to make the margin for error slight.

LAHINCH
Card of the Old course

Hole	M	Par	Hole	M	Par
1	352	4	10	412	4
2	468	5	11	126	3
3	138	3	12	434	4
4	391	4	13	250	4
5	441	5	14	446	5
6	142	3	15	422	4
7	365	4	16	178	3
8	320	4	17	400	4
9	351	4	18	487	5
	2968	36		3155	36

Total 6123 metres, par 72
Course record • 68,
Martin Barratt, 1989

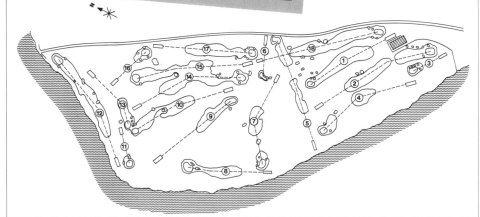

A general view showing the 10th and 13th greens in the foreground, the 14th on the left and the castle – a notable landmark – that gave the name to Lahinch's second course.

An enchanting short hole, the 11th is one of the few remaining reminders of the work of Alister MacKenzie.

A restored green position near the bridge over the river has transformed the 12th into a fiendishly difficult 4 but on the very short par-4 13th, doubling back to a small and tightly bunkered green, hangs hope of a birdie. The same applies on the 14th, mainly because the drive is more featureless owing to a change in the character of the ground. In this way, the finish suffers by comparison with the start but that is more a commentary on the quality of the earlier holes than a reflection on the last four which, if honest and by no means easy, may not please the connoisseur.

COUNTY SLIGO

Rosses Point belongs to a world of beauty and romance. In the heart of country made famous by the verse of Yeats, a feeling of remote splendour permeates a landscape vast and varied. Across an inlet to Drumcliff, Ben Bulben surveys a tranquil scene uninhabited and unspoiled.

It has its more angry moods as anyone familiar with seaside golf can well imagine but there are few more inspiring backgrounds for the game than County Sligo. It is the very opposite of courses where journeys to them hold little expectation. Long before Sligo is reached by a road winding gently down the Glencar Valley, there is growing certainty that Rosses Point, a few miles out of the old town, is something different.

Clubhouse and hotel form the centrepiece of a tiny hamlet that breathes golf, welcoming everyone with understandable pride to its delights. Cecil Ewing, a giant of a man in every sense who lived and died in Sligo, made my introduction and a great compliment it was. Although our round was blessed with summer sun it was easy to see how his game had been moulded, more by instinct than instruction, to a method geared to combat the winds. A narrow stance was the foundation that allowed a full turn of the shoulders and a perfectly timed action sped the ball on its way. It generated the power to flight shots as he wished, the firm sandy turf teaching the need for crisp striking with both long irons and short pitches.

How delighted he would have been that, in 1991, the Home Internationals were staged for the first time and won by Ireland, an event that receives a greater following there than in any of the other countries. Ireland's retention of the Raymond Trophy, won the previous year at Conwy, was the perfect way of celebrating the centenary of the Golfing Union of Ireland.

The opening at Rosses Point is inauspicious except as an immediate means of showing off its

glories. The 1st and 2nd are like steps on a magic ladder, the 2nd scaling quite an incline, but the breathtaking view from the 3rd tee is worth every effort to get there. Hills, green valleys, sea and sand merge into one enthralling canvas. No wonder that officers in the old Sligo militia considered they had stumbled on something exceptional a hundred years ago when they formed a club whose influence had much to do with the development of the game in the west of Ireland.

COUNTY SLIGO
Card of the course (championship tees)

Hole		M	Par	Hole		M	Par
1	Greenlands	347	4	10	Ben Bulben	351	4
2	Bar na Saide	278	4	11	Lissadell	366	4
3	Metal Man	457	5	12	Light House	448	5
4	Gan Gaineamh	150	3	13	Wrynne Point	162	3
5	The Jump	438	5	14	Mahon's Burn	394	4
6	Bomore	387	4	15	Through the Gap	367	4
7	Ewing's Profile	385	4	16	Knocknarea	196	3
8	The Churn	374	4	17	The Gallery	414	4
9	Cast a Cold Eye	153	3	18	Christy's Farm	336	4
		2969	36			3034	35

Total 6003 metres, par 71
Course record • 66, Francis Howley (A), 1991

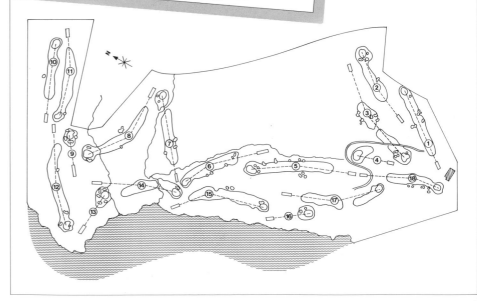

Peace and solitude at the short 16th on a links that provides glorious golf in a glorious setting.

The credit for the present course belongs mainly to Colt and Alison, their handiwork being particularly noticeable as the 5th drops down and a succession of challenging strokes broach lower land closer to the sea. Use is made at the 7th and 8th of streams in front of greens and the outward half ends with a fine short hole along a ridge flanked by trouble, contrived and natural.

The true golfing flavour of Rosses Point is yet to be sampled. Its greatness is highlighted on a seaside stretch of low sandhills, rumpled fairways and wild dune grasses.

The 10th leads down along the shore towards the church at Drumcliff; the 11th doubles back and the 12th, a par 5, heads for the sea. Next comes an enticing shot over a sandy inlet and another elevated tee shot on the 14th, a redoubtable par 4 rated among the finest in Ireland. The drive must open up a second shot that crosses a stream and a corner of the beach.

Completion of the coastal foray comes with the 15th and short 16th, the 17th then gliding gracefully up the gradual ascent to the clubhouse which, in the best Irish tradition, is hospitably warm. The annual West of Ireland Championship sees the best of all worlds, friendly competition on a superlative links in an incomparable setting. If you could ask for more, you would never find it.

221

INDEX